MW00450572

FAKING HISTORY

FAKING
HISTORY

Essays on Aliens, Atlantis, Monsters, and More

by

Jason Colavito

ALBANY

JasonColavito.com Books

2013

Copyright © 2013 by Jason Colavito

Published by Jason Colavito, Albany, New York

All Rights Reserved. No part of this book may be reproduced or transmitted by any means, electronic or mechanical, including photocopy, recording, or any other information storage and retrieval system, in any form whatsoever (except for copying permitted by U.S. copyright law or by reviewers for the public press), without the express written permission of the author.

Versions of the material included in this book first appeared on JasonColavito.com except as noted below:

"Who Really Discovered America?", "Who Lost the Middle Ages?", "Golden Fleeced," and "Did Native Americans Discover Europe in 60 BCE" first appeared in *Skeptic* magazine; "Of Atlantis and Aliens" first appeared in *Swans* magazine.

This book has been typeset in Charis SIL

ISBN-13: 978-1482387827
ISBN-10: 1482387824

www.JasonColavito.com

Contents

Introduction

'VE BEEN INTERESTED in fringe idea—ancient aliens, Atlantis, monsters—since I was a kid. In my first book, *The Cult of Alien Gods* (2005) I told the story of how my childhood discovery of the ancient astronaut books of Erich von Däniken prompted a teenage belief in alternative history that lasted until the house of cards came crashing down in my collegiate years. *The Sirius Mystery* author Robert Temple had claimed that an African tribe called the Dogon possessed anomalous knowledge of the Sirius star system, knowledge only aliens could provide. But I learned that anthropologists had found no such evidence, and the Sirius mystery crumbled. More research revealed still more distortions, omissions, and lies until nothing remained.

In early 2001, I began writing about what I had learned, just before I turned twenty. I published my thoughts about alternative history on my first website, *Lost Civilizations Uncovered*. In 2003, I made my most important discovery: that much of today's alternative history could be traced to the influence of the horror and science fiction writer H. P. Lovecraft, which I reported in my first professionally published article, "Charioteer of the Gods" (2004). It ran in *Skeptic* magazine, and I later expanded and updated it for *Dark Lore 7* (2012). I have included it in this anthology as Chapter 2. This article led to a book deal for *The Cult of Alien Gods*, which I thought would be my last word on ancient astronauts and alternative history. I continued writing articles for *Skeptic* magazine after this, but I turned my focus to my other love, horror fiction, producing a well-received study of the relationship between horror fiction and science as well as a critically acclaimed anthology of early horror criticism.

Then things changed. In 2009, the History Channel screened *Ancient Aliens*, a two-hour special intended as a pilot for a future series. I didn't watch it the night it debuted. Instead, I got a phone call from my father telling me that a friend of his had watched the show and saw my name in it. I turned on the show in a subsequent showing, and there I was, or rather a full-screen image of my "Charioteer of the Gods" with my name prominently displayed. The narrator was discussing von Däniken's 1968 book *Chariots of the Gods?* "But in spite of the book's enormous popularity—or perhaps because of it, von Däniken's theories were scorned by scientists, and jeered at by theologians." As scare quotes I never said scrolled across my name, the image inverted to deep black, and my name burst into an evil blood red—implying without words that the show took a negative view of my work.

Well, *that* wasn't good.

Ancient Aliens rekindled my passion for truth, and in the intervening years, I have investigated hundreds of claims made by every manner of alternative historian, from ancient astronaut writers to Atlantis believers, from pyramid mystics to mystery-mongers. I have published these investigations in the pages of *Skeptic* magazine, the *eSkeptic* online newsletter, as well as my website, JasonColavito.com, both as feature articles and among my daily blog posts. What you are about to read is a collection of fifty of my best essays on fake history and false claims, covering everything from Atlantis to Chupacabra to Stonehenge to UFOs, and even the demonic power of the humble dinner fork. All of these essays have been newly revised and updated for this edition, including full references.

Mark Twain once said, "Truth is mighty and will prevail. There is nothing the matter with this, except that it ain't so." I hope that the following essays make at least a tentative step toward giving the truth a fighting chance.

1. Of Atlantis and Aliens: Alternatives to History as Cultural Mirror

SOMETIME in the early history of ancient Greece, the Greeks came into contact with the Medes, an Iranian people living in Western Anatolia and the Caucasus. These people worshiped in holy places that they called *yazona* (= Persian *ayadana*), and the Greeks were greatly confused by this strange word. To them it sound very much like Iasonion, which they interpreted as altars sacred to the hero Jason (Iason in Greek), of Argonautic fame. From this "discovery" of a landscape studded with temples to Jason, the Greeks concluded that the Argonauts had conquered the Near East, and that the Medes were, by the same similarity of sound, the descendants of Jason's son Medus, by his wife, the sorceress Medea.[1] (The Persians, they thought, were descendants of Perseus.) The Greeks believed so strongly in this story that the Macedonian general Parmenio destroyed the sacred *yazona* wherever he found them to raise up his boss, Alexander the Great, over the mythic Jason, though he later atoned by restoring the Jason temple at Abdera.[2]

This object lesson in ancient hubris is a useful case study in how cultural assumptions and ethnocentric desires color the way even the most educated individuals interpret and understand the world around them. It also leads us to a deeper understanding of how the ad hoc explanations proposed for historical and cultural facts can open a window on the cultural expectations and values that popular theorists, especially those in the New Age and "alternative" archaeology movements, unconsciously foist onto history in their quest to rewrite the past to make it more palatable to the present.

Nowhere, perhaps, is this more obvious in the various theories proposed to explain the peopling of the Americas. Since the eighteenth century, mainstream scholars have understood that the Americas were populated from Asia, by peoples whose origins could be traced back to Siberia. But this fact, well-attested by archaeology, has been under near-constant assault almost from the first. Early opponents, almost all in the United States, stressed potential visitors from the high cultures of the Old World, including the peoples of Vedic India, the Phoenicians, and above all the Hebrews. An entire religion, the Church of Jesus Christ of Latter-Day Saints (the Mormons), was established on the belief that the Hebrews were the founding population of the Americas. Such theories were, in retrospect, designed to provide a suitably historic foundational myth for the United States, a country in search of an identity to replace the British history it had shed. The upshot of this myth was the Trail of Tears, which President Andrew Jackson specifically justified with appeal to lost founders who predated the Native Americans: "In the monuments and fortresses of an unknown people, spread over the extensive regions of the west, we behold the memorials of a once powerful race, which was exterminated, or has disappeared, to make room for the existing savage tribes."[3] This massacre, he said, was why removal of the Native Americans was not merely right but would restore America to its rightful heirs.

The growth pangs of the new nation soon gave way to imperial ambitions; the era of Manifest Destiny and America's entry onto the world stage required a suitably imperial mythology as precedent. In place of the Hebrews, former Minnesota congressman Ignatius Donnelly proposed the longest-lasting of American myths: the global empire of Atlantis, an expansionist power spreading civilization around the world, an almost transparent analogy for America's self-conception.[4] There was precedent for this, of course. The Spanish had previously claimed Atlantis as the founding population of America: "The Indies are either the island and firm land of Plato or the remnant of the same,"[5] Francisco López de Gómara had written in 1552, associating the new owners of the Americas, Spain, with a grand, mythic imperial predecessor. Atlantis recurred in Spanish writings for the next two centuries. It was, as always, the myth of the conquerors, beloved also in the British Empire and Imperial Germany, but of very little importance to the conquered.

The Atlantis theme, under another name, made its latest resurgence in the boom years of the 1990s, when the West celebrated the defeat of communism and stood astride the world like a colossus. In the last days of what George Will called the "holiday from history," British journalist Graham Hancock[6] capitalized on Western triumphalism by reviving the myth of an earlier, equally great, pre-Western civilization, which he declined to name but obviously meant as an analogue for Atlantis. His lost civilization was global, deeply spiritual, intellectually advanced, and composed of, it must be said, "lean, bearded white men" (specifically a "distinctively non-Indian ethnic type") who traveled to all the places where non-white people lived and gave them science, technology, and culture.[7] It is very difficult to read this theory—for which there is virtually no supporting evidence—as anything other than a reflection of the self-image of the "white" nations (America, Britain, Canada, Australia, etc.) in the moment of their shared Anglo-American cultural dominance.

Today, things are a little different. Western Civilization is plagued with a sense of decadence and decline diagnosed by Jacques Barzun in 2000[8] and exacerbated by 9/11, inconclusive warfare, and the economic crises of the past decade. The biggest economic story of the past twenty years has been the rise of China, and it is little wonder then that a few years ago in England, the fallen remnant of Empire, a retired submariner named Gavin Menzies[9] revived a forgotten claim by the German scholar Karl Friedrich Neumann (himself citing a 1761 French original) that an imperialist China had discovered and colonized America. When Neumann made this claim in the 1860s,[10] China was a colonial backwater, and the idea was seen as ridiculous and promptly forgotten, despite occasional revivals. It was no competitor for the glories of imperial Atlantis. Menzies' evidence differs from Neumann's (he favors a medieval date to Neumann's fifth-century one), though not in its low quality, but Menzies wrote in a different time, and his celebration of a resurgent China turned him into a celebrity and his claim into both a book and a multi-part PBS documentary. Atlantis has been all but forgotten in the *zeitgeist* (though not among various fringe communities, for whom no obscure idea is ever entirely forgotten[11]), a fatuous relic of imperial times, unfit for the current mood.

Instead, today we are experiencing a revival of a different kind of pseudoscience: the ancient astronaut theory, the claim that extraterrestrials arrived on the prehistoric earth and interacted with early humans, providing them with advanced culture. The government of China actively endorses this theory,[12] as did the Soviet government before it. In fact, the Soviets felt that the Chinese purposely supported the ancient astronaut theory as a way of channeling China's growing intellectual energy away from political reform.[13] The Soviets knew something about this; the Communist government endorsed the ancient astronaut theory from 1959 to 1970 as a secular alternative to religion because it provided a seemingly "scientific" explanation for angels, religious miracles, and the Bible that could be used for ideological purposes to undermine the religious ideas of the West.[14] To that end, the Soviet government allowed its scientists to fabricate evidence for ancient astronauts and disseminate that false evidence to the West, where it later appeared in the bestselling works of writers like Erich von Däniken and Zecharia Sitchin. Even the Russian-born French writer Jacques Bergier, a staunch believer in ancient astronauts, lamented in the 1970s that the Soviets "accept such evidence a little too easily, and it is not always very convincing."[15]

In 1970, the Soviet Academy of Physics put a stop to the nonsense and disclaimed the existence of ancient astronauts after a decade spent selling them to the West. This change of policy had been brewing since 1968, when the American embassy in Moscow noted that the country's media had suddenly turned on UFOs and ancient astronauts. New media reports debunking UFOs, the embassy wrote with great interest, made "no attempt to square this belief with previously published Soviet articles."[16] Perhaps one reason for the Soviet change of heart was the failure of ancient astronauts to displace religion in the West.

Right after the Soviets dropped them, ancient astronauts began a decade of unrivaled popularity in America, largely on the back of *Twilight Zone* creator Rod Serling's 1973 TV adaptation of an Academy Award-nominated German documentary about the theories of Swiss hotelier (and convicted embezzler) Erich von Däniken's *Chariots of the Gods* (1968). *In Search of Ancient Astronauts* was a cultural touchstone in the economically depressed decade of Watergate, oil shock, and fears of American decline. In the wake of *Time*'s famous question of whether God was dead, a sizable portion of the public embraced the idea of a superior race of saviors who could serve to restore traditional faith in God and His angels under another name.[17] But the idea wasn't new. Helena Blavatsky, the opportunistic founder of Theosophy, had imagined angels as extraterrestrial visitors from Venus in the nineteenth century, and the American preachers John Miller and George Van Tassel spent the 1950s and 1960s asking the public to worship aliens. Miller claimed God spoke through flying saucers like those in the Book of Ezekiel and Miller that Venusians were the true God of the Bible. For their troubles, both were monitored by the FBI as threats to national security and never achieved widespread popularity.

Not so Erich von Däniken. His theories, liberally borrowed (often verbatim) from Jacques Bergier, Louis Pauwels, and Robert Charroux (all of whom von Däniken eventually credited in a later edition of *Chariots* to stave off plagiarism charges), found him interviewed in *Playboy*, appearing with Johnny Carson on the *Tonight* show, and taking every opportunity to not just promote aliens but to advance his conservative political agenda. He took pains to stress that the ancient astronaut theory was fully compatible with traditional Christian religion[18] (despite his original contention that Jesus was an alien, deleted by his publisher[19]) and he lobbied then-president Gerald Ford to pander to UFO believers to secure re-election in 1976 and thus advance the conservative agenda for another four years. He urged the president to combat what he called "socialist dreamers" worldwide and to militarize space to protect Mars from communists.[20] Ford ignored the advice and lost the election, but von Däniken went on to become increasingly conservative, recently adopting the mantle of a prophet and promising that the aliens would return to judge the living and the dead for their "sins," including genetic engineering. He now claims the aliens will help us refute the liberal theories of global warming and human evolution.[21] The irony is that the ancient astronaut theory in Europe had been the tool of socialist New Agers like Jacques Bergier but in the U.S. had, through the agency of a Swiss, become a conservative counterweight to the New Age.

One of Von Däniken's bestselling rivals was Zecharia Sitchin, the late ancient astronaut theorist who claimed to be the only person on earth who correctly understood Sumerian, which he promptly confused with Akkadian (just as he confused Hebrew and Aramaic). Sitchin was less political than von Däniken, and as a result his theories, while less appealing to the mainstream media, have a smaller but more devoted following. In his "theory" the aliens were cosmic wanderers, traveling the universe in a mobile planet, obsessively collecting gold, manipulating other planets' politics, and reveling in their intellectual achievements and their cultivated separation from other species. The parallels to the anti-Semitic stereotype of the gold-hungry intellectual Jews who run the world in secret from their ghettos are so painfully obvious that only Sitchin, an Azerbaijani Jew who lived for years in Israel, could fail to see them. Sitchin unconsciously emphasized these parallels by drawing nearly all of his "evidence" for the aliens from Jewish texts and the Near Eastern myths the ancient Jews had interacted with.

A third contemporary theorist, Robert Temple, had some academics fooled with his claim that flying space frogs from Sirius gave civilization to the Sumerians, largely because of his ability to fill *The Sirius Mystery* (1976) with hundreds of footnotes to inaccurate and obsolete sources, which he misunderstood.[22] Several positive reviews by academics (though not archaeologists) gave Temple the patina of scholarship. But after his thesis was conclusively refuted by actual field research,[23] Temple descended into a New Age fog, imagining that the CIA, other world spy agencies, and "the hypnosis community" (don't ask) were stalking him across his home of London and they (not his scholarly shortcomings) were sabotaging his career.[24] While the U.S. government had investigated some ancient alien theorists with cult followings in the early 1960s, my own survey of all declassified CIA and other U.S. government documents finds no evidence of any interest in Temple or his Sirius "mystery."

The ancient astronaut theory had its heyday in the 1970s and gradually withered during the 1980s as economic prosperity drove away the spirit of ennui and returned America to a full-throated embrace of superpower status, reflected in renewed enthusiasm for the empire of Atlantis and its "lost civilization" mirror-images. But after 9/11 the heady confidence of the Atlantis empire-builders gave way to the aliens again, and the economic crisis of recent years opened the door to a renewed call for a mythic past of savior gods, especially those who could be expected to return to punish the wicked and reward the righteous, preferably by December 23, 2012, the (incorrectly assumed) end date of the Mayan calendar.

The rumblings of renewed interest in ancient astronauts began in the early years of the twenty-first century when the History Channel began running more frequent episodes of *History's Mysteries* exploring ancient astronauts, and other cable channels followed suit. By 2009, this spawned *Ancient Aliens*, a two-hour History Channel documentary (which, full disclosure, attacked me as a "skeptic") reintroducing the ancient astronaut theory. Ratings were so high that History commissioned *Ancient Aliens: The Series*, which has aired more than forty episodes since 2010 claiming alien intervention in everything from Stonehenge to the Revolutionary War. The program, led by charismatic "ancient astronaut theorist" Giorgio Tsoukalos (who, full disclosure, has actively disliked me since I interviewed him in college) and "lost civilization scholar" David Childress (who, again, full disclosure, has attacked me in print for labeling him an ancient astronaut theorist before he came out as such) offered speculation freed from facts, a comforting narrative about aliens as angels who would lift the souls of the dead to an extraterrestrial heaven (through a "quantum window" opened by human blood loss),[25] and a prophecy of the aliens' imminent return: "It's hard to know the future," Childress told viewers, "what's going to happen at the end of 2012—but it seems that perhaps the Mayans had some glimpse into the future that we have yet to find out."[26]

Freed from the earlier generation of writers' feints toward appropriating the legitimacy of science and scholarship, the new ancient astronaut theory of *Ancient Aliens* had become an all-out religious revival. (Creationists and fringe "spiritual" leaders were among its talking heads.) The "ancient astronaut theorists" asked viewers to worship the aliens and join them in condemning global warming, human evolution, and scientific inquiry as heresy against the aliens' agenda. The aliens are punishing us right now for our hubris with major earthquakes and hurricanes, the theorists, sounding like a wrathful Pat Robertson, said.[27] Instead, viewers were urged to equate the aliens with angels, pray for the aliens to spirit their consciousness to the aliens' plane of eternal bliss, and support traditional social and economic hierarchies as decreed by the aliens who were, in every sense that counts, gods.

The ancient astronaut theory, as depicted on *Ancient Aliens*, had collapsed in on itself. The twentieth century version of the theory had argued that ancient gods were really aliens; its modern religious version told *Ancient Aliens'* 1.5 million weekly viewers that the aliens were in fact their true gods. At least the Raëlians and Scientologists had the courtesy to admit upfront that their ancient astronaut theories were alternative religions. *Ancient Aliens'* slipshod pseudo-scholars wrap their faux-religion in the borrowed raiment of science and appear to pray for a future when they will be granted their rightful place as prophets, or kings.

Notes

[1] Strabo, *Geography*, 11.13-14; Justin, *Epitome*, 42.2-3.

[2] Justin, *Epitome*, 42.3; Strabo, *Geography*, 11.14.

[3] *Journal of the Senate*, Dec. 7, 1830, 24.

[4] Ignatius Donnelly, *Atlantis: The Antediluvian World* (New York: Harper and Brothers, 1882).

[5] Francisco López de Gómara, *Historia general de las Indias,* adapted from the translation appearing in Richard Eden, *The First Three English Books on America (?1511-1555 A.D.),* ed. Edward Arber (Westminster: Archibald Constable and Co., 1895), 347.

[6] In *Fingerprints of the Gods* (New York: Crown, 1995) and *Heaven's Mirror: The Quest for the Lost Civilization* (New York: Crown, 1998).

[7] *Fingerprints,* 45, 105. The white skin of the lost civilization's inhabitants is mentioned twelve times in *Fingerprints.*

[8] In *From Dawn to Decadence: 500 Years of Western Cultural Life* (New York: Harper Collins, 2000).

[9] In *1421: The Year China Discovered America* (Harper Perennial, 2004).

[10] Charles G. Leland, *Fusang: Or, the Discovery of America by Chinese Buddhist Priests in the Fifth Century* (London: Trübner & Co., 1875).

[11] The conservative Jewish scholar Richard Freund, for example, has employed pseudo-scientific methods to appropriate Atlantis as the Biblical kingdom of Tarshish in order to "prove" the Bible's King Solomon narrative true, a theory he shared in the 2011 National Geographic Channel documentary *Finding Atlantis.* (See Chapter 41.)

[12] The Chinese National Science and Technology Department staged an exhibition in Beijing in July 2012 endorsing supposedly 100-million-year-old extraterrestrial jade sculptures. See Yin Yeping, "Unraveling the X-Files," *Global Times* (China), June 25, 2012 and "Carved 'Aliens' in Ancient Times," *People's Daily Online,* July 18, 2012.

[13] See A. D. Dikaryov, "Unidentified Flying Objects (UFO) in Ancient China," *Narody Azii i Afriki,* July-August 1989.

[14] See James A. Herrick, *Scientific Mythologies* (InterVarsity, 2008), 49, 67.

[15] Jacques Bergier, *Extraterrestrial Visitation from Prehistoric Times to the Present* (New York: Regnery, 1973), 133.

[16] U.S. Moscow embassy airgram to U.S. Dept. of State, "Flying Saucers Are a Myth," February 20, 1968.

[17] The simultaneous return of religious conservatism can also be attributed to many of the same forces arising from a crisis of confidence in the secular culture of the 1960s and 1970s, and sparked, in part, by popular culture, particularly the movie version of *The Exorcist* (1973). See Michael W. Cuneo, *American Exorcism* (New York: Broadway Books, 2001).

[18] As he put it, "There's no reason to say Jesus came from space." (Erich von Däniken, interview with Timothy Ferris, *Playboy,* August 1974, 151.)

[19] "Pop Theology: Those Gods from Outer Space," *Time,* September 5, 1969.

[20] Erich von Däniken to Gerald Ford, January 8, 1976. This extraordinary document is housed in the National Archives in College Park, Maryland but was released upon my request, and I have posted it on my website, JasonColavito.com.

[21] See Erich von Däniken, *Twilight of the Gods* (Pompton Plains, NJ: New Page Books, 2009).

[22] See my "Golden Fleeced: The Misuse of the Argonaut Myth in Robert Temple's *Sirius Mystery*," *eSkeptic*, May 2010.

[23] See Walter E. A. Van Beek, "Dogon Restudied: A Field Evaluation of the Work of Marcel Griaule," *Current Anthropology* 32 (1992): p. 139-167.

[24] Robert Temple, *The Sirius Mystery: New Scientific Evidence of Alien Contact 5,000 Years Ago* (Rochester, VT: Destiny Books, 1998), 7-10; Robert Temple, "Who Was Moses," *New Dawn*, special issue 8, Winter 2009, 53.

[25] "Aliens and the Undead," *Ancient Aliens*, History Channel, October 26, 2011.

[26] "The Doomsday Prophesies," *Ancient Aliens*, H2, February 17, 2012.

[27] "Aliens and Mega-Disasters," *Ancient Aliens*, H2, March 2, 2012.

2. The Origin of the Space Gods[1]

I. Aliens in the Mythos

ONE OF THE most dramatic ideas found in H. P. Lovecraft's weird fiction known as the Cthulhu Mythos is the suggestion that extraterrestrial beings arrived on earth in the distant past, were responsible for ancient works of monumental stone architecture, and inspired mankind's earliest mythologies and religions. In the 1970s, this basic premise was resurrected as the "ancient astronaut theory," a fringe hypothesis that gained widespread popularity thanks to Swiss hotelier Erich von Däniken's book *Chariots of the Gods?* (1968) and its television adaptation, *In Search of Ancient Astronauts* (1973), hosted by Rod Serling, of *Twilight Zone* fame. According to research done by Kenneth L. Feder, at the height of von Däniken's popularity in the 1970s and '80s one in four college students accepted the ancient astronaut theory, but twenty years later less than ten percent did.[2]

Though mainstream science does not recognize extraterrestrial intervention in human history, the theory continues to receive exposure on cable television documentaries, in magazines, and in a plethora of books.

Providence, Rhode Island author H.P. Lovecraft (1890-1937) has been justly hailed as a master of the horror story, and his work claims a place beside Edgar Allan Poe and Stephen King in the pantheon of the genre. Born into a wealthy family in 1890, Lovecraft's life was a series of reverses and declines as his family lost their fortune and his parents succumbed to madness. He was a precocious and self-taught scholar who read voracious-ly and devoured as much literature as he could read. He read the novels of H.G. Wells, whose *War of the Worlds* told of the coming of alien creatures to earth. He also read the eighteenth-century Gothic masters of horror, and above all Edgar Allan Poe. He also read works of pseudoscience and mysticism for inspiration.

When he set about writing his own works, he began to blend the mod-ern world of science fiction with his favorite tales of Gothic gloom. Love-craft tried to bring the Gothic tale into the twentieth century, modernizing the trappings of ancient horror for a new century of science. Lovecraft published his work in pulp fiction magazines, notably *Weird Tales*, though some of his works were not published until after his death in 1937. Throughout the 1940s and 1950s, science fiction and horror magazines reprinted Lovecraft's tales numerous times, and he became one of the most popular pulp authors.

Lovecraft's works banished the supernatural by recasting it in materi-alist terms. He took the idea of a pantheon of ancient gods and made them a group of aliens who descended to earth in the distant past.

Across his works, Lovecraft provided a number of different explana-tions for the arrival ancient visitors on the primeval earth. In "The Call of Cthulhu," the Old Ones, including the tentacled, star-born Cthulhu, are said to have come "to the young world out of the sky" and to have raised mighty cities whose remains could be seen in the cyclopean stones dotting Pacific islands. These Old Ones brought with them images of themselves (thus inventing art) and hieroglyphs once legible but now unknown (the origins of writing). They spoke to humans in their dreams, and established a cult to worship them (the origins of religion). They appeared as, and were treated like, monstrous living gods, so great were their mystical powers.

> Old Castro remembered bits of hideous legend that paled the speculations
> of theosophists and made man and the world seem recent and transient
> indeed. There had been aeons when other Things ruled on the earth, and

They had had great cities. Remains of Them, he said the deathless Chinamen had told him, were still be found as Cyclopean stones on islands in the Pacific. They all died vast epochs of time before men came, but there were arts which could revive Them when the stars had come round again to the right positions in the cycle of eternity. They had, indeed, come themselves from the stars, and brought Their images with Them. These Great Old Ones, Castro continued, were not composed altogether of flesh and blood. They had shape—for did not this star-fashioned image prove it?—but that shape was not made of matter. When the stars were right, They could plunge from world to world through the sky; but when the stars were wrong, They could not live.[3]

In later stories, Lovecraft added new details and altered his previous conception of the Old Ones to provide a richer and more developed picture of alien intervention in earth life. In *At the Mountains of Madness*, Lovecraft presents his most complete vision of the extraterrestrial origins of human life. Here, the Old Ones were now a separate species of alien creature at war with Great Cthulhu and his spawn, who only arrived eons later. The Old Ones were "the originals of the fiendish elder myths" of ancient mythology,[4] and they raised great cities under the oceans and on the primitive continents. These beings arrived on earth after colonizing other planets, and they created life on earth a source of food. These artificial primitive cells they allowed to evolve naturally into the plants and animals of the modern world—including primitive humanity, which they used as food or entertainment.

Elsewhere, Lovecraft described his ancient visitors as maintaining a presence on the modern earth, and like the Nephilim of the Bible, they begat children with earth women in *The Dunwich Horror, The Shadow Over Innsmouth,* and "Medusa's Coil." In "The Horror in the Museum," it is suggested that the monstrous creatures once worshipped as gods were not all extraterrestrials, and that some may have come from alternate dimensions. In *The Shadow Out of Time*, the extraterrestrial Great Race is one of countless species spanning the universe, and their mental powers let them project themselves backward and forward in time, gathering intelligence and knowledge for their library and, in places, imparting their own wisdom. Most to the point, in his ghostwriting of William Lumley's "The Diary of Alonzo Typer" the title narrator learns from the pre-human *Book of Dzyan* that aliens from Venus came to earth in spaceships to "civilize" the planet.

Human knowledge of these aliens is fragmentary and obscure. Evidence exists in the form of anomalous ancient artifacts of pre-human manufacture, garbled folklore and mythology, and written texts like the *Necronomicon, Nameless Cults,* and the *Book of Eibon,* which hint at but do not fully disclose the extraterrestrials' nature and habits.

Many critics of Lovecraft have noted that his vision for the Mythos changed over time, as the godlike and semi-supernatural Cthulhu of "The Call of Cthulhu" gradually gave way to the fully material aliens of *At the Mountains of Madness*; in time faux mythology gave way to faux science in the Mythos. Many Mythos writers, beginning with August Derleth, were dismayed by the contradictions in Lovecraft's writing (e.g., Cthulhu is an Old One in "Cthulhu" but merely their "cousin" in "The Dunwich Horror"; the Old Ones change identity several times, too), and they have attempted to systematize the Mythos. However, Lovecraft's writings reflect the way real myths develop, with changes and contradictions and anomalies. This is compounded by the fact that Lovecraft did not write as an omniscient narrator but rather presented his Mythos through the eyes of scholars and writers who had only part of the story and therefore could not offer the whole truth. Even in the *Necronomicon* Abdul Alhazred (it is implied) was privy only to hints and rumors and interpreted the Mythos through the guise of the Near Eastern mythologies he knew. "These viscous masses were without doubt what Abdul Alhazred whispered about as the 'Shoggoths' in his frightful *Necronomicon,* though even that mad Arab had not hinted that any existed on earth except in the dreams of those who had chewed a certain alkaloidal herb."[5]

In other words, Lovecraft's Mythos tales show us a fragmented, shifting, and uncertain view of the alien beings reflected through the biases and prejudices and mental limits of those who encounter them.

* * *

II. Ancient Astronauts before Lovecraft

The idea that life could exist on other worlds was not unique to Lovecraft, of course, and the concept had a long history dating back to early Greek philosophers who speculated on the nature of beings on other worlds. Anaxagoras (c. 500-428 BCE) proposed that life began from "seeds" that littered the universe; Anaxarchus (c. 340 BCE) thought there to be an infinity of worlds, and Epicurus (c. 341-270 BCE) felt life existed on many planets across the vastness of space. These philosophers, though, did not propose the visitation of these aliens to the earth.

The most important early writer to propose extraterrestrial visitation on earth was Madame Helena Blavatsky (1831-1891), the founder of Theosophy, a Victorian-era amalgam of Spiritualism, Eastern religions, and good old-fashioned hokum. In *The Secret Doctrine*, Theosophy's most important text, Blavatsky noted Greek speculation about life on other worlds and asserted that the ancients had first-hand knowledge of the fact of extraterrestrial existence. She speculated that the beings on the innumerable inhabited worlds may have "influence" or "control" over the earth. She also asserted that spiritual beings originating on the moon contributed to the metaphysical development of earth life:

> The first race of men were, then, simply the images, the astral doubles, of their Fathers, who were the pioneers, or the most progressed Entities from a preceding though *lower* sphere, the shell of which is now our Moon. But even this shell is all-potential, for, having generated the Earth, it is the *phantom* of the Moon which, attracted by magnetic affinity, sought to form its first inhabitants, the pre-human monsters.[6]

But for her any alien intervention is a sideline to the epic history of evolutionary and spiritual developments of an assortment of earth creatures who grew from primal ooze to Aryan supremacy on the lost continents of Hyperborea, Lemuria, and Atlantis.

Blavatsky's disciple W. Scott-Elliot expanded on hints in the Theosophical cosmos by creating a race of divine beings inhabiting Venus. In *The Lost Lemuria* (1904), Scott-Elliot claimed that beings that evolved on Venus but had reached a spiritual or "divine" stage of development came to earth and taught the inhabitants of Lemuria the arts of civilization and gave them wheat and fire.[7] A critical difference between the lords of Venus, Blavatsky's moon creatures, and Mythos beings (and indeed modern ancient astronauts) is that the Theosophical Venusians and lunarians are not envisioned as true extraterrestrials (in the modern sense) from distant star systems but as incarnations of spiritual beings who share a mystic connection to earth creatures and feel a spiritual calling to aid their brethren on earth. Here, the Venusians are inhabitants of Venus in the same sense that the angels of God were once thought to inhabit Venus, Mars, and the other crystalline spheres that surrounded the earth. As Scott-Eliot put it:

> The positions occupied by the divine beings from the Venus chain were naturally those of rulers, instructors in religion, and teachers of the arts, and it is in this latter capacity that a reference to the arts taught by them comes to our aid in the consideration of the history of this early race, continued.[8]

In 1919, the great collector of anomalous trivia, Charles Fort, published the *Book of the Damned,* in which he speculated that old stories of demons could be related to "undesirable visitors from other worlds,"[9] though he did not draw a firm connection between devils and aliens. He also suggested that other worlds may have communicated with ours in the distant past, left behind advanced technology, or attempted to colonize the earth.[10] "If other worlds have ever in the past had relations with this earth, they were attempted positivizations: to extend themselves, by colonies, upon this earth; to convert, or assimilate, indigenous inhabitants of this earth."[11]

However, Fort made no claim that such things actually happened, only that they *may* have happened, and at any rate there is no way to tell whether the creatures were alien, trans-dimensional, spiritual, or even imaginary—perhaps the result of telepathy, communications from the spirit realm, or from myriad other sources.

H. P. Lovecraft read both *The Book of the Damned* and Scott-Elliot's compilation volume *The Story of Atlantis and Lost Lemuria* (1925), and from these fragmentary ideas about prehistoric extraterrestrial visitation imagined (more-or-less) flesh-and-blood aliens arriving on earth in the distant past and all that this implied.

III. Ancient Astronauts after Lovecraft

Lovecraft's Mythos became one of the touchstones of modern horror literature and a powerful theme in horror, fantasy, and science fiction, where the idea of alien visitors in the deep past continues to enjoy popularity in contemporary works like *Stargate*, *The X-Files*, *Doctor Who*, *Alien vs. Predator*, and hundreds of other movies, books, and television shows. However, Lovecraft's alien gods also spawned the decidedly non-fiction (if not factual) ancient astronaut theory, which continues to convert new adherents today.

The names of Lovecraft's alien gods, like Cthulhu, Yog-Sothoth, and Shub-Niggurath, began to crop up in other stories during Lovecraft's lifetime. Lovecraft himself started this practice by inserting these names, or variants on them, into stories he ghostwrote or revised for other authors. In his revision of Zelia Bishop's "The Mound," for example, Lovecraft slipped his alien god Cthulhu into the story under the variant name Tulu, giving magazine readers what they thought were independent stories featuring references to the same ancient gods. By the 1960s, several dozen authors were using elements of what came to be called "The Cthulhu Mythos" in stories they wrote for science fiction and horror magazines.

Lovecraftian fiction became increasingly popular in Europe, where the French embraced him as a bent genius, much as they embraced Edgar Allan Poe. In France, the Russian expatriate Jacques Bergier and the writer Louis Pauwels read Lovecraft and were inspired by his cosmic vision. Bergier claimed to have corresponded with Lovecraft in 1935, though no letters survive. He spent much of the 1950s promoting Lovecraft in the French media, including the magazine he and Pauwels edited, *Planète*, and working to bring Lovecraft's work out in French editions. *Planète*'s editors held Lovecraft as their prophet, and their reprints of his stories helped to popularize him and the Cthulhu Mythos in the French imagination.

Digging into Lovecraft's Theosophical and Fortean source material, Bergier and Pauwels wrote *Le Matin des magiciens* (1960) (published in English as *The Morning of the Magicians*) and presented the first fully-fledged modern ancient astronaut theory. In it, they presented the themes found in Lovecraft as nonfiction, speculating about such alternative history touchstones as the "true" origin of the Egyptian pyramids, ancient maps that appear to have been drawn from outer space, advanced technology incongruously placed in the ancient past, and the other staples of later ancient astronaut theories. They note that ancient mythologies are replete with gods who visit earth in fiery chariots and return to the sky. These, they state, may have been alien visitors in spaceships.

Pauwels and Bergier drew on unrelated writings from a number of French and other authors who wondered to a greater or lesser extent whether modern UFO sightings might have antecedents in prehistory, but they combined this 1950s space-age speculation with a Lovecraftian cosmic vision and a New Age sensibility that translated Cthulhu into an ancient astronaut in a way that shiny atom-age extraterrestrials in spacesuits never could.

Morning of the Magicians became one of the most important sources for Erich von Däniken, the Swiss writer whose *Chariots of the Gods?* (1968) brought what had hitherto been a theory known only to Theosophists, Lovecraft aficionados, and fringe theorists into the cultural mainstream. Von Däniken did not mention Pauwels and Bergier in his works, however, until a lawsuit forced him to disclose the sources he closely paraphrased in *Chariots*. The bibliography of *Chariots* thereafter listed the French writers' book in its 1962 German translation, *Aufbruch ins dritte Jahrtausend*. Tens of millions of copies of *Chariots* and its sequels sold, and the ancient astronaut theory became a cultural phenomenon, appearing in movies, on Johnny Carson's *Tonight Show*, in *Playboy*, and practically anywhere people were talking about the past.

Other authors were inspired by von Däniken's theories, including Robert Temple (whose *Sirius Mystery* argued that amphibious aliens from Sirius taught Sumerians civilization) and Zecharia Sitchin (whose *Twelfth Planet* argued that aliens from a "wandering" planet called Nibiru conquered ancient earth to steal its gold and other precious metals). By the end of the 1970s, there was an entire network of authors and promoters then known as the Ancient Astronaut Society (later the Archaeology, Astronautics and SETI Research Association, or AAS RA; now the Ancient Alien Society). As of this writing, the H2 channel broadcasts *Ancient Astronauts: The Series*, a weekly program that explores the work of von Däniken and other ancient astronaut theorists. The program was seen by more than two million viewers each week when it aired on the History Channel before it moved to sister station H2 in 2012. The ancient astronaut theory also appeared in movies and television series, ranging from the various incarnations of *Stargate* to Ridley Scott's *Prometheus* (2012), a film that the famed *Alien* director explicitly modeled on von Däniken's 1970s bestsellers: "NASA and the Vatican agree that is almost mathematically impossible that we can be where we are today without there being a little help along the way... That's what we're looking at (in the film), at some of Eric von Daniken's ideas of how did we humans come about."[12]

So what made so many believe aliens visited our ancestors?

IV. The Evidence for Aliens

The ancient astronaut theory, as it developed in the hands of Pauwels and Bergier, von Däniken, and others, uses a combination of suggestive archaeological, mythological, and artistic evidence. Though believers interpret nearly every piece of ancient history as supporting the ancient astronaut theory, in outline, the most important evidence is as follows:

Archaeological

Believers maintain that ancient cities and monuments the world over display three important properties that speak to their non-human origins. First, many are composed of stones that weigh so much that it seems impossible for ordinary humans to have moved them. For example, the blocks making up the Great Pyramid of Egypt weigh as much as fifty tons each, and the stones of the Incan fortress of Sacsayhuaman weigh as much as two hundred tons. Further, believers hold that these ancient sites are laid out and constructed with a precision that is unmatched by all but the most modern of contemporary constructions. The Great Pyramid, for instance, is said to be placed on a base within 0.049 inches of flat; its sides are oriented to the cardinal directions within three minutes of arc, something unmatched in nearly all modern constructions. Such engineering is said to be possible only with alien help, either as the builders themselves or as teachers who imparted the knowledge of such building techniques.

Second, believers argue that ancient sites and artifacts encode scientific data that should be unknown to Stone Age peoples. The Great Pyramid, to take a familiar example, is said to be an accurate scale model of the northern hemisphere of the earth thousands of years before Eratosthenes first estimated the planet's circumference. It is also said to be placed in the exact center of the earth's land masses. The monumental pyramids of the ancient Mexican city of Teotihuacan are often said to be a scale model of the solar system.

Third, anomalous artifacts represent advanced technology of possibly inhuman origin. The famous "Baghdad battery" is a small jar that may have held electrodes that when exposed to vinegar could have produced a small electrical charge. Small golden bees from Mexico may be depictions of ancient airplanes. A sparkplug may have been found inside a billion-year-old rock known as the Coso artifact.

Mythological

Ancient myths and legends record the arrival of the aliens and their deeds upon the earth. Believers in the ancient astronaut theory are united in their belief that myths and holy books are factual accounts of events that happened in the real world. The apocryphal Book of Enoch is a favorite, along with the legend of the Jewish prophet ascending to heaven in a fiery chariot. The Biblical vision of Ezekiel, who saw a fiery apparition of interlocking wheels, is said to represent an encounter with a flying saucer.

The destruction of Sodom and Gomorrah in fire and brimstone is suggested to be an account of aliens dropping an atomic bomb. Elsewhere, mythological appearances of savior gods such as Oannes in Sumer, Osiris in Egypt, Quetzalcoatl in Mexico, and Viracocha in Peru are thought to be factual accounts of anthropomorphic aliens bringing civilization to benighted ancient tribes. Hindu mythology is an especially rich source of proof because of its descriptions of flying machines, ray guns, and explosions that resemble atomic detonations.

And of course, like the Old Ones in *At the Mountains of Madness*, the gods who created humans and other earth life in myth and religion are here interpreted as aliens that genetically engineered earth life for their inscrutable purposes. They also manage earth life, like the Old Ones who wipe out unfavorable races, by sending floods or annihilating trouble spots with nuclear weapons.

Artistic

Ancient art shows images of the aliens and their advanced technology, according to believers. Aboriginal cave art in Australia depicts beings with circles around their heads, obviously the helmets of space-faring aliens. Similarly, ancient Japanese statuary of rotund monsters actually shows aliens in bulky spacesuits. Medieval paintings are said to contain images of flying discs or aerodynamic chariots that resemble flying saucers and rocket ships. The lid of the tomb of the Mayan king Palenque does not show the king in the underworld but rather depicts him at the controls of technological device, perhaps a rocket ship. An image of a lotus blossom in the Egyptian temple of Dendera is really a depiction of a light bulb, complete with power cord and filament. Ancient maps are believed to show a) earth as depicted from space, b) the world as it existed in the Ice Age before human civilization, c) Antarctica centuries before its discovery in 1818.

V. The Science

Archaeologists, paleontologists, anthropologists, and other scientific

professionals were less than impressed by the web of suggestion and interpretation that masqueraded as a scientific hypothesis. Since the mid-
1970s, skeptics have produced articles, books, and documentaries aimed
at debunking the ancient astronaut theory and explaining its "evidence" as
a series of misinterpretations, misrepresentations, and ignorance of scientific research. It would be impossible to thoroughly explore the scientific
arguments against the ancient astronaut theory in anything short of a
book (for which, see my 2005 book, the *The Cult of Alien Gods*[13]), but the
general lines of argument run like this:

Archaeological

No evidence of extraterrestrial technology has ever been found on
earth, and no artifact can conclusively be tied to a planet other than earth.
Such claims are exaggerations, misinterpretations, or frauds. For example,
the alleged Coso artifact is not a billion-year-old bit of advanced technology but a 1920s spark plug encrusted in solidified crud mistaken for ancient
rock. Ancient monuments show every sign of being constructed by the
ancient people who lived around them, as demonstrated by the artifacts
found in, around, on top of, and under ancient sites. Construction of buildings—even highly precise and heavy ones—can be accomplished with
large numbers of people working together.

Mythological

Ancient myths do not have a direct correlation with events in the distant past. Instead, they are complex web of symbolism, religious belief,
historical events, and imagination. There may be some distorted truth behind myths (as the discovery of Troy proved for Homer's *Iliad*), but they
cannot be interpreted as literal accounts of historic happenings. Nor are
the myths themselves consistent across time. The myth of Jason and the
Golden Fleece, for example, shows significant changes to major events
between its earliest recorded forms and the best-known version, written by
Apollonius of Rhodes many centuries later. In the earliest forms of the
myth, it is unclear whether the Golden Fleece was even present—a far cry

from those like Robert Temple or Erich von Däniken who assumed that one version of the myth stood for all, could be considered definitive, and could be interpreted literally as evidence of alien intervention. Mythology must be seen in its cultural context, and any interpretation must account for changes, distortions, and mutations that accrue over time as oral stories are retold, come into contact with stories from other cultures and lands, and eventually take on a written form. This is not unlike the contradictory variants of Mythos legends found in Lovecraft's own stories.

Artistic

Again, ancient art should not be taken as a literal recording of events happening before the artists' eyes. Many works of prehistoric art, such as cave paintings, depict shamans engaged in rituals designed to imbue them with the powers of the netherworld and their spirit animals. These cannot be taken literally but must be seen in cultural context and in terms of the visions of strange shapes and forms humans see when in shamanic trance states. Other pieces of ancient art, like the Dendera light bulb or Palenque's coffin lid, must be viewed in light of other artistic depictions from the period, not by itself, in order to understand the symbolism and artistic conventions used in the work. Neither seems so much like ancient depictions of technology when compared to other Egyptian depictions of the lotus, or Mayan funerary art. No one piece exists in isolation, and an interpretation based only on what something "looks like" instead of its place in the broader cultural picture will lead to mistaken correlations.

VI. Conclusions

The novelist and Lovecraft scholar Richard L. Tierney noted the potential correlations between Lovecraft's story "The Mound" (with Zealia Bishop) and actual Mesoamerican and Native American legends and traditions, and he identifies Yig, father of serpents, with the Aztec god Quetzalcoatl, the feathered serpent. At Teotihuacan, the Mexican city so old and mysterious that even the Aztecs themselves knew it only as a ruin belonging to the gods who descended from the sky, Tierney humorously identifies the sculptures of tentacled Tlaloc the rain god and serpentine Quetzalcoatl on Quetzalcoatl's temple as representations of Cthulhu and Yig.[14] Thus is the ancient astronaut theorists' evidence for aliens transformed again into proof of the Mythos. This, of course, was meant in jest, but the same reasoning transformed ancient achievements into alien interventions.

In 1982, Charles Garofalo and Robert M. Price wrote an article for *Crypt of Cthulhu* noting the similarities between the Mythos and Erich von Däniken's ancient astronaut theories. They concluded that despite the high degree of correlation between von Däniken's evidence and claims and Lovecraft's fictional conceits, direct influence was impossible because von Däniken denied ever having read or heard of Lovecraft.[15] As we have seen, though, the influence need not be direct. The connections between those who propose ancient astronauts as fact and those who write of them as (science) fiction are myriad, and the web of influence runs in many directions. Perhaps someday the Great Race will swap minds with some of us and tell the world how aliens once ruled the past, but until that happens, Cthulhu will have to rest in his tomb and the ancient astronauts will have to stay in their fictional chariots.

Notes

[1] This article contains some material that originally appeared in "Charioteer of the Gods," *Skeptic* 10.4 (2004). This version first ran in *Dark Lore 7* (Daily Grail, 2012).

[2] Kenneth L. Feder, "Skeptics, Fence-Sitters, and True Believers: Student Acceptance of an Improbable Prehistory," in Garrett G. Fagan (ed.), *Archaeological Fantasies* (New York: Routledge, 2006), 78.

[3] H. P. Lovecraft, "The Call of Cthulhu," in *The Fiction* (New York: Barnes & Noble, 2008), 367.

[4] H. P. Lovecraft, *At the Mountains of Madness*, in *The Fiction*, 769.

[5] Ibid., 771.

[6] Helena Blavatsky, *The Secret Doctrine*, Vol. 2: Anthropogenesis (Point Loma, California: The Aryan Theosophical Press, 1917), 115.

[7] W. Scott-Elliot, *The Lost Lemuria* (London: Theosophical Publishing Society, 1904), 34-44.

[8] Ibid., 36.

[9] Charles Fort, *The Book of the Damned* (New York: Boni and Liveright, 1919), 66.

[10] Ibid., 118, 124, 164.

[11] Ibid., 164.

[12] Scott Roxborough, "Ridley Scott, Michael Fassbender, Noomi Rapace Tease 'Prometheus' at CineEurope," *The Hollywood Reporter* [online], June 28, 2011.

[13] Jason Colavito, *The Cult of Alien Gods: H. P. Lovecraft and Extraterrestrial Pop Culture* (Prometheus, 2005).

[14] Richard L. Tierney, "Cthulhu in Mesoamerica," *Crypt of Cthulhu* no. 9 (1981).

[15] Robert M. Price and Charles Garofalo, "Chariots of the Old Ones?", in Robert M. Price (ed.), *Black, Forbidden Things: Cryptical Secrets from the "Crypt of Cthulhu"* (Mercer Island, WA: Starmont House, 1992), 86-87.

3. Pauwels, Bergier, and Lovecraft

IN MY FIRST BOOK, *The Cult of Alien Gods,* as well as in the preceding chapter of this book, I outline a series of mostly uncontested facts that demonstrate the direct connection between the horror author H. P. Lovecraft and the ancient astronaut theory as developed by Erich von Däniken and those inspired by him. These facts are as follows:

- Many modern ancient astronaut theorists were directly inspired by Erich von Däniken's *Chariots of the Gods* (1968), though this was not the first or only ancient astronaut theory, merely the most popular. Most others took inspiration from *Morning of the Magicians* (1960) by the French writers Louis Pauwels and Jacques Bergier. Most acknowledge this debt.

- In writing his book, Erich von Däniken drew on *Morning of the Magicians* to such a degree that he was forced by threat of lawsuit to acknowledge his borrowings in later editions of *Chariots of the Gods.*

- Louis Pauwels and Jacques Bergier were both fans of Lovecraft and found inspiration for their ancient astronaut theory in Lovecraft's writing.

Really, that's it. Everything else is window-dressing around these three key facts.

However, critics who disagree with my theory have frequently contested that I have failed to sufficiently demonstrate that Pauwels and Bergier were inspired by Lovecraft to create their ancient astronaut theory despite the well-established connections between the French authors and the American horror writer. For these critics, Lovecraft is merely a sidelight in a story that travels exclusively through non-fiction works, from Charles Fort and Theosophy to Pauwels and Bergier and thus to modern theorists. But this ignores the evidence.

Bergier, for example, asserted throughout his life that he had been a correspondent of Lovecraft (no letters survive), and both he and Pauwels translated and published the first French editions of Lovecraft's work. Nor am I the only writer to have noted such a connection; in *Lovecraft: A Study in the Fantastic* (1984), Maurice Lévy took issue with the French writers' implication that Lovecraft considered reality to be plastic when he was in fact a scientific materialist. In 2003, Gary Valentine Lachman discussed in *Turn off Your Mind* how Bergier championed Lovecraft in the 1940s and 1950s. Both of these works predate my own.

I believe that a direct quotation from the earlier *Morning of the Magicians* should settle any lingering doubt about the connection and firmly establish once again that the two French writers not only knew Lovecraft prior to writing *Morning* but drew on his work in developing their own.

> As an example of militant action in favour of the greatest possible degree of open-mindedness, and as an initiation into the cosmic consciousness, the works of Charles Fort have been a direct source of inspiration for the greatest poet and champion of the theory of parallel universes, H. P. Lovecraft, the father of what has come to be known as Science-Fiction to which he has contributed some ten or fifteen masterpieces of their kind, a sort of Iliad and Odyssey of a forward-marching civilization. To a certain extent, we too have been inspired in our task by the spirit of Charles Fort.[1]

From this passage, we can clearly establish a few key facts about Pauwels and Bergier in 1960:

- The two authors both knew of and thought highly of Lovecraft prior to writing *Morning of the Magicians*.
- The two authors considered Lovecraft to have embodied real theories ("greatest...champion of theory") in his fiction.

From Lovecraft, the authors explored Lovecraft's own sources, including Charles Fort, and from those sources and Lovecraft therefore developed their own version of the earlier authors' ancient astronaut theories. Had they come to Fort unmediated, there would be no reason to acknowledge the connection to Lovecraft, which they again make when discussing Arthur Machen, another author whose work the two French writers encountered via mentions in the work of Lovecraft.

This should establish the connection between Pauwels and Bergier beyond doubt. The French writers did not rely on Lovecraft as a primary source in *Morning of the Magicians* because they were (or believed they were) writing non-fiction and recognized that Lovecraft's work was fictional. They did, however, acknowledge his inspiration for leading them back to the sources he drew upon, including Fort and Theosophy, which the French writers used as Lovecraft had to develop their own work. Unlike Lovecraft, they thought they were creating fact, not fiction.

Bergier well understood that there was an obvious parallel between the Cthulhu Mythos and the ancient astronaut theory, one striking enough that he came to feel that he had to address the question in *Extraterrestrial Visitations from Prehistoric Times to the Present* (1970; English trans. 1973), a deeply weird book, perhaps the strangest ancient astronaut book I've ever read. The unnamed translator of the book, whoever he or she was, clearly had no real understanding of the material being translated, making an already obscure text that much more bizarre. Thus, in the first excerpted passages below, the name of Lovecraft's Old Ones is a bit butchered.

> Perhaps the [alien] Intelligences will be forced to wipe out our species [...] In any case, the Intelligences seem far removed from H. P. Lovecraft's Great Old Men, who created life on the earth by mistake or as a joke."[2] (referencing *At the Mountains of Madness*)

"[A lost] civilization could have been in [...] the extreme south: Antarctica. The ghosts of H. P. Lovecraft and Erle Cox [...] will rejoice when the traces of an advanced civilization in the Antarctic are discovered. It will be one more case of clairvoyance by inspired writers."[3] (referencing *At the Mountains of Madness* and Erle Cox's 1919 novel *Out of the Silence*, about the buried remains of a lost civilization)

"...there once existed a city in the desert, El Yafri, built of enormous cyclopean blocks [...] and the city should not be confused with Irem, H. P. Lovecraft's doomed city..."[4] (referencing "The Nameless City," but unaware that Irem, or Iram, is from the Qur'an 89:6-14)

"This book is as much a factual accounting as possible. However, among its readers there will certainly be some science-fiction fans who would like to know what the connection is between the mysteries we have described in this chapter and the myths created by H. P. Lovecraft [...] Much of [Lovecraft's work] relates so directly to the mysteries we have just described that there are still people who go to the Biblioteque Nationale or to the British Museum and ask for the *Necronomicon*! [...] It is not impossible that at least a part of Lovecraft's myth may be verified when the Empty Quarter is opened to exploration."[5] (referencing "The Nameless City")

Throughout, Bergier makes plain his debt to science fiction in general and H. P. Lovecraft in particular for inspiring his investigations into prehistory; even where unnecessary, Bergier emphasizes parallels between Lovecraft and the ancient mysteries he relates.

Extraterrestrial Visitations is a deeply European book, beginning with the author's insistence that he held an "exclusively rationalist position" even as he then proceeds to pile speculation upon speculation, often without any factual support, in the name of inductive reasoning. He assumes the reader is already familiar with the mysteries he discusses, leaving out conventional references, background information, and anything more than allusions to Victorian newspaper clippings and Fortean speculation. As a result, the text is frequently obscure, understandable only with a deep familiarity with the ancient mystery genre—and with Lovecraft.

Bergier devotes a chapter to the infamous case of Dr. Gurlt's cube, which he describes as being a 60 million year old perfect cube made of iron, with two opposite faces slightly curved. It had been found in a mine in Austria in 1885, and Bergier made three false claims about it: first, that it is perfect in form; second, it is an extraterrestrial recording device meant to transmit information about earth to outer space; and third, that a conspiracy is responsible for having made the object "disappear" from the Salzburg Museum so scholars like Bergier could never confirm its extraterrestrial origins.

Weirdly for someone writing in 1970, Bergier was completely unaware the object was analyzed in Vienna in 1967 when he wrote of how badly he wanted modern science to examine it. It is in all probability, as Dr. Gurlt suggested in 1886, a lump of meteoric iron. The rock itself is not a cube in any recognizable sense, much less a device of perfect machine manufacture, what he called "*data collectors* of the same type as magnetic bands, but much more highly perfected." It is instead a small, pockmarked stone of very roughly square shape when viewed from one angle, but appearing round when viewed in profile, with a deep ridge impressed around its circumference.

Furthermore, the ancient astronaut writer Peter Kolosimo argued that it could not have disappeared from the Salzburg Museum in Austria because it's actually in the *Salisbury* Museum, in Britain. (After consulting his original Italian text, I'm not so sure this isn't Kolosimo's translation error for Salzburg—not least because the name of the British museum is the "Salisbury and South Wiltshire Museum," though it does have a fine collection of geological specimens. I also don't see how the cube would have traveled from Britain to Vienna and back in 1967 without any record.)

Anyway, I don't want to waste too much time on the facts, since they speak for themselves. What interests me is the way Bergier's discussion of Dr. Gurlt's cube echoes Lovecraft. The "cube" Bergier persists—against evidence—as viewing as an extraterrestrial device of perfect geometry, which he claims must have been a recording device meant to take note of "everything that has taken place on our planet in the past ten million years."

> Their owners can no doubt retrieve them at great distance by means of a magnetometer; for the objects, when they receive a certain signal, must be able to indicate their exact position through an answering signal transmitted by magnetic resonance. [...] What is to be hoped is that the next angled object discovered will be carefully examined, especially with a mind to extracting its signals.[6]

This weird theory—unique to Bergier, so far as I know—is, to me, quite closely modeled on Lovecraft's Shining Trapezohedron from "The Haunter of the Dark" (1935). The Trapezohedron is, like Bergier's imaginary version of Gurlt's cube, a "crazily angled stone" of extraterrestrial manufacture that sends and receives signals to other intelligences across the cosmos, "a window on all time and space." It is also a relic of prehuman times (Triassic, though, rather than Paleogene):

> It was then, in the gathering twilight, that he thought he saw a faint trace of luminosity in the crazily angled stone. He had tried to look away from it, but some obscure compulsion drew his eyes back. Was there a subtle phosphorescence of radio-activity about the thing? What was it that the dead man's notes had said concerning a *Shining Trapezohedron*? [...] Of the Shining Trapezohedron he speaks often, calling it a window on all time and space, and tracing its history from the days it was fashioned on dark Yuggoth, before ever the Old Ones brought it to earth. It was treasured and placed in its curious box by the crinoid things of Antarctica, salvaged from their ruins by the serpent-men of Valusia, and peered at aeons later in Lemuria by the first human beings. It crossed strange lands and stranger seas, and sank with Atlantis before a Minoan fisher meshed it in his net and sold it to swarthy merchants from nighted Khem. The Pharaoh Nephren-Ka built around it a temple with a windowless crypt, and did that which caused his name to be stricken from all monuments and records.[7]

Based on these close similarities, I would suggest that Bergier's alternative explanation for Gurlt's cube is dependent upon Lovecraft's Trapezohedron. The most telling point is the last sentence of Bergier's that I quoted above. Despite spending his chapter discussing objects shaped like cubes, spheres, and cylinders, he refers to them collectively as "angled object[s]." This tells me that he had as his model the "crazily angled" Trapezohedron, and not the regular geometric forms of the "real" alien communication devices he purports to discuss.

As Bergier's 1970 book demonstrates, he clearly saw a connection between ancient mysteries and the "myths created by H. P. Lovecraft," and saw Lovecraft as having led him to the ancient mysteries he wrote about.

Notes

[1] Louis Pauwels and Jacques Bergier, *The Morning of the Magicians*, trans. Rollo Myers (New York: Stein and Day, 1964), 104.

[2] Jacques Bergier, *Extraterrestrial Visitations from Prehistoric Times to the Present* (Chicago: Henry Regnery Company, 1973), 8.

[3] Ibid., 67.

[4] Ibid., 86

[5] Ibid., 95-96.

[6] Ibid., 29, 34.

[7] H. P. Lovecraft, *The Fiction*, ed. S. T. Joshi (New York: Barnes & Noble, 2008), 1009, 1010.

4. Cthulhu vs. Xenu: The Case of H. P. Lovecraft and Scientology's Cosmology

I N THE FIRST months of 2011, two stories in the news turned attention toward the Church of Scientology, the faith founded by science fiction writer L. Ron Hubbard in 1952 and long rumored to involve secret teachings about space aliens who came to earth 75 million years ago. The first was a major article in the *New Yorker*'s February 14 edition detailing alleged abuse and poor working conditions at the hands of the church and its leaders.[1] The second was the rumor that film director Guillermo del Toro wanted the most famous Scientologist of all, Tom Cruise, to star in a big screen adaptation of H. P. Lovecraft's 1931 story of the discovery of an ancient extraterrestrial civilization, *At the Mountains of Madness*. While the *Mountains of Madness* movie project fell apart, interest in Scientology did not.

As some noted at the time of the Tom Cruise rumors, Scientology and Lovecraft share eerie parallels. Lovecraft's (fictional) extraterrestrials came to earth in the distant past and had a profound and largely dark influence on early humanity (see chapter two), and this idea bears a resemblance to Operating Thetan Level III (OT-III), the (supposedly nonfictional) cosmological doctrine L. Ron Hubbard created circa 1967 for Scientology. Lovecraft's version, to my mind, is the more subtle and convincing of the two.

It is a fact that Hubbard was a science fiction writer active in the same years that Lovecraft's stories were first published (the late 1930s—some Lovecraft tales were published after his 1937 death) and writing for the same types of pulp magazines in which Lovecraft's stories appeared. However, the two authors' outlets overlapped only at *Astounding Stories* (known after 1938 as *Astounding Science-Fiction*), the magazine that published *At the Mountains of Madness* in 1936. This story, however, includes the same type of cosmic sweep as Hubbard's cosmology, though both approach the concept in very different ways. Hubbard developed Dianetics (the precursor of Scientology) for *Astounding Science Fiction* in 1950, and science fiction luminaries such as L. Sprague de Camp and *Astounding* editor John W. Campbell were friends of Hubbard and also well-versed in Lovecraftian fiction.

I admit that in the past I have shied away from exploring the possible connections between Lovecraft and Scientology, both because of the church's infamous litigiousness and also because I had not studied the Scientology materials needed to make judgments. I should note here that I have no special knowledge of the secret doctrines of Scientology, and I do not know what the group teaches its followers beyond the publicly available information that has been widely reported since its disclosure during legal proceedings in the 1980s and 1990s. The 2011 *New Yorker* article reported what the court document and news accounts of the 1980s and 1990s had made public: that Hubbard claimed an ancient astronaut named Xenu (or Xemu), onetime president of a galactic confederation of overpopulated planets, came to earth 75 million years ago and buried a billion or more aliens beneath volcanoes and killed them with hydrogen bombs. Their souls (or thetans) are said to now infest human hosts, causing many problems—problems that only Scientology's "technology" can solve. According to testimony from Warren McShane, the president of the Scientology subsidiary, the Religious Technology Center, in the case of *Religious Technology Center v. F.A.C.T.Net, Inc., et al.* (1995), this information, "the discussion of the—of the volcanoes, the explosions, the Galactic confederation 75 million years ago, and a gentleman by the name Xemu there.

Those are not trade secrets."[2] Since this material is in the court records, it would seem to be fair game for analysis and criticism.

There are some superficial similarities between Lovecraft's and Hubbard's visions of our alien past. Both wrote that extraterrestrials came to earth tens of millions of years ago, and both wrote that earth had been a part of a galactic system of inhabited worlds before a cataclysm caused the aliens to retreat. Hubbard's Galactic Confederation was something like a cosmic United Nations, while Lovecraft had a messier conception of a multiplicity of alien races treating earth as one planet among many to conquer and on which to spawn. Both authors also wrote about buried evidence of alien civilizations: in Hubbard's case, alien implant or reporting stations at Las Palmas in the Canary Islands, a Martian station in the Pyrenees, and Xenu's prison[3]; for Lovecraft, sunken or buried cities such as Cthulhu's R'lyeh, the Old Ones' Antarctic city, or the Great Race's Australian metropolis. Hubbard's Xenu is said to be "in an electronic mountain trap where he still is." Of the other aliens, "'They' are gone," Hubbard wrote.[4] Similarly, Cthulhu lives on, trapped in his undersea city of R'lyeh. Of the other aliens in Cthulhu's retinue, "Those Old Ones were gone now, inside the earth and under the sea."[5] The differences are also telling. Cthulhu is trapped (in the original version) by purely natural forces (later August Derleth would make Cthulhu the victim of cosmic punishment), while Xenu is imprisoned by his rebellious lieutenants, like Kronos placed in the Greek Tartarus at the hands of Zeus.

Additionally, both wrote about the ability of minds to travel millions or billions of years across time and millions or billions of miles across space for encounters with the aliens. For Lovecraft, this took several forms. In "The Whisperer in Darkness," human brains were removed from their bodies and placed in metal canisters for interstellar travel. In "Through the Gates of the Silver Key," Randolph Carter's mind travelled from body to body across the planets and the eons, while in *The Shadow Out of Time*, Nathaniel Wingate Peaslee had his own mind traded with that of a member of the Great Race of Yith from 250 million years ago. The Great Race, of course, had learned to migrate from age to age by projecting their minds into other species' bodies, rendering the Grace Race close to immortal. For Hubbard, the initiate into Scientology's highest secrets is able to project his mind into the stars. According to David G. Bromley and Mitchell L. Bracey, Jr., the official Scientology doctrine is that the dead Hubbard lives on in bodiless form, researching spirituality on another planet,[6] just as Randolph Carter's mind visits the cosmic oneness that is Yog-Sothoth and studies magic in the body of a wizard on the planet Yaddith. Similarly, the Scientology "thetans" are also disembodied spirits who persist from age to age, like the roving minds of the Great Race. In both Lovecraft's and Hubbard's conceptions, this idea derives from nineteenth-century occult ideas of astral projection, which Lovecraft encountered in such sources as Walter De Le Mare's *The Return* (1910). Hubbard was also familiar with astral projection, having written about the practice early in his career in the science fiction story "The Dangerous Dimension" (1938), which he described as an updated, science-fiction form of astral projection.[7]

Both writers even had similar ideas about madness-inducing literary secrets. In "The Call of Cthulhu," Lovecraft's narrator describes the way madness results should anyone put together the pieces of the true history of aliens on earth, including hints from the *Necronomicon* and other written texts:

> The most merciful thing in the world, I think, is the inability of the human mind to correlate all its contents. We live on a placid island of ignorance in the midst of black seas of infinity, and it was not meant that we should voyage far. The sciences, each straining in its own direction, have hitherto harmed us little; but some day the piecing together of dissociated knowledge will open up such terrifying vistas of reality, and of our frightful position therein, that we shall either go mad from the revelation or flee from the deadly light into the peace and safety of a new dark age.[8]

In parallel, Hubbard claimed to Forrest J. Ackerman that his book *Excalibur* was so dangerous that those who had read it had committed suicide or had gone insane.[9] Hubbard himself said that he had written the book after receiving a message from the stars when he "died" for eight minutes during a dental examination,[10] and the Church of Scientology claimed that four people who read the book went insane.[11] Scientology would also declare that anyone who learned of Xenu without proper preparation would catch pneumonia and die.[12] Such claims are unique neither to Lovecraft nor Hubbard, though. In 1895, for example, Robert W. Chambers wrote of the fictitious play *The King in Yellow*, which he said would cause madness should anyone read its final act.

However, Hubbard's cosmic vision is very different in detail and in tone from that of Lovecraft. Lovecraft imagined a grand cosmos of a multiplicity of diverse aliens and incorporeal entities that were utterly inhuman and incomprehensible, that treat humans as elephants might treat earthworms. By contrast, Hubbard's aliens are essentially human in all but name, possessed of human vices and motivations. Lovecraft's cosmos is also much less dependent than Hubbard's on the tropes of space opera and Golden Age science fiction (presuming, of course, you take Hubbard's cosmology as a literary text rather than revelation).

While both writers actively worked to create a new mythology, they did so in very different ways. Lovecraft's artificial mythology was self-consciously fake, created for fun, and intended to create a deep background that presumably stood behind early fertility cults and shamanic faiths. Nor was the materialist, atheist Lovecraft shy about declaiming the falsity of his fake gods:

> Regarding the dreaded *Necronomicon* of the mad Arab Abdul Alhazred—I must confess that both the evil volume & the accursed author are fictitious creatures of my own—as are the malign entities of Azathoth, Yog-Sothoth, Nyarlathotep, Shub-Niggurath, &c. Tsathoggua & the *Book of Eibon* are inventions of Clark Ashton Smith, while Friedrich von Junzt & his monstrous *Unaussprechlichen Kulten* originated in the fertile brain of Robert E. Howard. For the fun of building up a convincing cycle of synthetic folklore, all of our gang frequently allude to the pet daemons of the others—thus Smith uses my Yog-Sothoth, while I use his Tsathoggua. Also, I sometimes insert a devil or two of my own in the tales I revise or

ghost-write for professional clients. Thus our black pantheon acquires an extensive publicity & pseudo-authoritativeness it would not otherwise get. We never, however, try to put it across as an actual hoax; but always carefully explain to enquirers that it is 100% fiction.[13]

Hubbard, by contrast, meant his artificial mythology to be taken as truth. Like Lovecraft's black pantheon lurking behind classical mythology, Hubbard would claim that Christianity emerged when a "madman" discovered Xenu's 75 million-year-old "R6" implant within his soul around 600 BCE.[14] This implant apparently included images of God and the Devil, high technology, and crucifixions, inspiring the Christian faith six centuries later and leaving humans predisposed to accepting a (false) Christian message. In both cases, therefore, the aliens are the originators or manipulators of religious thought, with humans mistakenly worshipping entities that did not have their best interests in mind.

It would go far beyond the evidence to suggest Hubbard borrowed his cosmology from Lovecraft, but the core concepts of ancient aliens, buried civilizations, and mental transfer across time are all ideas that Lovecraft wrote about in stories that Hubbard almost certainly would have read years or decades before developing OT-III. Nevertheless, the reported revelations of OT-III are much more similar to Golden Age SF space opera projected into the past than anything Lovecraft would have written. (Hubbard even called the Xenu story "very space opera" in his handwritten OT-III notes.) It is, quite frankly, impossible to imagine Cthulhu engaging in palace politics the way Xenu's lieutenants are said to have conspired against him. The closest parallel in Lovecraft is the war between the Old Ones of Antarctica and the spawn of Cthulhu in *At the Mountains of Madness*, but this takes much more of the form of a Darwinian survival of the fittest than a palace coup or even a Greek Titanomachy. It would seem that Hubbard's ancient aliens are the direct result of needing the aliens to exist in the past to provide a creation story for Scientology rather than any actual interest in saying something profound about ancient history, while

Lovecraft's aliens have a immense prehistory because the enormity of time and the transience of humanity were two of Lovecraft's major themes.

I previously established in *The Cult of Alien Gods* (Prometheus, 2005) and in Chapter 2 of this book that Lovecraft was the primary force marrying Theosophy's idea of planets inhabited by ascended masters and human souls waiting to be born (itself derived from medieval notions of planets as the seats of various ranks of angels) to science fiction's non-spiritual extraterrestrials in order to create the modern myth of ancient astronauts. In this limited sense, later works like Scientology's OT-III (taken again as a literary text) can be thought of as influenced by the ancient astronaut myth Lovecraft developed in the 1920s and 1930s. However, the more accurate thing to say is that both Lovecraft and Hubbard drew on the heritage of nineteenth century scientific romances and occult speculation, creating similar end products from the same source material. (Both, for example, were influenced by occultism—Lovecraft through the works of Arthur Machen and thus the Hermetic Order of the Golden Dawn, while Hubbard was involved with the Rosicrucians and Aleister Crowley's Ordo Templi Orientis, either to infiltrate the orders as Scientology claims or to practice magic as Russell Miller argued.[15]) That Lovecraft created his alien gods decades before Hubbard gives him priority in imagination.

It would be interesting to think that in some parallel world, a less scrupulous Lovecraft, had he lived past 1937, might have turned his artificial mythology into a profitable religion, leaving Hubbard's Xenu and friends to eke out an existence solely the pages of pulp fiction. Of course, in that world we would have dramatic exposés of the real origins of Cthulhu, and that would take all of the fun out of the Cthulhu Mythos.

Notes

[1] Lawrence Wright, "The Apostate: Paul Haggis vs. the Church of Scientology," *The New Yorker*, February 14, 2011.

[2] *Religious Technology Center v. F.A.C.T.Net, Inc., et al.* 95-B-2143. US District Court, 1995.

[3] "OT-III Scholarship Page," *Operation Clambake* [online]; Russell Miller, *Bare-Faced Messiah: The True Story of L. Ron Hubbard* (Michael Joseph, 1987), 206.

[4] "OT-III Scholarship Page."

[5] H. P. Lovecraft, *The Fiction*, ed. S. T. Joshi (New York: Barnes & Noble, 2008), 366.

[6] David G. Bromley, and Mitchell L. Bracey, Jr., "The Church of Scientology: A Quasi-Religion," in *Sects, Cults, and Spiritual Communities: A Sociological Analysis*, edited by William W. Zellner and Marc Petrowsky (Westport, CT: Praeger, 1998), 144.

[7] "The Golden Age," *The L. Ron Hubbard Site* [online], Church of Scientology, 2004.

[8] Lovecraft, 354.

[9] "L. Ron Hubbard," *Secret Lives*, Channel 4 (UK), (November 19, 1997).

[10] Martin Gardner, *Fads and Fallacies in the Name of Science* (Mineola, NY: Dover, 1957), 272.

[11] George Malko, *Scientology: The Now Religion* (New York: Delacorte Press, 1970), 39.

[12] Mikael Rothstein, "'His Name Was Xenu...He Used Renegades.': Aspects of Scientology's Founding Myth," in *Scientology*, ed. James R. Lewis (New York: Oxford, 2009), 369.

[13] Letter to William Frederick Anger, August 14, 1934; reproduced at "Quotes about the *Necronomicon* from Lovecraft's Letters," *HPLovecraft.com* [online], April 13, 2004.

[14] L. Ron. Hubbard, audio recording of "Class VIII Course, Lecture #10, Assists," October 3, 1968, "Hubbard Audio Collection," *Operation Clambake* [online].

[15] Miller, *Bare-Faced* Messiah, 112-130.

5. Was Cthulhu a King of Atlantis?

Y *CULT OF ALIEN GODS* and its supporting materials—including chapter two of this book—take a materialist view of the Cthulhu Mythos, assuming (correctly, by all rational laws of nature), that the Cthulhu Mythos is the invention of H. P. Lovecraft and has no basis in fact whatsoever beyond the building blocks from Theosophy, the *Arabian Nights*, and the *Encyclopaedia Britannica* that Lovecraft used to develop it.

But have you wondered what would have happened if *The Cult of Alien Gods* or chapter two of this book had been written by an "alternative" theorist? Fortunately, we don't have to wonder. It really happened. By a weird coincidence, at the same time I was writing *The Cult of Alien Gods* in 2004, occultist Tracy R. Twyman wrote her own funhouse-mirror version of my Lovecraft connection theory called "Dead but Dreaming: The Great Old Ones of Lovecraftian Legend Reinterpreted as Atlantean Kings."[1]

Whereas I looked at the connections between Lovecraft and ancient astronaut authors through the lens of the influence of (artificial) ideas, Twyman instead suggested that Lovecraft was carrying forward an esoteric tradition drawn from the Book of Enoch and the lost continent of Atlantis by way of Sumerian mythology. (This last point is obviously derived from the Sumerian-influenced hoax *Necronomicon* of Simon, which she acknowledges later.) She suggests that the "fall" of Cthulhu (i.e., his imprisonment in R'lyeh) descends from the Book of Enoch and the "universal" tale of Atlantis. Cthulhu, she claims, bears a striking resemblance to Oannes, the fish-man wrongly identified in Lovecraft's day with Dagon and later with ancient astronaut flying space frogs (see Chapter 25). I don't see it, personally. Cthulhu is an octopus-headed dragon, while Oannes is a man in a fish suit. Cthulhu has wings and claws; Oannes doesn't. The descent of R'lyeh into the abyss, she says "parallel[s] precisely the tales of the Nephilim, the Titans, and the war in Heaven between God and Lucifer, as well as the fall of the Atlantean empire," with the promised return of Cthulhu a cipher for the Apocalypse of Revelation.

At no time does Twyman seem to understand that she has the order of events backward. The prophesied return of Cthulhu resembles Revelation (and Ragnorak) because Lovecraft was Biblically literate and used the Biblical narrative as a base in order to subvert it. The imagined "fall" of Cthulhu, however, bears only a superficial resemblance to Atlantis, and even that was intentional. Lovecraft tried to create a (fictional) analogue to Plato's Atlantis narrative as an answer to the Theosophists and their silly claims about Venusians running occult schools on Lemuria. Plato's Atlantis sinks because of the Atlanteans' sins; the Nephilim fall because they are evil. Cthulhu and R'lyeh sink beneath the waves—just because. Geology happens. There is no moral good or evil implied. It just happened. This is decidedly *not* parallel but rather a subversion of the traditional Classical and Biblical narratives Lovecraft knew very well.

But Twyman is so blinded by ideology that she cannot fathom that Lovecraft was conscious of his own material; she truly believes that R'lyeh is a secret Atlantis and that it sank because of—seriously—Noah's Flood. She thinks the Old Ones' reign was "glorious" like that of Atlantis, Lemuria, or Thule because she cannot parse Lovecraft's complex narrative and takes his intentionally Biblical words at face value. The Old Ones' reign was one of violence, blood, and death; it is considered glorious by a delusional cult.

That same literal-mindedness leads her to read deep secrets into the Esoteric Order of Dagon practicing in an old Masonic Hall. Unable to believe that Lovecraft knew enough of the Freemasons (and Masonic conspiracy theories) to purposely use them to lend weight to the fictive Dagon cult, she instead reads this as proof that the real-life ancient cult of Dagon (whom she views as Satan) is in league with the flesh-and-blood Masons!

This is not enough, of course. She takes the hoax *Necronomicon* of Simon as a genuine representation of Sumerian myth, and based on its forced and false parallels between Lovecraft's deities and Sumer's (which exist only because Lovecraft used Classical, Biblical, and Arabian myths as inspiration, and these share an uneasy heritage with Mesopotamia) she suggests that the Sumerian (actually Babylonian) practice of identifying gods with planets (like the Romans did—Jupiter, anyone?) meant that the "gods" were from outer space or another dimension, like Cthulhu!

Her article shades into Lovecraftian Magick, the weird practice of taking Lovecraft as a conduit of truths from another sphere and then trying to summon his monsters. The late Kenneth L. Grant actually argued that Lovecraft unconsciously channeled the *Necronomicon* from another dimension and that therefore one could summon Cthulhu using appropriate spells. Since we are all still alive, this is obviously untrue. It was, however, a survival of Theosophy's unique insight that it could claim science fiction as prophecies of Theosophy by declaring that sci-fi writers merely received their ideas from the plane of ether, where Theosophy's extraterrestrial gods spend their time when not cruising earth's skies in flying chariots.

Twyman's article reads like a parody of my own work. Instead of seeking out the facts as they exist here on the earth, among real people, she dances across the clouds making "connections" at random, ignorant of the human motives behind them and unwilling to acknowledge that even a single piece of writing is the result of conscious decisions rather than the passive receipt of inspiration from the level beyond human.

Lovecraft's "Call of Cthulhu" acknowledges and subverts Atlantis and Armageddon—and this was intentional. Similarly, Lovecraft's "Dunwich Horror" purposely acknowledges and subverts the life of Christ. By failing to recognize intentionality and the role of the author as creator of his own narrative, Twyman can propose a global, universal, self-reproducing set of myths and legends. But this is a chimera. Hmm. I better watch myself. She might take that literally and think I'm channeling hybrid monsters from the plane of ether!

Notes

[1] Published online by DragonKey Press in October 2004 and later republished as an eBook in 2011.

6. How Rod Serling's *Night Gallery* Gave Us *Ancient Aliens*

T MIGHT BE a bit heretical, but I enjoyed the *Night Gallery* more than Serling's more famous series, *The Twilight Zone*. It's probably that my aesthetic sensibility runs more Gothic than sci-fi, and I preferred monsters to aliens, castles and mansions to rockets and asteroids. That said, *Night Gallery* is a difficult show to love unconditionally. Like any anthology, its segments vary in quality, and few anthologies varied as wildly as *Night Gallery*, largely due to the tension between the putative star of the series, Rod Serling, and the producer, Jack Laird.

At the time of *Night Gallery*'s inception, Serling had no interest in resuming the day-to-day running of a TV series, largely due to his bad experiences with CBS during the *Twilight Zone* years. He later realized it was a mistake to give control to Laird and the NBC network. Laird, to put it as gently as possible, was a populist in the worst sense of the term and pushed the show toward a campy, sensationalist tone that stood in tension with Serling's more restrained take on the macabre. The result was a series that could reach dizzying heights (for 1970s TV, anyway) and fall to such painful lows as short one-joke comedy segments in which vampires visit blood banks, vampires need to hire a babysitter, or a cannibal tries to hire a maid. Needless to say, Laird was behind the misbegotten comedy bits, which severely undercut the stronger segments by their sheer campy awfulness. But even Laird was a bulwark of quality against interference from

NBC and Universal Studios, who demanded lower quality, more action, more gore, and more shock. By the third season, Serling was little more than a paid host for a program that was churning out some of the worst genre television committed to film. (Just try watching the segments "Fright Night" or "Hatred unto Death.")

But at its best, *Night Gallery* offered dark, moving portraits of fear and the macabre, usually in the Gothic mode, many drawn from classic pulp magazine stories that Serling loved as a young man. Adaptations of *Weird Tales* authors Seabury Quinn, Clark Ashton Smith, August Derleth, and H. P. Lovecraft gave a pulp-literary cast to the show's greatest efforts. To the best of my knowledge, in 1971 *Night Gallery* became the first TV show to produce straight adaptations of Lovecraft stories: "Pickman's Model" and "Cool Air." (*The Dunwich Horror*, a straightforward adaptation of Lovecraft's tale, had bowed in movie theaters the previous year.) Such segments as "A Death in the Family," "Class of '99," "Green Fingers," and "Miracle at Camafeo" are both dramatically satisfying and as memorable as the best of *The Twilight Zone*. Even the critically-despised third season had a few hits, like the Smith adaptation, "The Return of the Sorcerer."

By late 1972, the writing was on the wall for *Night Gallery*. The network had cut the program from an hour to half an hour, and both NBC and the production company, Universal, ordered the show to feature more monsters, more mayhem, and more "promotable" stories; in other words, nothing too challenging for audiences. The new direction was failure, and the miserable run of duds for the final season ground to an ignominious end in May 1973 (production had ended some months earlier), when the final episode groaned its way to a sclerotic conclusion.

Serling had become disenchanted with the program, referring to the third season as "shit," and he publicly disavowed any responsibility for the show that bore his name (its official title was *Rod Serling's Night Gallery*). He had written twenty scripts for the second season, but contributed just four in the third. As the last episodes aired, the studio began repackaging the show for syndication, chopping up and butchering episodes to fit into half-hour slots. When that failed to produce enough episodes for syndication, they added 25 truncated episodes of the 1972 psychic-investigator drama *Sixth Sense* to the package, but to make them fit with *Gallery*, they paid Serling handsomely to film new introductions for these episodes. Serling essentially blackmailed them for cash, knowing they couldn't syndicate without his intros. With that he washed his hands of the *Gallery*, and network series.

This meant that in late 1972, he was ending his series commitment and open to suggestions for his next project. His longtime producer, Alan Landsburg, came to him with some excitement, babbling about ancient aliens to a skeptical Serling. Landsburg convinced Serling that ancient astronauts were real, and he proposed a project to bring the story to the masses.[1] In his 1974 book, *In Search of Ancient Mysteries*, Landsburg presents his conversion to ancient astronautics as his own *sui generis* brainstorm, but in fact Landsburg had seen an Oscar-nominated 1970 German documentary about Erich von Däniken's *Chariots of the Gods,* probably in the English dubbing made in Britain. Landsburg's proposal wasn't so much to rewrite history as to make good money reediting the documentary for American audiences with Serling as the narrator. He called the new version *In Search of Ancient Astronauts,* and it aired on NBC on January 5, 1973, two days after a new *Night Gallery* episode. Two sequels followed in 1975: *In Search of Ancient Mysteries* and *The Outer Space Connection.*

Serling was no stranger to ancient astronauts. He knew about them from fiction, especially the works of H. P. Lovecraft, which he had read and loved years earlier and which were also a major influence on *Night Gallery,* thanks to both his and *Gallery* producer Jack Laird's fandom. Therefore Serling was primed to accept the message that aliens had once visited the ancient earth. Even so, he initially thought the idea suitable only for fiction (not unlike, say, his reverse-ancient astronaut script for *Planet of the Apes*) until Landsburg provided "evidence" in the form of the Nazca lines to convince him.

With Serling's familiar voice lending the awe any mystery of *The Twilight Zone* and *Night Gallery* to ancient astronauts, *In Search of Ancient Astronauts* and its successors were ratings successes. The programs propelled sales of von Däniken's books and helped make him a 1970s celebrity. With no actors to pay, documentaries made for cheap programming. Therefore, Landsburg made plans to turn his documentaries into a television series, and he wanted Serling to continue as narrator. Serling, however, died in June 1975, and Leonard Nimoy, who had acted in and directed for *Night Gallery*, stepped into the role. The series, called *In Search of...*, ran from 1976 to 1982 in syndication.

The NBC documentaries and the *In Search of...* series drove public interest in ancient astronauts and prehistoric mysteries. More people watched the NBC specials than would ever read ancient astronaut books (there were only three networks and PBS for most TV viewers in those days), and the TV shows gave credibility to von Däniken's ideas, despite PBS's *Nova* making a valiant effort to discredit the idea by adapting a BBC *Horizon* episode.

Without the failure of *Night Gallery* in its third season, Serling likely wouldn't have had the time or inclination for *In Search of Ancient Astronauts*. Without the participation of one of the network's stars, NBC would have been much less likely to air the documentary, or for audiences to watch it. Without the documentary, von Däniken's book sales would have been much less robust, his star much dimmer. Without a celebrity author and TV credibility, the ancient astronaut theory might have faded into just another weird idea on the lunatic fringe.

Instead, von Däniken's residual fame led to a *Chariots of the Gods* documentary special on ABC in 1996 (to compete with NBC's successful documentaries advocating Atlantis and creationism), a spate of cable TV documentaries in early 2000s, and the History Channel's 2009 *Ancient Aliens* documentary, which in turn served as the pilot for *Ancient Aliens: The Series*. In an ever-more-fractured television landscape, appeals to the fond memories of popular old ideas were a shortcut to ratings. If only NBC and Universal had left *Night Gallery* to its devices, we might have had more quality classic horror and no *Ancient Aliens*.

But that was hardly all *Night Gallery* gave us. It also helped inspire the claim that the world would end in 2012 because the Maya said so. Or, rather, 2011, following an incorrect date first proposed by the Mayanist Michael C. Coe in 1966, misinterpreting the Maya calendar. Coe thought the Maya calendar similar to the cyclical time of Hinduism, and he speculated that the end of the calendar cycle would have been viewed like the end of the Hindu *kalpas,* when the world was destroyed and reborn.

Coe's incorrect 2011 date was later corrected to 2012, but not before it showed up in Alan Landsburg's ancient astronaut film *The Outer Space Connection* (1975) and its accompanying book. In the documentary, narrator Rod Serling informs viewers that ancient astronauts will return to earth on December 24, 2011, the date predicted by the Mayan calendar:

> An inscription tells us that the modern period will end December 24, 2011 A.D. We may presume that they [the aliens] were computing the length of a space voyage and marking the exact date of return. They may return to seek the fate of the colony left on earth. Perhaps at Uxmal they will find answers we have never been able to divine.

As *In Search of Ancient Astronauts* had done for the ancient astronaut hypothesis, Landsburg's *Outer Space Connection* helped spread fictitious Mayan Apocalypse beliefs beyond the New Age fringe since the film, like its predecessor, was broadcast on NBC to an audience comprising around a third of all TV viewers. The result would be a florescence of 2012 beliefs in the late 1970s, lasting down to the inevitable disappointment that followed the failure of the apocalyptic predictions at the end of 2012.

It continues to amaze me how a single writer, making a single claim, can set off a chain reaction that echoes down the ages as later writers repeat, expand, and misunderstand the original. Here Coe is at fault, but his scholarly speculation would have been forgotten if Landsburg hadn't been casting about for new material to make a sequel to his adaptation of Erich von Däniken's *Chariots of the Gods,* which was itself a success because of Rod Serling, who only narrated the film due to the disaster that was NBC's and Universal's treatment of his *Night Gallery,* leading to its untimely cancellation despite strong ratings. So, thanks to the failure of *Night Gallery* we not only got ancient astronauts and eventually *Ancient Aliens* but *also* the 2012 apocalypse myth. Truly, this was the most consequential series cancellations of its time. It's the law of unintended consequences at work. I for one think we'd have all been better off with more *Night Gallery* and much less apocalypse and aliens.

Notes

[1] Rod Serling, foreword to *In Search of Ancient Mysteries*, by Alan Landsburg and Sally Landsburg (New York: Bantam, 1973), viii-ix.

7. The Green Children of Banjos

I DID NOT REMEMBER the story of the "green children" of Banjos, Spain until I read about them in Jacques Bergier's *Extraterrestrial Visitations* (see Chapter 3), but a quick Google search finds that these mysterious beings are apparently a mainstay of the alternative history and mystery-mongering genres. They appear in *The Big Book of Mysteries* by Lionel and Patricia Fanthope (2010), Charles Berlitz's *World of the Incredible but True* (1992), Colin Wilson's *Enigmas and Mysteries* (1976), and John Macklin's *Strange Destinies* (1965). The story concerns the appearance of two children, green in color, who were found near the village of Banjos in Catalonia in 1887 speaking a strange tongue and refusing to eat anything but beans.

They also appear in Karl Shuker's *The Unexplained* (1996), a book I read when I was fifteen, so I must have read the story and promptly cared nothing for it, probably because Shuker provides a correct (though incomplete) solution to the mystery—one we will get to anon. It is, I suppose, a testament to the stupidity of this story that it left no impression on me.

"There is only one, well established case of a green child," Bergier wrote, referring to the 1887 incident. This, though, is not even close to true. Rather than belabor the point, here's the reason it isn't true. It's a point-for-point duplicate of a medieval legend of the Green Children of Woolpit recorded by Ralph of Coggeshall and William of Newburgh:

BANJOS CHILDREN	WOOLPIT CHILDREN
Location: Non-existent Spanish Village	Location: Woolpit, Suffolk
Date: 1887	Date: before 1188
Number of children: 2, a boy and a girl	Number of children: 2, a boy and a girl
The children were found in a cave by farmers at harvest time	The children appeared in the village at harvest time
The children spoke a language that was not Spanish	The children spoke a language that was not English
The children wore metallic clothes	The children wore unusual clothes
The children were taken to the house of mayor Ricardo de Calno	The children were taken to the house of nobleman Richard de Calne
The children refused all food except beans	The children refused all food except beans
The color of their skin gradually became white	The color of their skin gradually became white
The boy sickened and died	The boy sickened and died
The girl stated that they came from a land of perpetual twilight	The girl stated that they came from a green land of perpetual twilight
The girl stated that they had heard a loud noise and were pushed through a portal to Spain	The girl stated that they had heard bells and fell into a trance before arriving in England
The girl died five years later	The girl became a servant and a slut, but eventually married and lived a long life

The Banjos story appears first in Macklin's *Strange Destinies*, but not only is it inspired by the Woolpit story, it is a very close paraphrase of Thomas Keightley's version from *The Fairy Mythology* (1850), with the geographic details changed. Here's Keightley's version:

"Another wonderful thing," says Ralph of Coggeshall, "happened in Suffolk, at St. Mary's of the Wolf-pits. A boy and his sister were found by the inhabitants of that place near the mouth of a pit which is there, who had the form of all their limbs like to those of other men, but they differed in the colour of their skin from all the people of our habitable world; for the whole surface of their skin was tinged of a green colour. No one could understand their speech. When they were brought as curiosities to the house of a certain knight, Sir Richard de Caine, at Wikes, they wept bitterly. Bread and other victuals were set before them, but they would touch none of them, though they were tormented by great hunger, as the girl afterwards acknowledged. At length, when some beans just cut, with their stalks, were brought into the house, they made signs, with great avidity, that they should be given to them. When they were brought, they opened the stalks instead of the pods, thinking the beans were in the hollow of them; but not finding them there, they began to weep anew. When those who were present saw this, they opened the pods, and showed them the naked beans. They fed on these with great delight, and for a long time tasted no other food. The boy, however, was always languid and depressed, and he died within a short time. The girl enjoyed continual good health; and becoming accustomed to various kinds of food, lost completely that green colour, and gradually recovered the sanguine habit of her entire body. She was afterwards regenerated by the layer of holy baptism, and lived for many years in the service of that knight (as I have frequently heard from him and his family), and was rather loose and wanton in her conduct. Being frequently asked about the people of her country, she asserted that the inhabitants, and all they had in that country, were of a green colour; and that they saw no sun, but enjoyed a degree of light like what is after sunset. Being asked how she came into this country with the aforesaid boy, she replied, that as they were following their flocks, they came to a certain cavern, on entering which they heard a delightful sound of bells; ravished by whose sweetness, they went for a long time wandering on through the cavern, until they came to its mouth. When they came out of it, they were struck senseless by the excessive light of the sun, and the unusual temperature of the air; and they thus lay for a long time. Being terrified by the noise of those who came on them, they wished to fly, but they could not find the entrance of the cavern before they were caught."

This story is also told by William of Newbridge,[1] who places it in the reign of King Stephen. He says he long hesitated to believe it, but he was at length overcome by the weight of evidence. According to him, the place where the children appeared was about four or five miles from Bury St. Edmund's: they came in harvest-time out of the Wolf-pits; they both lost their green hue, and were baptised, and learned English. The boy, who was the younger, died; but the girl married a man at Lenna, and lived many years. They said their country was called St. Martin's Land, as that saint was chiefly worshiped there; that the people were Christians, and had churches; that the sun did not rise there, but that there was a bright country which could be seen from theirs, being divided from it by a very broad river.[2]

Note that Keightley writes that "when some beans just cut, with their stalks, were brought into the house, they [the children] made signs, with great avidity, that they should be given to them." Macklin writes that "beans cut or torn from stalks were brought into the house, and they [the children] fell on them with great avidity." Garth Haslam discussed this on an older version of his Anomaly Info site, which has unfortunately been taken offline.

The long and short of it is that the evidence shows that Macklin fabricated the 1887 encounter from a medieval fairy story, and later authors simply repeated him point for point without bothering to check the source. (It is possible that Macklin merely copied from another hoaxer, but no earlier version of the Banjos story has emerged.) Ridiculously, when some alternative writers discovered the earlier medieval version, they then concluded that the Macklin account must be true because the aliens were repeatedly testing humanity! Suffice it to say that there are no records of any children being found in Catalonia in 1887, or for the existence of Banjos at all.

It does, however, make me wonder what Jacques Bergier thought "well established" means.

Notes

[1] *Guilelmi Neubrigensis, Historia, sive Chronica Rerum Anglicarum,* Oxon. 1719, lib. i. c. 27. (Keightley's note.)

[2] Thomas Keightley, *The Fairy Mythology,* new edition (London: H. G. Bohn, 1850), 281-283.

8. Getting It Wrong: When Myths and Legends Lie

ACCORDING TO ancient astronaut pundits, we are supposed to believe that ancient myths and legends are literal records of extraterrestrial intervention, while alternative historians argue that these same myths and legends instead record the intervention in the human past of an advanced, lost civilization on the order of Atlantis. Both groups, of course, selectively interpret myths and legends to support their preconceived points of view.

But what does it really mean to say that we must take myths and legends literally? Let's look at a few and then compare them to the stories these speculators won't tell you about.

Before his death in 2012, Philip Coppens of *Ancient Aliens* made the case that we should take as evidence of extraterrestrial dispensation the Famine Stela, a Ptolemaic-era monument recording a dream supposedly experienced by the architect Imhotep two millennia earlier, in which a god tells Imhotep that he (the god) will give Egypt rocks aplenty. This, Coppens said, is proof of the alien origins of architecture. We are also told by Erich von Däniken and others that the Book of Ezekiel is a literal record of the descent of a flying saucer in Biblical times. *Ancient Aliens* star Giorgio Tsoukalos tells us that a fourteenth-century Arab text's description of the supernatural inspiration for Egypt's Great Pyramid five thousand years earlier is proof of an extraterrestrial master-plan (see Chapter 30).

On the other hand, Atlantis theorists from Ignatius Donnelly on down inform us that Plato's *Timaeus* and *Critias* are to be taken as history, not allegory, and followed to the letter to find Atlantis, except where such literalism interferes with the selective changes they wish to induce to fit Atlantis to their pet theory. *Fingerprints of the Gods* author Graham Hancock tells us that pre-Columbian legends of savior gods are to be taken as literal records of the lost white race of Atlantis visiting the Americas (whereas ancient astronaut writers prefer to see them as aliens, and earlier Christian missionaries as wandering European saints or the devil in disguise).

While no two theorists agree on exactly what such myths mean, all agree on one thing: ancient people are not capable of making things up, or reporting false information. Their stories are derived from real life and are therefore a reliable guide to the past.

So what do these theorists make of the following stories?

- The Roman walls of southern Germany were believed down to the twentieth century to have been built by the Devil.
- Roman amphitheaters of southern France and Toledo were for many centuries called "palais de Gallienne," after Galiana, the (fictional) Moorish wife of Charlemagne, who they falsely believe built or lived in them.
- "Caesar's Camp" in Sussex was traditionally described as a Roman fortress but proved to have been built by the Normans.

These tales misattribute known constructions to wrong builders. But, you may say, so what? This is Roman material, so it isn't relevant. Let's have a few more.

- The Bolewa of Nigeria have a tradition that their chief's sacred sword was carried from Yemen many centuries ago and is therefore extremely valuable. Upon examination, it proved to have been made in Prussia only a few decades before.

- The Arabs of the Sudan, prior to the colonial era, claimed that their chain armor had been captured from the Crusaders and brought by the Arabs from the Holy Land. In fact, was imported from Germany in the late 1700s.

- The Arabs of Jordan had a tradition ascribing the Treasury building at Petra (the one seen in *Indiana Jones and the Last Crusade*) to Pharaoh from the Bible, even though Petra's buildings are obviously later than dynastic Egypt.

Pshaw! Arabs. Not relevant to aliens or Atlantis, despite Jacques Bergier's claim that the Qur'an's story of Iram of the Pillars was an extraterrestrial act of explosive destruction.

Fine, let's have some more, and this time let's include both prehistory and supernatural power, ancient alien writers' favorite themes:

- Prehistoric African stone works of known medieval construction are still ascribed to the work of spirits or demons in folk traditions.

- The dolmens of France and Britain, known by archaeological findings to be the tombs of Bronze Age notables, were believed down to the twentieth century to have been built by fairies.

- The hill forts of Ireland were down to the middle twentieth century popularly held by tradition to be the work of the Danes, despite actually being prehistoric in origin.

- Stonehenge, a late Neolithic/early Bronze Age construction, was routinely ascribed to the magic powers of Arthur's wizard Merlin down to the early modern period.

(All of the above examples, excepting Stonehenge, are drawn from Lord Raglan's *The Hero*, wherein he provides full citations for each.[1])

So, I ask ancient alien speculators and lost civilization hypothesizers this: If these folktales, myths, legends, and traditions proved wrong in the face of known historical facts, what warrant do we have for assuming that *your* selections from myth, legend, and tradition are true? If you do not believe the fairies built the British dolmens, or Charlemagne's wife built Roman amphitheaters, how can we trust a medieval Arab writer that the pyramids were inspired by sky beings, or a Ptolemaic stela that an Egyptian god bequeathed the rocks used to build the first pyramid? In short, why do you get to pick and choose what the rest of us should accept as true, and based on what objective criteria?

Notes

[1] Lord Raglan, *The Hero: A Study in Tradition, Myth and Drama* (Mineola, New York: Dover, 2003).

9. The Greek Mythic Memory

I N THE PREVIOUS chapter, I looked at some of the ways folklore, mythology, legends, and traditions have gotten the facts wrong and asked the question of how we can therefore trust that alternative history writers' selections are somehow unquestionably true. Today I'd like to continue by examining the work of Sir John Boardman, a retired Oxford professor of Classical archaeology. His 2002 book *The Archaeology of Nostalgia*[1] explains clearly how the ancient Greeks used the shards left over from the preceding Mycenaean civilization to fabricate an ancient past that never was.

First a few facts: The Mycenaeans were a Greek-speaking civilization that flourished from roughly 1600 to 1200 BCE. The civilization collapsed, and four hundred years known as the Greek Dark Ages followed. During this period, there was no writing, populations migrated, whole cities vanished or were transformed, and even the gods themselves emerged in new forms. For example, Drimios, the son of Zeus, vanished from the pantheon; Paean, the god of healing, merged with Apollo; and Zeus superseded Poseidon as the most honored of the gods. The exact degree of continuity and change between Mycenaean and Homeric Greece is open to dispute and is one of the most fascinating questions in Greek religion.

Boardman explains that the Greeks did not retain a historical memory of the Mycenaeans in the sense that we would consider history. Nevertheless, they saw around them the ruined cities of the Mycenaeans, whom they considered the Heroes, the men of old, the men of renown. [Note to the literarily impaired: Yes, I am making a Biblical allusion.] They found their artifacts, especially their bronze weapons, armor, and implements.

(In the next chapter, we'll look at how alternative authors' efforts to take Greek myth literally result in the actual destruction of historical knowledge, and I'll discuss the mythic association of specific places with legendary heroes who could not possibly have lived there.)

The ancient Greeks considered the Heroes to be giants for three reasons: 1) Mycenaean cities seemed so massively large that only giants—specifically Cyclopes—could have built them. 2) They believed that the world was in gradual decay, so earlier generations were therefore larger and more robust, and 3) they found the bones of prehistoric elephants and assumed they were the skeletons of the Heroes themselves.

Ancient astronaut writers have frequently asserted that ancient descriptions of "giant" skeletons are to be taken as literal proof of alien-human hybrid creatures of giant size. However, Boardman (following Adrienne Mayor[2]) makes very clear that nearly all the ancient descriptions of "giant's bones" observed *in situ* have nearly 1-to-1 correlation with locations where modern excavators have discovered the remains of fossil elephants and other megafauna.

Boardman also describes artifacts that the Greeks misinterpreted by filtering them through myth. At the Temple of Artemis at Ephesus there was displayed a Neolithic greenstone axe from 2000 BCE, which was taken to be a thunderbolt from Zeus, a "sacred stone that fell from the sky" as the Biblical writers were well aware.[3] A similar axe head gave rise to an entire cult of Zeus at Labraunda in Libya.[4] Bronze Age armor from the Mycenaeans found its way into the treasury of Alexander the Great, who considered it a relic of the Trojan War.[5] Elsewhere, Bronze Age arms were attributed to Herakles, Diomedes, Agamemnon Aeneas, and Odysseus and great effort was taken to preserve the ancient spears, swords, and shields from disintegration.

The Greek case is somewhat different from those described in the previous chapter because the Greeks retained a vague, shadowy understanding of the Mycenaeans, and although their Heroic identifications were literally incorrect they did correctly attribute such relics to a bygone civilization. We know that some continuity must have existed because Homer discusses a boar's tusk helmet[6] that was for a long time thought fictional. But archaeologists found several of them in Mycenaean graves and could thus conclude that they ceased to be made at least two centuries before Homer composed the *Iliad*. *Something* of the past survived—but note we only know this *because archaeology confirmed it.*

Here's the rub: The Greek mythic memory is the exception that proves the rule. The Greeks remembered something of the past, but freely mixed fragments of history with myth, misinterpretation, and imagination. Because we have archaeology to confirm or deny the claims of the Greeks, we can see how the myths and legends were distorted, what they got right and what they got wrong. Martin Nilsson recognized the Mycenaean origins of Greek mythology, but even he admitted that it is only the confirmation of archaeology that allowed such connections to be seen; the stories, on their own, were no substitute for history. As Lord Raglan wrote, if myths require outside confirmation to prove them true, the myth is therefore unnecessary as proof. A myth absent outside confirmation is essentially worthless; it can tell us what people *believed* at the time of the telling, but not whether their beliefs were correct.

So, when ancient astronaut writers ask us to take myths as truth, we are within our rights to ask for confirmation: Why is this true? Why is this story closer to the Greek memory of Mycenae than the (literally) fairy tales of fairies building the Irish dolmens?

Notes

[1] John Boardman, *The Archaeology of Nostalgia: How the Greeks Re-Created Their Mythical Past* (New York: Thames & Hudson, 2002).

[2] Adrienne Mayor, *The First Fossil Hunters: Paleontology in Greek and Roman Times* (Princeton: Princeton University Press, 2000).

[3] Acts 19:35

[4] Plutarch, *Greek Questions* 45

[5] Arrianus, *Alexandri anabasis* 1.11.7-8

[6] *Iliad* 10:260-5. "Meriones found a bow and quiver for Ulysses, and on his head he set a leathern helmet that was lined with a strong plaiting of leathern thongs, while on the outside it was thickly studded with boar's teeth, well and skilfully set into it; next the head there was an inner lining of felt" (translated by Samuel Butler).

10. How Alternative History Methods Destroy Knowledge

ONE OF THE most maddening things about alternative historians and ancient astronaut theorists is the way they insist on literal interpretations of ancient texts. For example, Ezekiel's vision is seen as a firsthand report of a UFO, Phaeton's fiery crash of the sun chariot is seen as an eyewitness account of a crashed flying saucer, and of course Plato's Atlantis is taken for historical fact. Let's look at an example of how this rejection of textual criticism, superficially an appealing way to make new discoveries, actively destroys knowledge when applied in practice.

Our example comes from a strange incident in the adventures of Jason, the Greek hero who captured the Golden Fleece after making a great journey to the East. In later Greco-Roman religious practice, this hero somehow acquired a series of temples across the East as well as a mountain in Iran, Mt. Jasonium.[1] He was also recognized as the conqueror of Armenia before the Trojan War.[2] Taken at face value, as alternative historians prefer, such tales imply either that Jason was seen as a god (or, heaven help us, an alien) or that the Greeks had conquered much of the Near East long before Alexander.

But taking the texts at face value actively destroys knowledge. The real story is so much more interesting.

The origin of the tale can be found in the Persian religious structures called *ayazana* or *ayadana*, the exact nature of which archaeology has yet to clarify. They may be related to (or the same as) the fire altars of the Zoroastrians, as mentioned in 2 Maccabees 1.19-34. There is no doubt, however, that they were religious precincts of some sort, since the Persian king Darius was recorded in a Persian inscription as restoring the "*ayazana*" the usurper Gaumata the Magus destroyed, while this word is translated in the contemporary Akkadian and Elamite versions of the text as the "temples" or "places of worship."[3]

When the Greeks first visited areas under the influence of Persian religion, they apparently misheard the Median dialect version of the *ayadana*, **yazona*, as Jasonia (sound it out—it's close if we remember that in Greek Jason was called "Iason"), and they applied their pre-existing myth of Jason's great eastward voyage to explain the presence of these sacred sites across the East. Similarly, the effort to apply the myth to the geography of the Medes' territory (now Iran), identified as a land visited by Jason, led to Mt. Damavand becoming Mt. Jasonion (Greek) or Mt. Jasonium (Latin). Thus, Strabo writes "that the memorials of Jason are, the Jasonian heroa, held in great reverence by the Barbarians, (besides a great mountain above the Caspian Gates on the left hand, called Jasonium)."[4] Lest this connection seem speculative, it should be remembered that the Medes' empire extended into Cappadocia in Asia Minor, almost to the very site at Cape Jason where the most famous Jasonium stood.

After this, it is a short hop to the strange story found only in Pompeius Trogus (as epitomized by Justin) that Jason "set out on a second voyage for Colchis, accompanied by a numerous train of followers (who, at the fame of his valour, came daily from all parts to join him), by his wife Medea, whom, having previously divorced her, he had now received again from compassion for her exile."[5] Then, to make amends to Medea's father for stealing the Golden Fleece and treating his daughter badly, he "carried on great wars with the neighbouring nations; and of the cities which he took, he added part to the kingdom of his father-in-law, to make amends for the injury that he had done him in his former expedition."[6] This, Trogus and Justin affirm, is the reason that that Jasonia exist across the East, in honor of Jason's conquest of the entire region. So powerful was this myth that, according to Justin, one of Alexander's generals destroyed the Jasonia where he found them so the mythic figure could not rival Alexander. Of course this "second voyage" never happened; it was a post-hoc explanation meant to give a mythic background to the confusion of terminology found in Iran and Armenia.

But if we were content to accept the ancient writers at face value, none of this knowledge about early Greek interactions with the East would have come to light. Instead, we would be searching for evidence of pre-Greek temples to Jason that never existed, and evidence of Bronze Age Greek invasions of Armenia and Iran that never happened. This actually happened from the eighteenth century to the early twentieth century, producing much speculation and few facts. This is how "alternative" readings of ancient texts actively destroy knowledge and retard a real understanding of the past.

Notes

[1] Strabo, *Geography*, 11.13-14.

[2] Strabo, *Geography*, 11.14; Justin, *Epitome*, 42.2-3.

[3] Behistun inscription, 1.61-6.

[4] *Geography*, 11.13.10.

[5] *Epitome* 42.2.

[6] *Epitome* 42.3.

11. Ancient Aliens and Atlantis

IN AN ARTICLE on the *Legendary Times* website carrying the official byline of the official ancient astronaut research organization, the Archaeology, Astronautics & SETI Research Association (now the Ancient Alien Society), and therefore representing the official position of the premiere Paleo-SETI research society, Atlantis never existed!

> And there could not have been any Atlantis (i.e. a very advanced civilization comparable to ours) either, or else we would find traces of its infrastructure worldwide—not to mention the untenable theory of a geologically recently sunken continent.[1]

Now, I agree with this statement 100%, but I suspect it comes as news to many ancient astronaut theorists, especially David Hatcher Childress, whose bread and butter has been promoting extreme claims that imaginary civilizations like Lemuria, Mu, Atlantis, and the "Rama Empire" reigned in the deep past, mostly on vanished continents. Additionally, the "alternative archaeologists" who appear on *Ancient Aliens*, including *Fingerprints of the Gods* author Graham Hancock, must be shocked to learn that the leading ancient astronaut research organization considers their research moot.

Of course, the ancient astronaut theory, being no theory in the scientific sense, refuses to simply reject findings (however ridiculous) that contradict the theory. Instead, they are incorporated in a completely different form:

> Whenever findings, imitations of findings or descriptions thereof [i.e. of an Atlantis-like civilization] appear in old cultures, they seem to come up suddenly as if "dropped from the sky". But where were the manufacturing sites if not on Earth?[2]

Thus, after rejecting Atlantis for lack of evidence, the AAS RA simply relocates it into the depths of space. The very fact that no evidence for it exists somehow has become evidence that a force not from this earth was responsible! But here's the really interesting thing. The AAS RA is run by Giorgio Tsoukalos, who is a consulting producer on *Ancient Aliens*, on which he appears as the primary talking head.

On the *Ancient Aliens* episode "Underwater Worlds" (November 11, 2010), so-called "ancient astronaut theorists" argued about the existence of Atlantis and its possible connection to aliens. Despite the official position of the ancient astronaut theory's main organization that Atlantis never existed, AAS RA head Giorgio Tsoukalos appeared on the program to promote his theory that Atlantis was in fact an extraterrestrial spacecraft using what he claimed were genuine Greek myths of bronze islands that fell from the sky—UFOs.

At first blush this theory seems impossible. The Greek philosopher Aristotle doubted the ability of even small rocks—meteors—to fall from the sky and instead believed them to be the tops of exploded volcanoes, but the Roman Pliny did believe in falling space rocks. In neither case, however, did these ancient authors suggest that whole islands were descending from the heavens. This would have been a blatant impossibility, since in the mythological scheme of things the Greek sky was itself a dome made of bronze[3] or iron.[4]

In order to make the case that Atlantis was a UFO, *Ancient Aliens* provided two pieces of evidence. Let's take them in order. First, according to the narrator of the program, "One myth tells of the Titan goddess named

Asteria who fell from the sky and became an island." But is this what the myth really says? Surprisingly, the show has it almost right. But not quite.

According to the Greek mythographer Apollodorus, "Of the daughters of Coeus, Asteria in the likeness of a quail flung herself into the sea in order to escape the amorous advances of Zeus, and a city was formerly called after her Asteria, but afterwards it was named Delos."[5] While Hyginus, the Roman mythographer, gives it slightly differently in his *Fabulae*: "Though Jove [= Zeus] loved Asterie, daughter of Titan, she scorned him. Therefore she was transformed into the bird ortux, which we call a quail, and he cast her into the sea. From her an island sprang up, which was named Ortygia. This was floating."[6]

Notice that *Ancient Aliens* leaves out the part about the bird, lest the real myth seem to stray too far from the idea that the island was an alien spaceship. Nor in myth does Asteria become an island before falling into the sea. Further, other "ancient texts" make clear that the island of Asteria (or Ortygia, or Delos, depending on the source) fell "like a star," meaning that the ancients were attempting to liken the island to meteors (as the well-known phenomenon of shooting stars), not to aliens, since Asteria was (surprise!) the goddess of falling stars. Thus, the non-extraterrestrial explanation for this myth is both obvious and evident: The goddess of falling stars was associated, poetically but not unnaturally, with an island that was one of the falling stars. No UFOs necessary. And since other islands were said to have grown from such origins as a clump of sod[7] or the union of the sun god and a nymph, we can discount the idea of a widespread sky-island tradition as the origin of Greek islands.

But then things get weird. Immediately following the narrator's mention of Asteria, Giorgio Tsoukalos says:

In Ancient Greece we have a number of myths which describe islands— bronze, gleaming islands—that fell from the sky and landed in water. I don't think that Atlantis therefore was an actual, stationary, physical island. Atlantis, according to Plato, disappeared in one night with a lot of fire and a lot of smoke. See, I don't think that Atlantis sank. I think that Atlantis lifted off.

Let's leave aside the inconsistency of taking Plato's allegorical dialogues literally for the age and description of Atlantis while arguing that Plato's plain statement of its sinking should be discounted. I must admit that here I am at a complete loss. I cannot find a reference to "bronze, gleaming islands" anywhere in Greek mythology. The closest I can find is the "island of bronze" in the 1963 Ray Harryhausen movie *Jason and the Argonauts*, but this was not an island made of bronze but rather one that housed bronze statues. There are some myths that are sort of in the ballpark:

- The island of Corfu was said to have been formed from an adamantine sickle that fell from the sky, the sickle Cronus (Kronos) used to castrate his father, Uranus (Ouranos). This wasn't an island when it fell and it wasn't bronze, though it is the only myth I could find that was relatively close to Tsoukalos' claims. The myth derives from the island's characteristic sickle shape.

- In the *Odyssey*[8] Aeolus had a floating island surrounded by cliffs and a wall of bronze. But this wasn't a falling bronze island. It floated because he was the god of wind and therefore lived in the air.

- During the Gigantomachy Athena killed Enkelados by "hurling" the island of Sicily through the air to crush him. But again the island wasn't made of bronze, nor did it fall from the sky.

- The Aloadi (Aloads) imprisoned the war god Ares in a bronze jar before attacking the gods in the heavens by piling mountains atop one another, but while this myth has the sky and bronze and moving landforms, it lacks an island or falling things.

- Ares also had an island on which lived birds with feathers that shot out like arrows, but this isn't even close.

- Icarus with his wax wings fell out of the sky, and an island was named for him. But he wasn't bronze, nor is the island of Icaria.

Now, I am the first to admit that Greek mythology is a sprawling, ramshackle mess in which a few bronze islands might well have hidden from my survey. But I cannot find "a number of myths" of falling bronze islands, or even a single one. They do not exist in the many manuals and handbooks of Greek myth I consulted, nor any of the ancient authors who would have been expected to record such happenings. So, while it is possible that these bronze islands exist in Greek myth, the burden at this point falls on Giorgio Tsoukalos to show that they are more than the product of his admittedly fertile imagination.

Notes

[1] Archaeology, Astronautics and SETI Research Association, "Paleo-SETI: Interdisciplinary and Popularized," *Legendary Times* [online], no date.

[2] Ibid.

[3] *Iliad* 17.425.

[4] *Odyssey* 15.329.

[5] *Library,* 1.4.1; translated by James Frazer.

[6] Fabula 53; translated by Mary Grant.

[7] Pindar, *Pythian* 4.

[8] *Odyssey* 10.1-4.

12. The Ancients and Outer Space; or, Aliens Are Bad Teachers

O NE OF THE TENETS of the ancient astronaut theory is that the extraterrestrials gave ancient humans detailed knowledge about outer space. According to most ancient astronaut theorists (AATs) this is evident in the Book of Enoch, where Enoch is taken up into the sky and instructed on the geography and movements of the heavens,[1] which they interpret as an actual trip to outer space. Additionally, in *The Sirius Mystery* (1976, rev. ed. 1998), Robert Temple argued that the aliens provided the Sumerians with detailed knowledge of the Sirius star system, including its binary (or even triune) nature, and the planet in that system from which the extraterrestrials had ventured to earth. This knowledge, he said (building on a reference in Santillana and von Dechend's *Hamlet's Mill*[2]), was retained by the African Dogon tribe down to the present day.

Therefore, in examining ancient Near East mythology, we should expect to see an understanding of outer space from the extensive knowledge the aliens supposedly gave the Sumerians and others. At the most basic level, this should mean that the ancients understood that space was a vast empty territory beyond the earth which could be reached by traveling high enough into the sky, with no barriers between the earth, the planets, the stars, and the galaxies beyond.

So what do the Sumerians say about the sky?

The Sumerians believed the sky to be a dome of some sort, since they claimed it had a zenith. They all called tin the "metal of heaven," and many scholars follow S. N. Kramer[3] in suggesting that the Sumerians viewed the sky as made of tin. Thus, instead of revealing knowledge of deep space, instead the Sumerian belief appears to be that the sky was a tin dome covering the earth. Surrounding this was an ocean, with the dome of heaven suspended within like an air bubble in gelatin.

Well, no matter. Robert Temple's sources were Babylonian rather than Sumerian (the priest Berossus), so perhaps the Babylonians are the place to look for this knowledge.

According to the Babylonian *Enuma Elish*, the sky is a solid barrier raised like a roof over the earth[4] in which there were gates through which the sun passed.[5]

Maybe the Egyptians can do better.

According to the Pyramid Texts, the sky was conceived as a solid mass that required support from gods who hold it up. Max Müller argued based on several texts that the Egyptians believed the sky to be a dome made of iron from which the stars were suspended on cables. They knew it was crafted from iron because meteorites that crashed to earth were made of iron and must therefore have been pieces of the dome.

Well, this isn't going well. Let's try the Greeks.

The two oldest extant Greek sources are Homer's *Iliad* and *Odyssey*. According to the *Iliad*, the dome of heaven was a solid roof of bronze,[6] while the *Odyssey* claims that the heavens were instead made of iron.[7] Other myths make evident that the sky was conceived as a solid dome, or else Atlas would have had nothing to hold. The stars, the Greeks thought, were fixed in the dome of the heaven.[8]

But certainly the Book of Enoch at least means that the Jews had special knowledge of the heavens.

In Genesis 1:6-8, God separated the water above from the water below by creating a vault within the waters, just as in the Babylonian and Sumerian creation stories. Since there was water above the sky, the sky, called the "firmament"—the Hebrew term meaning literally the "solid sky"—

must be solid to hold back these waters from merging again with the waters below. St. Augustine elucidated this position, which Christians adopted. Crucially, Jewish apocryphal literature makes clear that the ancient Jews speculated whether the firmament were composed "of clay, or of brass, or of iron."[9] Origen, the Christian father, writes in his first homily on Genesis: "*Omne enim corpus firmum est sine dubio, et solidum*"—that without doubt the firmament was both firm and solid.

Apparently Temple's flying space frogs did a poor job educating the Sumerians or any other group. So where, exactly, do AATs think the ancients imagined their aliens coming from?

Notes

[1] 1 Enoch 72-82.

[2] Giorgio de Santillana and Hertha von Dechend, *Hamlet's Mill: An Essay Investigating the Origins of Human Knowledge and Its Transmission through Myth* (Boston: Nonpareil, 1998), Appendix 1: "It goes without saying that we need not subscribe to the author's [Germaine Dieterlen's] opinion that the Mande peoples invented 'their own systems of astronomy...'"

[3] *The Sumerians* (Chicago: University of Chicago Press, 1963), 112-113.

[4] 4.137-138: "He [Marduk] slit Tiâmat open like a flat (?) fish [cut into] two pieces, / The one half he raised up and shaded the heavens therewith..." (trans. E. A. Wallis Budge).

[5] 5.9-11: "He [Marduk] opened great gates under shelter on both sides. He made a strong corridor on the left and on the right. He fixed the zenith in the heavenly vault (?)" (trans. E. A. Wallis Budge).

[6] *Iliad* 17.425.

[7] *Odyssey* 15.329.

[8] e.g. Aristotle, *De caelo*, 2.8, 3.1.

[9] 3 Baruch 3:7.

13. Ancient Atom Bombs?

I. The Myth of Ancient Atomic Warfare

IN FEBRUARY 2008, global dignitaries gathered to inaugurate the Svalbard Global Seed Vault, a repository for plant life designed to withstand nuclear war so survivors could restart civilization with healthy seeds. Magnus Bredeli-Tveiten, who oversaw construction of the vault, told the Associated Press that he expected it to last as long as the 4,500-year-old pyramids of Egypt. However, for a certain percentage of the public, ancient civilizations like Egypt are just one key to a nuclear war that already happened—thousands of years ago.

Believers maintain that in the distant past either extraterrestrials or a lost civilization like Atlantis detonated nuclear weapons, producing terrible devastation. This disaster was recorded, they say, in the Bible, Hindu scriptures, and world mythologies. Sodom and Gomorrah felt the sting of nuclear weapons when "the LORD rained down burning sulfur on Sodom and Gomorrah—from the LORD out of the heavens."[1]

An ancient Indian epic was said (erroneously, as we shall see) to describe a "single projectile charged with all the power of the universe. An incandescent column of smoke and flame as bright as ten thousand suns rose in all its splendor." To believers, these sound like eyewitness accounts of nuclear bombs being dropped from above. To skeptics, these sound like imaginative interpretations of the equivalent of prehistoric science fiction.

No mainstream scientist or historian endorses the idea of prehistoric atomic bombs, and nearly all experts believe the evidence cited to support the idea is misinterpreted at best and fraudulent at worst. For example, believers hold that deposits of 28-million-year-old glass found buried in the deserts of Libya are the result of ancient atomic bombs that melted the desert sand. In fact, according to geologist Evelyn Mervine, the glass (while still not completely understood) is likely the result of either a meteorite impact or volcanic action.

Textual Literalism

One of the key tenets of the modern ancient astronaut or lost civilization craze is the belief that ancient scriptures are the literal testament of what has gone before. For this reason young-earth creationists still claim that the earth is only 6,000 years old, and others take literally the harrowing adventure the Hebrew patriarch Enoch was said to have had in heaven. But this textual literalism tends to be highly restricted, confined to specific texts, typically those that are least familiar or accessible to the average reader and thus most difficult to check.

From the very beginning of the ancient astronaut movement, Hindu mythology, exotic to Western eyes, has been a mainstay of ancient astronaut theories. Ancient Vedic epics, running into the hundreds of thousands or even millions of words each were perfect for out-of-context quoting since ancient astronaut writers could be fairly certain no one would be able to find and check their accuracy. These theorists wish us to believe that ancient Indian Vedic literature is every bit as true as a modern-day news report. "Researchers" like self-proclaimed "real life Indiana Jones" David Hatcher Childress fervently argue that the flying machines and powerful weapons described in the Indian Vedas were actual airplanes and even nuclear weapons.

It is this latter claim of ancient atomic warfare that has sparked the interest of many internet conspiracy mongers, and these ancient atom bombs are a mainstay of the History Channel-style "ancient mystery" documentaries. As of this writing, claims of prehistoric nuclear warfare continue to be repeated in newly-published books of "alternative" history, and are broadcast frequently on *Ancient Aliens*, seen by more than a million people in the United States and many more worldwide.

It is therefore important to examine this strange theory critically to see where it came from and why anyone would believe aliens used nuclear bombs on prehistoric humans.

II. The First Ancient Atomic Bomb Theories

Obviously, the earliest references to the theory that ancient sites were destroyed by atomic or nuclear weapons do not predate the creation of those weapons in 1945. After the United States developed the first working atomic bombs, J. Robert Oppenheimer, the father of the atomic bomb, used a line from ancient Indian epic the *Bhagavad Gita* to reflect on the enormous power of the Bomb: "Now, I am become Death, the destroyer of worlds." He spoke these words not at the time of the detonation in July 1945, but twenty years later, on a television documentary, *The Decision to Drop the Bomb.* From this, an apocryphal story arose that Oppenheimer had told students in 1952 that the Manhattan Project produced the first atomic weapon "in modern times." There is no evidence that Oppenheimer ever said this, and his reference to the *Bhagavad Gita* was meant as a poetic reflection, not a serious scientific reflection on ancient weaponry.

Among fringe thinkers, an allegedly scientific paper by two researchers named David W. Davenport and Ettore Vincenti is said to have recorded the scholars' belief that an archaeological site they investigated in India, the famous city of Mohenjo Daro, was destroyed in ancient times due to a nuclear blast. However, the authors' 1979 book, *2000 a.C. Distruzione atomica* (Atomic Destruction in 2000 B.C.), was not a scientific paper but another work of pseudoscience, unrecognized by academia. There is to date no evidence of nuclear explosions prior to 1945.

Instead, the earliest reference to prehistoric nuclear warfare appears to be the Soviet mathematician and ethnologist Matest M. Agrest, who argued in 1959 that Sodom and Gomorrah had been destroyed by nuclear bombs from alien spaceships. This claim was brought to the attention of the other side of the Iron Curtain through *The Morning of the Magicians*

(1960), a French work by Louis Pauwels and Jacques Bergier which outlined one of the earliest complete (nonfiction) versions of the modern ancient astronaut theory (see chapter two) and offered outlandish claims
about ancient nuclear warfare.[2] We will examine their specific claims
about ancient India momentarily, but first we turn to the other alleged
prehistoric bomb blast—the one from the Bible.

Biblical Bombs

Those who support the theory of ancient atom bombs tend to be believers in a lost civilization like Atlantis or in extraterrestrial intervention
in ancient history, the so-called "ancient astronaut" theory popularized by
Swiss hotelier Erich von Däniken in the 1960s and '70s with his book
Chariots of the Gods? (1968), its sequels, and movie adaptation as *In Search
of Ancient Astronauts* (1973), narrated by Rod Serling of *Twilight Zone*
fame. It was von Däniken who introduced mainstream audiences to the
idea (borrowed from the French writer Robert Charroux, as well as Pauwels and Bergier) that the "aliens" had blown up Sodom and Gomorrah
with atom bombs. Pauwels and Bergier quote what they say is a description from the Dead Sea Scrolls about the nuclear effects of the Sodom
bomb,[3] but I have been unable to find this passage in published versions of
the scrolls. It appears to be a lightly paraphrased and re-ordered version of
the Genesis account, translated from its original tongue to French to English with modern terms like "explosions" added in. No references are
given. As we shall see, this is not the only case where Pauwels and Bergier
offered an unusual translation to support their belief in ancient atomic
warfare.

Von Däniken argued in *Chariots of the Gods?* (1968) that atom bombs
destroyed Sodom and Gomorrah, the biblical cities of sin: "since the dropping of two atomic bombs on Japan, we know the kind of damage such
bombs cause. . . Let us imagine for a moment that Sodom and Gomorrah
were destroyed according to plan, i.e. deliberately, by a nuclear explosion."[4] From his offhand remark, asked as a question rather than stated as
fact, a whole sub-genre of ancient warfare grew, usually without reference

to the earlier and (slightly) more serious versions proposed by Pauwels and Bergier or Agrest. However, this remark was, well, remarkably ill-considered. Here is what Genesis says about the destruction of the two cities:

> By the time Lot reached Zoar, the sun had risen over the land. Then the LORD rained down burning sulfur on Sodom and Gomorrah—from the LORD out of the heavens. Thus he overthrew those cities and the entire plain, destroying all those living in the cities--and also the vegetation in the land. But Lot's wife looked back, and she became a pillar of salt. Early the next morning Abraham got up and returned to the place where he had stood before the LORD. He looked down toward Sodom and Gomorrah, toward all the land of the plain, and he saw dense smoke rising from the land, like smoke from a furnace. So when God destroyed the cities of the plain, he remembered Abraham, and he brought Lot out of the catastrophe that overthrew the cities where Lot had lived.[5]

This description is notable for its brevity, but even this brief mention has little in common with an actual atomic or nuclear blast. When atomic bombs go off, the majority of their destructive power derives from the blast wave—a wall of wind that knocks down all around it. No mention of this blast wave—the most prominent effect of a nuclear blast—shows up in Genesis. Theoretically, with Lot so close to the site of the destruction, he should have felt the blast. While nuclear weapons can set off fires, this is entirely dependent on the amount of flammable material and the distance from the blast site; whereas in the biblical description the dominant motifs are first, a rain of burning sulfur and second, heavy smoke and fire lasting into the next day. The clear implication, taking the story as literally as von Däniken would like, is that the two cities were destroyed by a shower of flaming rocks from the sky. This led some researchers to propose recently that cities were destroyed by an asteroid, though this is, like so many theories, unproven since neither Sodom nor Gomorrah has ever been found (though some Bronze Age candidates like Bab edh-Dhra have been proposed), or even proved to have once existed outside the Bible.

The Indian Connection

As I have noted, von Däniken's most important source was not scientific literature, or even first-hand observation; instead, von Däniken derived much of his information and wild speculation from a *The Morning of the Magicians*. Pauwels and Bergier misquote out-of-context passages from Vedic Indian literature to claim that India experienced atomic warfare ten thousand years ago.[6] We will explore their specific misquotation momentarily. For now, it is important to note that von Däniken read and repeated these claims for an international audience and continued the tradition of misinterpretation. The author gives a lengthy quotation in *Chariots of the Gods?* from the *Mahabharata*, the ancient Indian epic, which he likens to the devastating effects of a nuclear blast, suggesting that the ancient poem is a record of nuclear war in the distant past. The quotation describes what sounds like the effects of a nuclear blast:

It was as if the elements had been unleashed. The sun spun round. Scorched by the incandescent heat of the weapon, the world reeled in fever. Elephants were set on fire by the heat and ran to and fro in a frenzy to seek protection from the terrible violence. The water boiled, the animals died, the enemy was mown down and the raging of the blaze made the trees collapse in rows as in a forest fire. The elephants made a fearful trumpeting and sank dead to the ground over a vast area. Horses and war chariots were burnt up and the scene looked like the aftermath of a conflagration. Thousands of chariots were destroyed, then deep silence descended on the sea. The winds began to blow and the earth grew bright. It was a terrible sight to see. The corpses of the fallen were mutilated by the terrible heat so that they no longer looked like human beings. Never before have we seen such a ghastly weapon and never before have we heard of such a weapon.[7]

However, this quotation is translated into English from an 1889 German translation of the Sanskrit original, with no indication of where in the 1.8 million words of the epic the quotation came, or in what context this amazing weapon worked. In Book 7, I found what I believe to be the same passage in the standard Ganguili translation:

> The very elements seemed to be perturbed. The Sun seemed to turn round. The universe, scorched with heat, seemed to be in a fever. The elephants and other creatures of the land, scorched by the energy of that weapon, ran in fright, breathing heavily and desirous of protection against that terrible force. The very waters being heated, the creatures residing in that element, O Bharata, became exceedingly uneasy and seemed to burn. From all the points of the compass, cardinal and subsidiary, from the firmament and the very Earth, showers of sharp and fierce arrows fell and issued, with the impetuosity of Garuda or the wind. Struck and burnt by those shafts of Açwatthāman that were all endued with the impetuosity of the thunder, the hostile warriors fell down like trees burnt down by a raging fire. Huge elephants, burnt by that weapon, fell down on the Earth all around, uttering fierce cries loud as those of the clouds. Other huge elephants, scorched by that fire, ran hither and thither, and roared aloud in fear, as if in the midst of a forest conflagration. The steeds, O king, and the cars also, burnt by the energy of that weapon, looked, O sire, like the tops of trees burnt in a forest fire. [...] Burnt by the energy of Açwatthāman's weapon, the forms of the slain could not be distinguished.[8]

The context for this passage makes clear that the speaker is describing an imaginary weapon composed of fiery arrows that rain flame down onto the ground. Unlike an actual nuclear weapon, which produces a mushroom cloud, vaporizes the area beneath it, and then dissipates, this weapon is specifically said to be like a "smokeless fire." It causes the sky to fill with clouds that rain blood, but instead of vaporizing those it hits, instead, it causes the air to boil, setting alight all around it. In an actual nuclear explosion, the blast force is the force that kills once one passes the hypocenter. And anyone who survived to describe the blast would by definition have been in the region where the blast wave overtook any flame. Outside the small area where the actual explosion occurs, the thermal radiation from a nuclear blast is intense, but brief, lasting perhaps one or two seconds. It can cause severe skin burns (but not light a person aflame). Thermal blasts can ignite highly flammable materials, though these do not include elephants or trees; nor would it boil the rivers and seas.

All of this is irrelevant, however, since the description makes clear that the weapon is no bomb but instead a type of imaginary sky-cannon, shooting flames like arrows or thunderbolts to the ground below. The context notes that the weapon is wielded by an individual, who fires it. It is not dropped like a bomb.

But this type of creative interpretation pales against the wholesale rewriting of Indian myth to suit the needs of the ancient astronaut theory that we find in *The Morning of the Magicians* and the unscrupulous writers who altered and mangled even its dubious scholarship. In *Morning*, two passages from the *Mahabharata* are cited as proof of ancient atomic warfare. In later works, like those of David Hatcher Childress, these two distinct passages from a prose translation of the epic are conflated into a single block of text and then rewritten as poetry in order to show that ancient Indians knew the effects of radiation poisoning; of course no such passage exists in the *Mahabharata*. It is instead a misquotation of a mistranslation. The flawed transmission of this passage is so complex that the entire next chapter of this book is devoted to exploring this one passage, but suffice it to say for now that the "radiation poisoning" passage originally referred to the scavenging of corpses by vermin.

The false version of this passage appears time and again in alternative works—more than three dozen times in print and thousands more online. In a half dozen books, Childress alone repeats the same alleged passage from the *Mahabharata*, gleefully explaining that the excerpt describes in precise detail the exact pattern of radiation poisoning seen after a nuclear event—something ancient people could not possibly have known yet recorded in their literature. Childress is not the only author to rely on this false quotation, merely the most prolific, but he has an important reason for needing it to be true.

*   *   *

III. The Tesla Death Ray

David Hatcher Childress is perhaps the most famous proponent of the atomic warfare theory. Childress calls himself a "lost science scholar," and claimed in his book *Extraterrestrial Archaeology* that the moon and nearby planets contain pyramids, domes and spaceports visible by telescope and satellite. (Full disclosure: Childress publicly criticized my discussion of his theories in my 2005 book *The Cult of Alien Gods* as inaccurate because it linked him with those who believe in alien visitations in the remote past. He claimed at that time that ancient anomalies were the work of a lost super-civilization, but he returned to the alien intervention theory in 2009 when he joined the History Channel's *Ancient Aliens* television series.) He has a profound respect for the scientist Nikola Tesla, who Childress believes invented antigravity, time-travel, death-ray, and thought machines. Childress is also prone to seeing conspiracies, arguing in his book *The Fantastic Inventions of Nikola Tesla* that the U.S. government conspired to suppress the discoveries made by Tesla to protect big business. Incidentally, Childress claims only to be the posthumous co-author of *Fantastic Inventions* with Tesla as the main author.

To promote his turn-of-the-millennium book *Technology of the Gods* (2000), Childress released a chapter on ancient nuclear weapons to *Nexus* magazine, the "alternative" magazine founded in 1987 to report unconventional and occult stories, or what owner Duncan Roads calls "suppressed information": "It was a magazine that addressed itself to the alternative fringe of society and thus it carried many 'alternative' points of view on the subjects of health, human rights, the environment, human potential and suppressed information. I revived this magazine by deleting all articles on the new age, the occult, environment and similar subjects, and by concentrating on what I call 'suppressed information.'"[9]

Childress begins his article by discussing a geological anomaly: namely that the same glass-like fusion of sand which occurs on the land beneath a nuclear blast can also be found in ancient strata dating back up to 8,000 years. Hatcher provides the scientific explanation, and then he rejects it: "The general theory is that the glass was created by the searing, sand-melting impact of a cosmic projectile. However, there are serious problems with this theory...."[10]

Childress rejects the theory because he says there is no evidence of an impact crater. The 1988 work of A.A. Qureshi and H. A. Khan concluded that a crater would no longer be visible because the glass did not form 8,000 years ago, as Childress would have it, but much longer ago: "Based on these studies a meteoritic impact, which caused the fusion of Nubian sand or sandstone and resulted in the formation of Libyan desert glass 28.36 m.y. [million years] ago, has been recognized."[11] A 1988 study by A.V. Murali et al. found traces of the actual meteor in the Libyan glass.[12] Childress also ignores another possibility. Childress himself admits that there have been impacts which did not produce craters, like the Tunguska Event of 1908, of which mainstream science holds that an asteroid hit Siberia and vaporized without leaving any trace except flattened trees and an explosion so loud it could be heard in Moscow and so bright that midnight was bright as noon in London.

A whole mythology has grown up around the Tunguska Event. Many explanations exist, ranging from the scientifically-accepted asteroid theory to the crash of a UFO and the resulting detonation of its nuclear reactor. How anyone knows whether UFOs are nuclear-powered is not explained. One fringe theory that fits well with Childress' conspiratorial view of Tesla is the Tesla ray. True-believer Oliver Nichelson says, "The idea of a Tesla directed energy weapon causing the Tunguska explosion was incorporated in a fictional biography (1994), by another writer, and was the subject of a *Sightings* television program segment."

Nichelson continues: "Given Tesla's general pacifistic nature it is hard to understand why he would carry out a test harmful to both animals and the people who herded the animals even when he was in the grip of financial desperation. The answer is that he probably intended no harm, but was aiming for a publicity coup and, literally, missed his target."[13] Nichelson then gives his version of how Tesla directed an energy-ray across the globe to blow up a relatively uninhabited section of Siberia.

So what does the Tunguska Even have to do with ancient atomic warfare?

Well, the answer lies in the literary career of David Hatcher Childress, author of books on both antediluvian nuclear weapons and the so-called Tesla Death-Ray. Childress needs the Tunguska event to be something other than an asteroid to bolster his theories. In the course of his work, Childress became convinced that Tesla had only "rediscovered" technology that had existed in ages past, much as Ignatius Donnelly asserted in his *Atlantis: The Antediluvian World* (1882). Therefore, Childress asks: "[I]s it possible that the vitrified desert is the result of atomic war in the ancient past? Could a Tesla-type beam weapon have melted the desert, perhaps in a test?"[14]

IV. Big Theories, No Evidence

Childress built on the mangled quotations from *The Morning of the Magicians* and the supposedly scientific report from Davenport and Vittore to develop his own "evidence" from the same sources: "If one were to believe the *Mahabharata*, great battles were fought with in the past with airships, particle beams, chemical warfare and presumably atomic weapons. . . [B]attles in the latter days of Atlantis were fought with highly sophisticated, high-tech weapons." Needless to say, for Childress, Atlantis is not only real but an active competitor for ancient India, which he calls the Rama Empire: "The Rama Empire, described in the *Mahabharata* and *Ramayana*, was supposedly contemporaneous with the great cultures of Atlantis and Osiris [Egypt] in the West. Atlantis, well-known from Plato's writings and ancient Egyptian records, apparently existed in the mid-Atlantic and was a highly technical and patriarchal civilization."[15]

There is neither proof of Atlantis existing outside of Plato's mind, nor any evidence that the Atlanteans had high-tech weaponry. I know of no ethnographies describing the familial relations of Atlanteans. Osiris, we are told, is pre-dynastic Egypt. Childress' source? "Esoteric doctrine" unrevealed to the reader. It is, in fact, material derived from the Lemurian Fellowship, a New Age society Childress was once associated with. As for the Rama Empire, Childress says it began with "Nagas (Naacals) who had come into India from Burma and ultimately from the "Motherland to the East"—or so Col. James Churchward was told."[16] Churchward wrote about the lost continent of Mu in the early twentieth century. His books sold well, but were quickly shown to be a hoax when he could produce no evidence of the tablets where he read of the continent or the monks who gave them to him. (See Chapter 15.)

Of course, this is good enough evidence for Childress. He identifies Mu with Lemuria and uses material from the Lemurian Fellowship lesson manual to tell how the Ramas and the Atlanteans fought a great war which resulted in nuclear holocaust. Never mind that Lemuria was a failed nineteenth century scientific theory designed to explain the appearance of lemurs in both India and Madagascar before plate tectonics showed that the animals walked from one to the other when both were linked.

None of this made it into Childress' story, and he tells how the Atlanteans were angry that the Ramas had beat them in battle: "Assuming the above story is true, Atlantis was not pleased at the humiliating defeat and therefore used its most powerful and destructive weapon—quite possibly an atomic-type weapon!"[17] As has been shown, the above story is not true and there was neither Atlantis nor Lemuria to fight with any weapons at all, let alone nuclear ones.

Childress cites L. Sprague DeCamp's assessment of ancient oil-based weapons like Greek Fire to bolster the claim of sophisticated stone-age weapons. DeCamp, it should be noted, was one of the disciples of the American horror author H. P. Lovecraft, whose mythos of Great Cthulhu helped spawn the ancient astronaut theory when Pauwels and Bergier used him as inspiration for *Morning of the Magicians* (see Chapter 2). Childress then brings in another ancient astronaut supporter, Robin Collyns, to testify that on the authority of another Indian epic, the *Vaimānika Shāstra*, ancient peoples had plasma guns powered by electrified mercury. The *Vaimānika Shāstra* is no ancient text; instead it was "channeled," supposedly between 1918 and 1923, but remained unknown until 1952 when G. R. Josyer "revealed" its existence. The text claims to be a transcript of an ancient poem composed in another dimension by a character from the *Ramayana*.

If that were not enough, Childress brings in moldy nineteenth-century tales of vitrified ruins in Death Valley, California to say that ancient atom bombs melted the bricks in those buildings. However, he also says that he could not prove they existed, let alone were the result of a nuclear blast. Nevertheless, they form an important piece of evidence for the author.

Remember what von Däniken said about Sodom and Gomorrah, that they were destroyed by a vengeful alien race? Childress also makes this claim: "Probably the most famous of all ancient 'nuke 'em' stories is the well-known biblical tale of Sodom and Gomorrah."[18] Childress apparently does not think it is that well-known, for he then quotes it in full. He then sets up a straw-man, smashing the paper-tiger argument that the cities were destroyed by plate tectonics. Obviously, this is false, and Childress knows it. He then claims there is but one hypothesis to explain the disappearance of the two cities: "Therefore we come back to the popular theory that these cities were not destroyed in a geological cataclysm but in a man-made (or extraterrestrial-made) apocalypse that was technological in nature."[19] Obviously, Childress neglects to recognize that there are other explanations, the simplest of which is that the cities and their destruction are the product of a fertile imagination.

The theory of Occam's Razor says we cannot accept this possibility without extraordinary evidence. Childress believes he has it. Quoting L. M. Lewis, the reader learns that Lot's wife (the pillar of salt) proves an atomic blast because the pillar still stood in the first century A.D. when Flavius Josephus saw it. Sodom, of course, was destroyed in 1898 BCE, according to Lewis. Therefore, had the salt pillar been anything but the remains of a nuclear blast, it should have vanished. Of course, he fails to note that the Dead Sea area produces new salt pillars on a regular basis. These are still called "Lot's wife" by the locals, but few are of any great age.

So where does this leave the theory of ancient nuclear activity?

There is no basis in fact for the empty assertions of alternative authors like von Däniken, Pauwels and Bergier, and Childress, but they are repeated by so many who read these authors that they take on a verisimilitude that endangers a rational view of the past. How can genuine mysteries be explored and the vast tapestry of ancient history displayed in its full color and glory when rampant and baseless claims throw dark stains on the delicate images of the past?

The final question we must ask is this: Why does this silly theory matter?

V. What It All Means

The first reason the claims about ancient atom bombs matter is that far too many people take them seriously. Recently, first the History Channel and then H2 have given von Däniken and Childress a weekly soapbox to opine unchallenged on the ancient astronaut theory, telling an audience that once reached two million viewers that aliens blew up ancient cities with nuclear weapons and genetically engineered early humans. These claims are utterly without compelling evidence, and do violence to our public discourse by misleading the public and using the power of television to circumvent the need for real evidence and sound theories.

What is more interesting, though, is not the alleged evidence for ancient atom bombs but rather *why* people come to embrace a belief in the existence of nuclear devastation in the remote past. Surely the History/H2 would not program *Ancient Aliens* if two million or more viewers weren't ready and willing to embrace the idea of aliens with atomic weapons.

Though the Atlantis legend has its origins in an unfinished work by Plato written more than 2,500 years ago, the modern version of the Atlantis legend begins with Ignatius Donnelly, an American politician who wrote *Atlantis: The Antediluvian World* in 1882 to prove that the lost continent was very real and was the origin of all European, Asian, and Native American civilizations. Donnelly was the first to equate Atlantis with the destructive power of advanced weaponry. In the book he discusses an event from the Bible when "a fire from the Lord consumed two hundred and fifty men" who led a rebellion against Moses.[20] Tellingly, though, Donnelly interpreted this event through the lens of the technology of his time: "This looks very much as if Moses had blown up the rebels with gunpowder."[21] He also thought gunpowder was responsible for explosions in India and Atlantis.

Though Donnelly believed Atlantis was roughly as sophisticated as the pre-industrial Europe of the eighteenth century, those who built on his work steadily expanded the wonders of the lost continent to include everything from lasers to antigravity devices to nuclear power, keeping the mythical Atlantis one step ahead of modern technology. By the time of von Däniken, Donnelly's quaint ideas about gunpowder had gone out the window. Instead, von Däniken argued that biblical explosions, like the one at Sodom, were effected "deliberately, by a nuclear explosion."[22] Granted, even nuclear scientists like J. Robert Oppenheimer, the father of the atom bomb, noted the (thematic, not literal) similarities between passages in the *Bhagavad Gita* and the destructive power of atomic weapons, but why was it that in the 1970s ancient texts started to seem like historical records of nuclear war?

Ironically, von Däniken provides the answer to this question, in a passage I quoted earlier: "[S]ince the dropping of two atomic bombs on Japan," he wrote, "we know the kind of damage such bombs cause and that living creatures exposed to direct radiation die or become seriously ill."[23]

Because the nuclear age had produced horrors on a scale previously unimaginable, and because nuclear war was a very real possibility during the Cold War (the Cuban Missile Crisis had occurred just six years before von Däniken published his first book), it made sense that some would begin to look for mythological and historical precedents for otherwise unprecedented events. This relationship between modern technology and the ancient atom bomb theory has kept it current even as so many other "alternative" beliefs of the '70s—like psychic spoon bending, EST, and pyramid power—have lost their currency.

In fact, the same day that the Svalbard Global Seed Vault opened, an article appeared on the *American Chronicle* website declaring that the destruction of Sodom and Gomorrah, Atlantis and the lesser-known lost continent of Mu were all the result of ancient atom bombs. Like von Däniken, writer Paul Dale Roberts immediately understood the connection between his reconstruction of the past and his concerns about the present: "The world is in dire straights (sic) ...With the threat of terrorism, crime, global warming, wars and the rumors of wars, new diseases arising, we are facing the Four Horsemen of the Apocalypse."[24]

Roberts's description of ancient atomic warfare leaned heavily on the work of the field's most popular author, David Hatcher Childress, who in the late 1990s connected the dots to events then in the news, the development of nuclear weapons in the 1990s in both Pakistan and India, countries that had previously fought several (non-nuclear) wars: "The echoes of ancient atomic warfare in south Asia continue to this day with India and Pakistan currently threatening each other," Childress wrote. "Ironically, Kashmir, possibly the site of an earlier atomic war, is the focus of this conflict. Will the past repeat itself in India and Pakistan?"[25]

Childress has appeared in countless television documentaries to testify to the advanced state of ancient technology, and cable channels like History, H2, and Syfy have been complicit in popularizing the story of ancient nuclear weapons, the myth of Atlantis, and the "reality" of ancient astronauts. The echo chamber of the internet reinforces these beliefs among the core of believers. And ancient mysteries sell better than science.

"I have to wonder," geologist Mervine wrote in 2005, "what inspires such crazy notions and how people such as Von Daniken and Childress manage to sell so many books. Certainly, far more copies of a single one of their books have been sold than, say, all the editions of my igneous petrology textbook."[26] For Mervine, the answer comes from the explanatory power of fringe theories, which offer a one-size-fits-all explanation for the otherwise complex and difficult tangles of ancient history. It's easier to say the aliens or Atlanteans did it than to study the intricacies of history.

While this may be true for the Atlantis theory or the ancient astronaut theory, for the specific case of ancient atom bombs, it seems that contemporary anxieties are being projected backward into the past. Until the first nuclear blast in 1945, no human civilization had possessed the power to completely destroy civilization, but imagining such a civilization in the deep past serves two powerful purposes.

First, it provides a morality tale for the modern world. A great civilization (human or alien) once had the power to destroy the world. They misused the power and destroyed themselves. We must therefore avoid their fate. Second, it provides a comforting ray of hope. Although early human civilization had been destroyed, we are still here today. Humanity can and will survive nuclear war, and the species will go on.

The story of ancient atomic bombs, therefore, is a morality tale with a promise for redemption. *It tells us that we will be ok even when the technology we create threatens to destroy us.* For this reason, the modern myth of ancient atom bombs continues to ricochet around the internet, cable television, and "alternative history" publishers and likely will for years to come.

Notes

[1] Genesis 19:24-25 (NIV)

[2] Louis Pauwels and Jacques Bergier, *The Morning of the Magicians*, trans. Rollo Myers (New York: Stein and Day, 1964), p. 122

[3] Ibid., 216-217.

[4] Erich von Däniken, *Chariots of the Gods? Unsolved Mysteries of the Past,* trans. Michael Heron (New York: Bantam, 1973), 36.

[5] Genesis 19:23-29 (NIV)

[6] Pauwels and Bergier, *Morning,* 122.

[7] Von Däniken, *Chariots,* 59-60.

[8] Drona Parva, sec. 201.

[9] Duncan Roads, "What Is NEXUS Magazine?", *Nexus Magazine* [online], no date.

[10] David Hatcher Childress, "The Evidence for Ancient Atomic Warfare," *Nexus Magazine* [online], 2000.

[11] A. A. Quereshi and H. A. Khan, "Recognition of Meteoric Impact by Fission Track Dating (FTD) Technique," *Geological Bulletin of the University of Peshawar* 21 (1988): 49-56.

[12] A.V. Murali, M.E. Zolenski, J.R. Underwood, and R. F. Giegengack. "Formation of Libyan Desert Glass," *Lunar and Planetary Science* 19 (1988): 817-818.

[13] Oliver Nichelson, "Tesla's Wireless Power Transmitter and the Tunguska Explosion of 1908," *Prometheus* [online], 1995.

[14] Childress, "The Evidence."

[15] Ibid.

[16] Ibid.

[17] Ibid.

[18] Ibid.

[19] Ibid.

[20] Numbers 16:31-41

[21] Ignatius Donnelly, *Atlantis: The Antediluvian World* (New York: Harper & Bros., 1882), 449.

[22] Von Däniken, *Chariots*, 36.

[23] Ibid.

[24] Paul Dale Roberts, "Messages from the Gods: Crop Circles," *Unexplained Mysteries* [online], April 12, 2008.

[25] Childress, "The Evidence."

[26] Evelyn Mervine, "Desert Glass," *Skeptic Report* [online], June 1, 2005.

14. The Case of the False Quotations

The very spring and root of honesty and virtue lie in the felicity of lighting on good education.

—Plutarch, *Of the Training of Children*

ANCIENT ASTRONAUT THEORISTS (AATs for short) have spent fifty years arguing that ancient Hindu texts present firsthand reports of prehistoric nuclear explosions. (See discussion in the previous chapter). However, a major problem with efforts at debunking AATs' claims is that most scientific debunkers focus on, logically enough, the science involved since the most prominent debunkers tend to be physicists, evolutionary biologists, astronomers, etc. Fewer are experts in history and the humanities, which AATs have exploited, basing much of their evidence on ancient texts and artwork that hard scientists are not always able to effectively debunk on the merits of individual cases. Even an archaeologist, by dint of specialization, may not have the broad cross-cultural knowledge to spot the mistake in a quotation from a sacred text from an unfamiliar culture or time period.

Here, I'd like to focus on a problem with texts used by the AATs to show exactly how a false belief arises, how it is sustained, and how a mixture of ignorance, half-truths, and misrepresentation creates fanciful new extraterrestrial "texts" out of very different originals. Our sample text will be an alleged "quotation" from the *Mahabharata* "reporting" on a nuclear explosion and its aftermath.

In 1960 Louis Pauwels and Jacques Bergier published *Morning of the Magicians*, their outrageous, Fortean compendium of conspiracies, misinterpretations, and lies. In that book, they drew on some weird Soviet "science" that suggested nuclear weapons had been used in ancient India. To support their claim, they quoted what they said was the Indian *Mahabharata*, an ancient Sanskrit epic poem from c. 400 BCE:

> In the *Mausola Purva*, we find this singular description, which must have been incomprehensible to nineteenth-century ethnologists though not to us today: "...it was an unknown weapon, an iron thunderbolt, a gigantic messenger of death which reduced to ashes the entire race of the Vrishnis and the Andhakas. The corpses were so burned as to be unrecognizable. Their hair and nails fell out; pottery broke without any apparent cause, and the birds turned white. After a few hours, all foodstuffs were infected. The thunderbolt was reduced to a fine dust."
>
> And again: "Cukra, flying on board a high-powered *vimana*, hurled on to the triple city a single projectile charged with all the power of the Universe. An incandescent column of smoke and flame, as bright as ten thousand Suns, rose in all its splendor... When the *vimana* returned to Earth, it looked like a splendid block of antinomy resting on the ground."[1]

In a review of the literature, I found that the spelling "Mausola Purva" turns up nowhere before the 1963 English translation of the *Morning of the Magicians*, and all later references with that spelling derive from later writers copying that book without checking the source. The conventional spelling since at least 1807 is Mausala Parva, and it is the sixteenth parva, or division, of the *Mahabharata*, which one would not know from reading *Morning*. Similarly, "Curka" is a misspelling of Sakra, another name for Indra, a misspelling found only in *Morning* and its derivatives. The misspelling occurred because nineteenth century French translations of the *Mahabharata* transliterated Sakra as Çakra, with the c-cedilla (Ç) having the sound of an "S." Pauwels and Bergier, or their publisher, mistakenly dropped the cedilla (the small hook) from the Ç, and misread the "a" as a "u." This error appears in both the 1960 French edition and the 1963 English translation.

According to Pauwels and Bergier and other AATs, these passages record the blinding explosion of nuclear weapons and accurately report the fallout from a nuclear blast, including radiation burns, the loss of fingernails, etc. As we shall see, this is not the case when we look at the original text. But for now, let's focus on the text these authors provide.

What we have so far is an English translation of a questionable French translation of a Sanskrit original. Now watch what happens when alternative history writer David Hatcher Childress, gets hold of this passage. In his *Lost Cities of Ancient Lemuria and the Pacific* (1988, repeated in 1992's *Vimana Aircraft*), he conflates the two passages into one continuous passage, and then he breaks it up into lines to make it look like original Sanskrit poetry, calling his mangled poetry "authentic verses":

Gurkha, flying a swift and powerful vimana,
hurled a single projectile
charged with all the power of the Universe.
An incandescent column of smoke and flame,
as bright as ten thousand suns,
rose in all its splendor.

It was an unknown weapon,
and iron thunderbolt,
a gigantic messenger of death,
which reduced to ashes the entire race of the Vrishnis and Andhakas.

The corpses were so burned
as to be unrecognizable.
Their hair and nails fell out.
Pottery broke without any apparent cause,
and the birds turned white.

...After a few hours, all foodstuffs were infected...
...to escape from this fire,
the soldiers threw themselves in streams
to wash themselves and all their equipment.[2]

Somehow the god Sakra, mistakenly called "Cukra" in *Morning,* has now become "Gurkha," the name of the famed Nepalese unit of the British colonial military. This, in turn occurred because Erich von Däniken, or his publisher, mistakenly transliterated Cukra as Gurkha in the German edition of *Chariots of the Gods?* when summarizing Pauwels and Bergier, possibly due to misreading the word as a French rendering of the famed Nepalese military units, the Gurkhas. The mistake was carried over into the English edition: "In the same book [the *Mahabharata*], in what is perhaps the first account of the dropping of an H-bomb, it says that Gurkha loosed a single projectile on the triple city from a mighty Vimana."[3]

Childress followed the spelling of von Däniken, even though von Däniken did not provide the text Childress reprints. Note that in Childress the material has been rearranged, lines altered, words dropped, and ellipses added, as though Childress were presenting a scholarly excerpt from a longer text. But he is not. This text appears in this alleged "translation" nowhere before *Morning of the Magicians,* and certainly not in the false poetic form given here, or in the rearranged and misleading conflation presented here. The origins of this "poetic" form are a bit obscure, but according to one bibliographic entry on a website and Childress's bibliography, it apparently originates in Charles Berlitz's *Mysteries from Forgotten Worlds* (1972), which presents "excerpts" from the *Mahabharata* (properly cited but not conventionally translated) but does not claim they are a continuous poem.[4] Berlitz is merely repeating Pauwels and Bergier, though with the inclusion of some unwarranted ellipses, apparently the inspiration for Childress's more numerous own. Joseph Rosenberger's *The Atlantean Horror,* a 1985 *novel* about an action hero who takes on impossible missions, uses the excerpts as a single poem. On page 25 of the novel, part (but not all) of the quote from *Morning of the Magicians* is set in verse (without ellipses) as a "prophecy" from Atlantis of nuclear war as Russians and Americans battle in Antarctica. The text, in poetic form, also appears in *The Journal of South Asian and Middle Eastern Studies,* but that was in 2007 (vol. 30), and is far too late. So, Childress either conflated the excerpts and rendered them into a poem, or he relied on a source unknown to me and unacknowledged in his work. More than 35 books and thousands of websites have published Childress's version of the text.

So now we have a conflated, rewritten version of an English translation of a questionable French translation of a Sanskrit original. "Authentic verses" indeed.

So, what exactly did this Sanskrit original say? Funny thing: It doesn't say anything about nuclear weapons. Turning to the *Mahabharata*, we find the following four wholly separate and either unrelated or distantly related passages (as given in the standard Ganguli translation):

> When the next day came, Camva actually brought forth an iron bolt through which all the individuals in the race of the Vrishnis and the Andhakas became consumed into ashes. Indeed, for the destruction of the Vrishnis and the Andhakas, Camva brought forth, through that curse, a fierce iron bolt that looked like a gigantic messenger of death. The fact was duly reported to the king. In great distress of mind, the king (Ugrasena) caused that iron bolt to be reduced into fine powder.[5]

Note that the supposed "bomb" in this section, from the Mausala Parva, is actually a bolt (like a scepter), that the king feared the bolt, and the king *destroyed it before it could be used.*

From a different section of the same parva comes the bit about supposed radiation poisoning, which has almost *nothing to do* with the previous passage about the iron bolt that was never used except that they were incidents in the lives of a particular people, over many decades:

> Day by day strong winds blew, and many were the evil omens that arose, awful and foreboding the destruction of the Vrishnis and the Andhakas. The streets swarmed with rats and mice. Earthen pots showed cracks or broken from no apparent cause. At night, the rats and mice ate away the hair and nails of slumbering men. [...] That chastiser of foes commanded the Vrishnis to make a pilgrimage to some sacred water. The messengers forthwith proclaimed at the command of Kecava that the Vrishnis should make a journey to the sea-coast for bathing in the sacred waters of the ocean.[6]

This destruction, incidentally, happens *three decades* after the destruction of the iron bolt, when the Vrishnis and Andhakas (and I am not making this up) killed each other by beating one another with pots and pans. Not exactly a nuclear bomb. Note that the supposed effect of radiation poisoning recorded in the Pauwels/Bergier/Berlitz/Childress text, the loss of nails, is a complete fabrication. In the original *mice and rats* ate the nails. Again, hardly a nuclear bomb.

The bit about Sakra riding the *vimana* comes from an entirely different parva, the Karna Parva, the eighth book of the *Mahbharata*, and again has *nothing to do* with the other passages:

> While the worlds were thus afflicted, Sakra, surrounded by the Maruts, battled against the three cities by hurling his thunder upon them from every side. When, however, Purandra failed to pierce those cities made impenetrable, O king, by the Creator with his boons, the chief of celestials, filled with fear, and leaving those cities, repaired with those very gods to that chastiser of foes, viz., the Grandsire, for representing unto him the oppressions committed by the Asuras.[7] [...]

> Thus equipped, that car shone brilliantly like a blazing fire in the midst of the priests officiating at a sacrifice. Beholding that car properly equipped, the gods became filled with wonder. Seeing the energies of the entire universe united together in one place, O sire, the gods wondered, and at last represented unto that illustrious Deity that the car was ready. [...] Then He called Nila Rohita (Blue and Red or smoke)—that terrible deity robed in skins,—looking like 10,000 Suns, and shrouded by the fire of superabundant Energy, blazed up with splendour. [...] The triple city then appeared immediately before that god of unbearable energy [Maheswara, or Siva], that Deity of fierce and indescribable form, that warrior who was desirous of slaying the Asuras. The illustrious deity, that Lord of the universe, then drawing that celestial bow, sped that shaft which represented the might of the whole universe, at the triple city. Upon that foremost of shafts, O thou of great good fortune, being shot, loud wails of woe were heard from those cities as they began to fall down towards the Earth. Burning those Asuras, he threw them down into the Western ocean.[8]

Note that Maheswara (Siva), not Sakra (or Cukra or Gurkha), is the driver of the car in the original; and also note that it is the Asuras (evil gods), not the Vrishnis who are the subject of these weapons. Note, too, just how much text it took Pauwels and Bergier to find a half-dozen lines they could string together to supposedly show nuclear weapons.

As should be clear, this passage is referring to the power of thunder in destroying the evil gods, the Asuras, parallel to the thunder-god Zeus using the thunder bolt to destroy the giants in the Gigantomachy of Greek mythology. Additionally, it is clear that the "weapon" is envisioned as an arrow (not an explosive), which pierces the cities and causes them to *fall down*, not to *evaporate* as Pauwels and Bergier and Childress assert.

Thus, I hope I have now shown at sufficient length that the AATs' methodology is little better than slapping together random sentences to create a false impression. Pauwels and Bergier seem to have intentionally mistranslated Sanskrit sentences into French to create a false impression, but were honest enough to allow that the sentences weren't related to each other and to leave in some baffling details, like the disintegration of the thunderbolt. But Berlitz, Childress, and their followers are content to mangle a bad English translation of a French mistranslation of a Sanskrit original without ever checking the original source material. Texts are conflated, separate incidents combined into one. No context is considered or analyzed. Details that do not support the AATs' ideas are eliminated with no indication that they were dropped. Mistranslations are purposely created, copied uncritically but changed at will to support the author's views, and repeated endlessly as revealed truth.

The *Mahabharata* is 1.8 million words long. These authors seem to have purposely used no references or citations to the actual text of the ancient epic, trusting that no one will be able to search through that much text to find the passages to which they have done so much violence. My guess, from the number of later writers who claim "Gurkha" as a Hindu god, is that most later copyists never consulted the original at all.

David Hatcher Childress asserts: "The public needs scientists and the scientists need the public. However, many times the lay person is the better source of information."[9] What exactly are we to think of this? As we have seen, Childress is a terrible source of information. He, those he copied from, and those who copy from him are at best guilty of ignorance and poor scholarship; at worst they intentionally altered texts and misrepresented history to fool their readers—all while claiming "scientists" are the ones hiding the truth.

Notes

[1] Louis Pauwels and Jacques Bergier, *The Morning of the Magicians*, trans. Rollo Myers (New York: Stein and Day, 1964), p. 122.

[2] David Hatcher Childress, *Lost Cities of Ancient Lemuria and the Pacific* (Stelle, IL: Adventures Unlimited Press, 1988), pp. 72-73.

[3] Erich von Däniken, *Chariots of the Gods? Unsolved Mysteries of the Past*, trans. Michael Heron (New York: Bantam, 1973), 58.

[4] Charles Berlitz, *Mysteries from Forgotten Worlds* (New York: Doubleday, 1972), pp. 214ff.

[5] Mausala Parva, sec. 1

[6] Mausala Parva, sec. 2

[7] Karna Parva, sec. 33

[8] Karna Parva, sec. 34

[9] David Hatcher Childress, *Atlantis and the Power Systems of the Gods* (Stelle, IL: Adventures Unlimited Press, 2002), p. 36.

15. The Naacal Tablets and Theosophy

THE WORD "NAACAL" originates in the work of the extremely imaginative Augustus Le Plongeon (1825-1906), the French antiquarian who explored the Maya ruins of Central America, stood in awe of their grandeur, and imagined them the motherland of all civilization. In his 1896 book *Queen Móo and the Egyptian Sphinx*, he wrote of the high priests of the Maya: "those **Maya** adepts (**Naacal**—'the exalted'), who, starting from the land of their birth as missionaries of religion and civilization, went to Burmah, where they became known as *Nagas*, established themselves in the Dekkan, whence they carried their civilizing work all over the earth"[1] (emphasis in original).

A British engineer name James Churchward (1851-1936)—falsely claiming to be a colonel—discussed lost civilizations with Le Plongeon and decided to invent his own lost world, drawing on Le Plongeon's ideas. He removed the Naacal from the Maya lands and placed them instead on Mu, a fictitious Pacific continent, in his 1926 book *The Lost Continent of Mu, Motherland of Man*. Churchward claimed that on a trip to India, he met an Indian priest, one of just three in all India who could read the lost language of Naacal. After assuaging the priest's doubts about his motives, Churchward gained access to tablets containing Naacal texts. The priest helped translated the texts, which revealed the "history" of Mu.

The Naacal tablets revealed for Churchward that 13,000 or more years ago Mu was, in essence, the Theosophical Lemuria (with which it is often identified), on which white Aryan humans ruled over a motley assortment of darker slave races, and they were also monotheistic creationists, rejecting Darwin's "monkey theories," in Churchward's words, thousands of years before they were proposed!

Of course no Naacal tablets have ever been brought to light, and they are obviously a fiction. In later books the discovery of the Naacal tablets miraculously moved from India to Tibet. In 2012, the late Philip Coppens claimed that Churchward's Naacal library really existed in India; of course, the evidence for managed to recede toward the horizon in direct proportion to the observer's effort to catch up to it.

Churchward was familiar with the tenets of Theosophy, and he seriously studied Madame Blavatsky's fictitious *Stanzas of Dzyan*, another lost text whose discovery exactly paralleled that of the Naacal tablets. Like Churchward a half century later, Blavatsky also claimed to have traveled to Tibet where she said that the Occult Brotherhood kept the ancient manuscripts of this pre-human text hidden away from prying eyes, written in the unknown language of Senzar, which she claimed was the original of Sanskrit. At any rate, with the help of the Occult Brotherhood, she "translated" the *Stanzas of Dzyan* in *The Secret Doctrine*, which revealed the mystical philosophy of the earliest humans.

> [These are] the records of a people unknown to ethnology; it is claimed that they are written in a tongue absent from the nomenclature of languages and dialects with which philology is acquainted; they are said to emanate from a source (Occultism) repudiated by science; and, finally, they are offered through an agency, incessantly discredited before the world by all those who hate unwelcome truths, or have some special hobby of their own to defend.

Blavatsky, translator extraordinaire, managed to translate these secret texts and, what's more, reveal them to the book-buying public without a hint of protest from the secret brotherhood. In this, she in turn was paralleling the earlier history of Mormonism. In 1830, Joseph Smith published the Book of Mormon, first written on never-seen gold tablets in an un-known language he termed "Reformed Egyptian" and telling the story of a lost race that once inhabited America. According to Smith, an angel named Moroni showed him where to find the tablets buried in a hill in upstate New York, taught him to translate the language contained therein, and took the tablets back up to the sky with him.

Churchward wrote in *The Children of Mu* (1931) that *Dzyan* was "the writings of a disordered brain, wandering about in fog."[2] However, he folded it into his Muvian cosmology by making it a "Hindu book written in Sanskrit about 1500 B.C."[3] (thus denying any special role for Blavatsky) and claiming that it was based on the Naacal writings he had himself translated, thereby placing himself above Blavatsky as a revealer of truth!

While I can't confirm that Churchward was directly copying Blavatsky, the parallels between the two make independence rather unlikely. Both claimed to have (a) traveled to India, (b) met with occult keepers of knowledge, (c) gained access to occult texts, (d) translated these texts from a forgotten language, (e) failed to bring the originals of the texts back for scientific study, (f) and claimed that the texts revealed secrets about human prehistory. The structural similarities in the narratives of discovery are impossible to miss, as are the parallels with the Book of Mormon, minus the sojourn in India. Where they differ is that Blavatsky kept this mostly spiritual, with the *Dzyan* stanzas merely blubbering about mystical mumbo-jumbo that she needed to explicate with occult infor-mation about Atlantis and Lemuria, while Churchward claimed that the Naacal tablets plainly laid out the history of Atlantis and Mu, without the later encrustation of Oriental philosophy.

From this, as well as Churchward's emphasis on the superiority of White Aryans and monotheism, it becomes possible to understand his Mu myth as an attempt to strip Theosophy of the Oriental trappings of its In-dian mysticism. (At the time, the cult was based in Benares, India and fo-cused on Hindu-derived occult traditions.) Perhaps he had had enough of the East during his years as a tea grower in Sri Lanka. His Mu would be Theosophy for the mind of the common (Anglo-American) man: pure, monotheistic, Aryan, and plainspoken in the Anglo-Saxon tradition. But Churchward's lost continent and Blavatsky's spiritual poetry pale in comparison to the claims of Joseph Smith a century earlier. In all three cases, curiously enough, the original tablets and texts disappeared and have never been found. (What a shock.) Therefore, it was no surprise when in the 1970s, in *Gold of the Gods*, Erich von Däniken claimed to have found a library of gold tablets on which the aliens had written their entire history in a lost language and then buried it in a cave in Ecuador. Of course every expedition to von Däniken's supposed cave turned up nothing and the author admitted he had made the whole thing up and had never been there (see Chapter 16).

Notes

[1] August Le Plongeon, *Queen Móo and the Egyptian Sphinx,* second ed. (New York: Author, 1900), xxiv.

[2] James Churchward, *The Children of Mu* (New York: Ives Washburn, 1945), 198.

[3] Ibid.

16. Neil Armstrong's Brush with Ancient Astronauts

NEIL ARMSTRONG WAS the first man on the moon, but fans of alternative archaeology and ancient astronauts also remember him as a member of the 1976 expedition that went in search of Tayos caves in Ecuador that Erich von Däniken claimed in *The Gold of the Gods* (1972) contained a vast library of metal books inscribed with the writings of an alien civilization. Von Däniken had claimed in *Gold* to have personally visited this metal library, but he was forced to admit that he had fabricated his account of the cave after its alleged discoverer, Juan Moricz, stated that he had never taken von Däniken to the cave.

In an interview with *Playboy* magazine in 1974, Von Däniken claimed his false personal account was *dramaturgisch Effekte* or "theatrical effect" (i.e. dramatic license) and that the cave really existed, though he would not travel there himself because he feared the Ecuadorian government would assassinate him for revealing too much information, and "I really don't care too much" about the only extraterrestrial artifacts that could prove his theories beyond doubt.[1]

In 1976, Scottish explorer Stanley Hall, a deep believer in alternative science and ancient astronauts, asked Armstrong, then a professor of aerospace engineering at the University of Cincinnati, to join him on a British military scientific expedition to Ecuador to investigate the Tayos caves, which von Däniken had claimed were carved at perfect right angles by aliens with laser beams. Armstrong, as Honorary President of the expedition, flew to Quito in August on a British Royal Air Force cargo plane along with Hall and the Black Watch and the Royal Highland Fusiliers regiment to explore the caves, though he was unaware of von Däniken's wild claims about them or Hall's alternative theories. It took only a day's exploration at Cueva de los Tayos to determine two essential facts. First, there was no metal library where von Däniken had claimed. Second, in Armstrong's own words: "It was the conclusion of our expedition group that they [the caves] were natural formations."[2] No lasers. No gold library. No aliens.

Newspapers had a field day, publishing headlines like "THE CHARLATAN MAKES A FOOL OF HIMSELF," and "DÄNIKEN UNMASKED!"

Von Däniken quickly went into damage control mode. Despite having conceded that his *Gold of the Gods* claims were fabrications in his 1974 *Playboy* interview, von Däniken reversed course, doubled down on the caves' reality, and suggested that Armstrong had been duped into debunking him: "He [Armstrong] knew nothing about his task of exposing Däniken," he wrote in *According to the Evidence* (1977). "Every expert knows that there are hundreds of different caves in Ecuador."[3] Armstrong did not set out with the purpose of debunking von Däniken, but he also did not shy away from asserting that the science he conducted was real and that his findings were sound. Von Däniken's new tactic was to claim that whatever cave anyone visited (and many tried), it was the wrong cave—even though he would never say what the "right" cave might be. He would later claim that Hall knew the exact position of the true cave and purposely went to the wrong one to protect the metal library from exposure to the wrong sort of people. (Presumably the ones who in von Däniken's imagination were waiting to assassinate him.)

Von Däniken became angry when the controversy would not go away, and he recognized that this was the beginning of the end for his time in the spotlight. A popular author could not withstand the double-whammy of confessing fabrication *and* being publicly debunked by a global hero. That's why he began striking out, demanding to know in *According to the Evidence*, "What are they [the media] still on about?"[4] and telling his dwindling readership that his 1972 claim was five years in the past, old news, and probably in a different cave anyway.

But the public had moved on. Von Däniken continued to write books, but they sold fewer copies, and he was no longer the media darling of the heady years of 1973-1975, when he was on the *Tonight* show, interviewed in *Playboy*, and the toast of the New Age intelligentsia. EST, pyramid power, Noah's Ark, and alien abductions had begun to take over the public imagination, and ancient astronauts were no longer interesting enough even for *In Search of...*, the 1976-1982 syndicated television program spun off from *In Search of Ancient Astronauts* (1973) and its two sequels, the film versions of von Däniken's own work. His theories appeared just once on the series after the Armstrong expedition, despite a prominent first season role. In 1978, a biography of von Däniken by Peter Krassa appeared, but even this laudatory tome was forced to ask if "von Däniken [was] at the end of the road."[5]

For the next twenty years, von Däniken was an afterthought in alternative history. He continued to pump out his twenty-five books, but increasingly few were ever translated into English. In 1996, he hit his low point, forced to concede that "alternative" history writers Graham Hancock and Robert Bauval had surpassed him in popularity with their lost civilization and ancient Egypt theories. So he wrote *The Eyes of the Sphinx*, among his last major works published by a large English language publisher (Penguin's Berkley) and the last for which he apparently wrote completely original text. (His later books contained increasing amounts of recycled text, much of it from *Eyes*.) It was a sad book, summarizing Hancock and Bauval and layering on aliens.

Von Däniken experienced a dramatic resurrection after 2009 on the back of *Ancient Aliens*, but the bitterness showed. In 2010, von Däniken, now a prophet claiming the imminent return of the aliens to punish his enemies, still felt anger at Armstrong and all those (like, ahem, me) who continued to cite him as proof that von Däniken had lied about the metal library. (Well, he *did* admit to lying after all...) In *History Is Wrong* (2010), von Däniken again asserted that despite his earlier lies, the metal library was real and the media and skeptics were his enemies:

> I am happy to laugh around and philosophize with my colleagues from the writing guilds, but I *do* have something against this constantly offended and indignant minority, which only takes the trouble to understand the minimum of a life's work necessary to be able to pass judgment on the rest of the things they can't actually be bothered to look into.[6]

What part of von Däniken's life's work is not understood? Which of his lies, fabrications, distortions, and untruths has been left unexamined? Erich von Däniken was diagnosed as a psychopath and pathological liar by a court-appointed psychiatrist during his embezzlement trial, and some dismiss him on those grounds, but skeptics have studiously examined his every claim because hypotheses are independent of the theorist. His biography and "life's work" is irrelevant; every claim has been found wanting.

For the record, before his death in 2008, Hall revealed the "true" location of the cave: 1° 56′ 00″ S, 77° 47′ 34″ W. If von Däniken is so certain that this site is a "kick in the teeth" (his words) to "conservative" archaeology and ethnology, I invite him to prove us all wrong and do what he never did in the 1970s: actually visit the cave and show us some real proof. It's what Neil Armstrong's expedition tried to do, and it is the honorable way to prove the assertion true. Your move, Däniken.

Notes

[1] Erich von Däniken, interview with Timothy Ferris, *Playboy*, August 1974, 58.

[2] Quoted in James R. Hansen, *First Man: The Life of Neil A. Armstrong* (New York: Simon & Schuster Paperbacks, 2006), 632. The preceding discussion is based in part on Hansen's account of Armstrong's expedition.

[3] Erich von Däniken, *According to the Evidence: My Proof of Man's Extraterrestrial Origins*, trans. Michael Heron (Souvenir Press, 1977), 293.

[4] Ibid., 291.

[5] Peter Kraasa, *Disciple of the Gods: A Biography of Erich von Däniken*, trans. David B. Koblick (London: W. H. Allen, 1978), 6.

[6] Erich von Däniken, *History Is Wrong* (New Page Books, 2012), eBook.

17. Santa Is an Alien Robot!

THE FOLLOWING Great Moment in Ancient Astronautics comes from Bruce Rux's 1996 book *Architects of the Underworld: Unriddling Atlantis, Anomalies of Mars, and the Mystery of the Sphinx*. Rux is a former actor, a follower of Zecharia Sitchin, and a conspiracy theorist who believes that Hollywood uses movies and TV shows about UFOs to aid the government in covering up alien visitation now and in the past, as detailed in his book *Hollywood vs. the Aliens* (1998). He also believes that ancient astronauts and current "grey" aliens are in fact robots sent by the real aliens from their home planet.

According to Rux, references to the Underworld in ancient mythology are code for the planet Mars. His evidence is that the Underworld is usually thought of as laying in the far west and is associated with the color red: "Since 'sea' or 'ocean' can also mean '[outer] space,' and there is no up or down in space, it is certainly possible that this Underworld is actually beneath the earth—another planet."[1] Since the Underworld's color is red (usually thought to represent the sunset), this planet must be the Red Planet, Mars.

The aliens' robots, who appeared to ancient humans as gods, created the doctrine of the bodily resurrection of the dead because they engaged in cloning and took tissue samples into deep space for cloning (since bodily transport requires too much fuel), an idea proposed by Erich von Däniken in the 1970s and developed by Alan Landsburg extensively in *The Outer Space Connection*, the book that claimed aliens would come back for the clones on Christmas Eve 2011. As we have seen, through some confusion about dates, this in turn gave rise to the December 2012 Maya Apocalypse panic (see chapter six).

By Rux's analysis, the color red is closely associated with white and black in alien cosmology, so therefore, such figures as (and I am not making this up) the Red Cross (red symbol on a white background), the country of Japan (red sun disc on a white flag), Easter Island's statues (which once wore red hats), and Santa Claus (because of his clothes) are all part of the aliens' secret plans directed from their Martian base.

Yes, you heard it right: the Red Cross, Japan, Easter Island, and Santa Claus are all part of an alien conspiracy overseen by the U.S. government, a secret guarded so carefully that only someone as clever as Bruce Rux was able to identify it.

So I guess that's where *Futurama* got its evil robot Santa idea. No, wait... wouldn't that be part of the conspiracy from *Hollywood vs. the Aliens*? My God, the aliens have gotten to Bruce Rux! His theory is actually *helping* the conspiracy! He must be one of Them!

Notes

[1] Bruce Rux, *Architects of the Underworld: Unriddling Atlantis, Anomalies of Mars, and the Mystery of the Sphinx* (Berkeley, California: Frog Books, 1996), 364.

18. Stonehenge: The Day Spa of the Gods

A S I'VE DISCUSSED quite a bit so far, ancient astronaut theorists and alternative historians ask us to take ancient texts literally in order to make discoveries about the ancient past. Thus, they take Plato's *Timaeus* and *Critias* literally as evidence for the existence of Atlantis. (Though, strangely, Euhemerus' equally fictional lost continent of Panchaea is roundly ignored.) This type of literalism, as I have show previously, prevents us from making real connections about events in the ancient past. Here is yet another case where ancient astronaut theorists' literalism leads us to the edge of incoherence when applied to an ancient text.

Our sample today comes from Diodorus Siculus' *Library*, where the historian describes the earlier work of Hecataeus of Abdera on a mysterious land far to the north:

> Hecataeus and some others have said that on the coasts opposite the Celtae, there is an island little less than Sicily, under the Arctic Pole, where they who are called Hyperboreans inhabit. They say that this island is exceedingly good and fertile, bearing fruit (i.e., crops of grass) twice a year. The men of the island are, as it were, priests of Apollo, daily singing his hymns and praises, and highly honouring him. They say, moreover, that in it there is a great forest, and a goodly temple of Apollo, which is round and beautified with many rich gifts and ornaments; as also a city sacred to him, whereof the most part of the inhabitants are harpers, and play continually on their harps in the temple, chanting hymns to the praise of Apollo, and magnifying his acts in their songs.[1]

Many modern historians believe this passage represents a description of Britain, with the round temple being Stonehenge on Salisbury Plain. If so, this would be a remarkable piece of literature, since Hecataeus lived in 300 BCE, roughly a thousand years after Stonehenge's heyday. (Not all archaeologists agree, however.) But if we adopt the ancient astronaut theorists' textual literalism, we are prevented from investigating the question of whether this passage refers in fact to Britain and Stonehenge because, since we must take this literally, we should be looking for an island the size of Sicily near the North Pole. An alien Arctic research station? Was the temple a biodome?

I don't think it would surprise anyone to know that there is no such island at the North Pole (it's water up there under the ice), or that there has been no weather warm enough to grow two rounds of annual crops since humans evolved. This line of investigation is stale. But if ancient astronaut theorists choose not to interpret this text literally, then we must ask what criteria they use to decide which texts are worthy of literal readings, and which must be read symbolically or figuratively?

Of course, this is a moot point for ancient astronaut theorists, since textual literalism means they also have to accept that Geoffrey of Monmouth was literally correct that the stones of Stonehenge were meant as a bathtub for African giants, a story which probably derives from an older story, that Merlin carried Stonehenge to Salisbury from Ireland:

"If you are desirous," said Merlin, "to honour the burying-place of these men with an everlasting monument, send for the Giant's Dance, which is in Killaraus, a mountain in Ireland. For there is a structure of stones there, which none of this age could raise, without a profound knowledge of the mechanical arts. They are stones of a vast magnitude and wonderful quality; and if they can be placed here, as they are there, round this spot of ground, they will stand for ever."

At these words of Merlin, Aurelius burst into laughter, and said, "How is it possible to remove such vast stones from so distant a country, as if Britain was not furnished with stones fit for the work?" Merlin replied: "I entreat your majesty to forbear vain laughter; for what I say is without vanity. They are mystical stones, and of a medicinal virtue. The giants of old brought them from the farthest coasts of Africa, and placed them in Ireland, while they inhabited that country. Their design in this was to make baths in them, when they should be taken with any illness. For their method was to wash the stones, and put their sick into the water, which infallibly cured them. With the like success they cured wounds also, adding only the application of some herbs. There is not a stone there which has not some healing virtue."[2]

Corrupt and confused as this legend is, it does correctly preserve a memory that Stonehenge's stones came not from England but from the Celtic fringe beyond the control of Anglo-Saxon monarchs. Though I'm pretty sure Stonehenge was never used as a spa.

Just remember that bit of "ancient text" the next time an ancient astronaut theorist tries to tell you that Stonehenge is an outpost for aliens, a Phoenician temple, or a remnant of Atlantis.

Notes

[1] Diodorus Siculus, *Library of History* 3.13, translated by H. Cogan in L. Gidney, *Stonehenge, Viewed by the Light of Ancient History and Modern Observation* (Salisbury: Brown and Co., 1873), 2.

[2] Geoffrey of Monmouth, *Historia Regum Britanniae* 8.10-11, translated in *The British History of Geoffrey of Monmouth*, trans. A. Thompson and J. A. Giles (London: James Bohn, 1842).

19. Are There Platinum Coffins Off Nan Madol?

RICH VON DÄNIKEN released a new book called *Evidence of the Gods: A Visual Tour of Alien Influence in the Ancient World* in 2012 under the auspices of New Page Books. *Evidence of the Gods* is another recycling job, this time rewriting much of the information that appeared in *In Search of Ancient Gods: My Pictorial Evidence for the Impossible* (1973; English trans. 1975). In the new book, von Däniken describes sarcophagi with platinum bars found in the waters off Nan Madol (Ponape or Pohnpei), the basalt island city in the Caroline Islands that was an inspiration for Cthulhu's R'lyeh. This is a revised version of the claim from *In Search of Ancient Gods* that a mysterious and unnamed source of platinum led to the metal becoming the island's main export under Japanese rule (1919-1945) despite no platinum being found in the island's rocks. In turn, this claim is a condensation of an even earlier claim from *The Gold of the Gods* (1972; English trans. 1973), which is given as follows, referencing an imaginary lost underwater city off Nan Madol:

> What the pearl divers did not find was discovered by Japanese divers with modern equipment. They confirmed with their finds what the traditional legends of Ponape reported: the vast wealth in precious metals, pearls and bars of silver. [...] The Japanese divers reported that the dead were buried in watertight platinum coffins. And the divers actually brought bits of platinum to the surface day after day! In fact, the main exports of the island—copra, vanilla, sago and mother of pearl—were supplanted by platinum! Rittlinger says that the Japanese carried on ex-

ploiting this platinum until one day two divers did not surface, in spite of their modern equipment. Then the war broke out and the Japanese had to withdraw. [...]

I do not believe in the metal or platinum coffins. Hexagonal or octagonal basalt columns, overgrown with mussels and coral, could easily be mistaken for coffins under the water. Never mind. The fact remains that Japan exported platinum from Ponape after its mandate in 1919.

Where did all this platinum come from?[1]

Note that this story makes no sense as reported since the U.S. did not occupy Ponape during World War II, and Japan was only dismissed from the island after surrendering in 1945. Thus, the outbreak of the War in 1939 (though Japan had been fighting in China for several years), or 1941 (with U.S. entry) has no direct correlation to withdrawal, and thus no effect on the cessation of platinum extraction a decade earlier, based on the date I'm going to establish below. Also: How were they breaking up the underwater, water-tight coffins to take back chunks?

Despite even the notoriously credulous von Däniken's doubt over the authenticity of the platinum coffins, David Childress repeated the story, almost verbatim, in (as is his practice) several of his books. From there, it has become part of alternative lore, appearing in hundreds of books and websites as evidence for space aliens, Atlantis, Lemuria, African supergeniuses, and other occult ideas. Somehow, in the telling the story has mutated from divers breaking off bits of the platinum coffins to modern versions where the coffins were raised up and then melted down and cast into bars for transport to Japan. No one has ever made public a single shipping manifest or other piece of documentation proving that any platinum actually left Ponape during the Japanese mandate.

Von Däniken derives this story not from firsthand knowledge but from the explorer and artist Herbert Rittlinger, in his 1939 book *The Measureless Ocean*, which puts a *terminus ante quem* on the story. Under the Treaty of Versailles in 1919, the Caroline Islands (including Ponape) were given to Japan as a mandate, taking them over from the defeated Germany. This puts a *terminus post quem* on the tale. This is the same Herbert Rittlinger who was a Nazi intelligence agent in Turkey for Hitler during World War II. His South Pacific trip is known to have occurred between his 1932 Turkish sailing jaunt and his 1936 Amazon sailing adventure. Therefore, the platinum, if it existed, was recovered entirely between 1919 and 1935, with an outside chance of extraction starting a few years earlier, since Japan was the occupying power on the island during World War I.

In 1920, the U.S. exported 1,102 ounces of unmanufactured platinum to Japan, according to the U.S. Geologic Survey, a number consistent with other years, implying that no new source of platinum had reached Japan at this point, at least none capable of severely affecting demand or international platinum prices, as the discovery of whole coffins made entirely of the rare metal would have done. In internet chatter, the "several pieces" of platinum claimed in 1939 have now become "several tons" of platinum, which would certainly have distorted world commodities markets if true. Only 3.6 million troy ounces (roughly 230 tons) of platinum are mined *on earth* each year, almost all of it in South Africa and North America.

Platinum was widely used throughout Southeast Asia, and as Japan colonized Southeast Asia in the 1920s and 1930s, the Japanese discovered immense amounts of platinum already in the hands of Southeast Asians, which, of course, they either confiscated outright or bought with inflated paper currency (military scrip). By the outbreak of World War II, the Japanese military had billions of dollars worth of platinum ingots, and the accused war criminal Yoshio Kodama alone had plundered millions of dollars' worth of platinum during the Japanese occupation of China. Whatever else this means, it clearly implies that Ponape was never a primary, or even important, source of platinum for Japan.

I can't find any evidence that platinum was ever exported from Ponape, and I ask alternative writers to please show us the shipping documents proving it existed and was exported. How can von Däniken know that platinum supplanted all other island exports if there are no export statistics showing this? Platinum does not appear in the list of exports for the island collected by the U.S. government in the 1920s, let alone as the chief export.[2] How would he know the amount and its value to know it exceeded the value of all other products? And what type of platinum was this? Uncombined native platinum, or something refined from a sulfide? Why is there no more platinum off Ponape? The story, as given by Rittlinger, says the Japanese merely "stopped" collecting it, in 1935, because of mysterious disappearances, not because they ran out of platinum. So, surely some should still be there.

The fact is that there is simply no mention of platinum on or around Ponape in any literature I could find prior to 1939 and no wild claims of aliens or super-civilizations prior to von Däniken's popularizing of the ex-Nazi intelligence officer's book in 1972. In fact, the *only* discussions of this story occur in "alternative" books, and none has any information not derived from the English translation of von Däniken's summary of Rittlinger in *Gold of the Gods*, except, weirdly, Childress, who actually tried to find the platinum coffins and failed. So, there you have it: Von Däniken doesn't believe they exist, and Childress couldn't find them. Yet somehow they keep rising up from their watery graves time and again thanks to the alternative world's endless penchant for recycling material. Rittlinger, a dedicated environmentalist, would at least be proud of the recycling effort.

Notes

[1] Erich von Däniken, *The Gold of the Gods*, trans. Michael Heron (New York: G. P. Putnam's Sons, 1973), 103.

[2] For example, the U.S. Hydrographic Office listed dried coconuts (copra) as the chief export in 1920 in report no. 165. By 1942, exports were given as coconuts, fish, and phosphates, according to *Life* magazine ("Jap Pacific Bases," December 14, 1942, p. 73).

20. The Believer Who Almost Became President

D ID YOU KNOW that an ancient astronaut theorist was almost president of the United States? It's true, and, as always, there's a weird connection to H. P. Lovecraft.

Our story opens in 1944, during World War II, when an ailing President Franklin Roosevelt was running for his fourth term as America's head of state. For the previous term, Henry A. Wallace had been serving as vice-president of the United States, and he served as the Secretary of Agriculture before that. Wallace recognized that Roosevelt was unlikely to survive his fourth term, and, of course, he wanted to remain on as vice-president with the near-certainty of succeeding to the top job. Party bosses were deeply troubled by the possibility of a Wallace presidency, and they worked behind the scenes to dump Wallace and replace him on the ticket with the more acceptable Harry Truman. What was it that made Wallace unacceptable? Ancient astronauts. Sort of.

Wallace never formally joined any theosophical groups, but he was deeply influenced by theosophical thinking. One of Theosophy's main tenets is that extraterrestrial spirit beings from Venus, the moon, and Mars came to the ancient earth and influenced the development of civilization on Lemuria and Atlantis. Wallace became deeply involved in the occult speculations of the Russian émigré artist Nicholas Roerich, who had joined Theosophy and developed his sub-discipline of Theosophy, called the Living Ethics or Agni Yoga, named for the Vedic fire god, Agni.

Roerich believed that World War I had been the apocalypse that signaled the end of the Hindu Kali Yuga and the start of the next phase of human evolution and civilization. He claimed that this new world age would be directed by a mysterious cult of Mahatmas living in isolated splendor deep in Shambhala in Central Asia. These, of course, answer to the "deathless Chinamen" who live in Central Asia in H. P. Lovecraft's "The Call of Cthulhu," and they derive from Theosophical traditions, as appropriated from Buddhism, in turn derived from the Hindu belief that Vishnu's incarnation as Kalki will rule the millennial kingdom of Shambhala thousands of years from now.

Agni Yoga preserved Theosophy's "astral plane," on which some of the extraterrestrial beings were thought to live. (Roerich believed he was in communication with some of these trans-dimensional creatures, called the "Hierarchy of Light.") It also retained Theosophy founder Helena Blavatsky's race theory, which held that extraterrestrials from Venus, the moon, and Mars incarnated as earlier races of human beings. Agni Yoga taught that a new incarnation was manifesting as the Sixth Root Race in the present. The movement also adopted Blavatsky's *Secret Doctrine*, with its tales of ancient astronauts, as one of its core texts.

Wallace met Roerich in 1929, years before FDR's election, and he quickly hit it off with the spiritual leader and painter, referring to him as his "guru." Roerich, for his part, opened a museum in New York City in 1930 to display his dramatic paintings, including some of Buddhist monasteries clinging to the snowy sides of the Himalayas. H. P. Lovecraft visited the museum shortly after its opening, and he was inspired by these strange vistas. "Surely Roerich is one of those rare fantastic souls," Lovecraft wrote in a 1930 letter, "who have glimpsed the grotesque, terrible secrets outside space & beyond time & who have retained some ability to hint at the marvels they have seen."[1] He modeled the Old Ones' frozen mountain city in *At the Mountains of Madness* on Roerich's paintings, which he explicitly cited in the story: "Something about the scene reminded me of the strange and disturbing Asian paintings of Nicholas Roerich, and of the still stranger and more disturbing descriptions of the evilly fabled plateau of

Leng which occur in the dreaded *Necronomicon* of the mad Arab Abdul Alhazred."[2]

Wallace was also quite taken with Roerich's esotericism, and he brought his occult beliefs to Washington after FDR's election and his appointment to head the Department of Agriculture. As Secretary of Agriculture he used his influence with the U.S. government to send Roerich on an official U.S. mission to Central Asia after FDR normalized relations with the Soviet Union in 1933. FDR also knew and liked Roerich, though he was not a believer in Roerich's occult musings. Officially, Roerich went to the USSR in 1934 to collect grasses; unofficially, he was there on a spiritual journey. Wallace was fascinated by botany and agronomy, and he was one of the most brilliant men ever to head the Department of Agriculture. With his favorite on an expedition to collect grasses, Wallace's special area of interest, expectations were high.

The expedition was a fiasco; Roerich collected just 20 plants during a 16-month trek across Central Asia. A second expedition, sent by the Department of Agriculture in the same period, collected 2,000 plants in less time. Worse, Roerich began making indiscrete statements to foreign leaders as though acting with the authority of the U.S. government. Wallace was humiliated, and after more than five years in thrall to Roerich, he finally broke with Roerich and rejected his Agni Yoga and his millenarian expectations. Wallace directed the American embassy in India to refuse aid to Roerich and forward all Roerich's communications directly to Wallace. He also held a press conference in which he accused Roerich of being a spy. Finally, he strongly encouraged the IRS to audit Roerich, which they did, producing a bill for nearly $50,000 in back taxes. Roerich, for his part, simply stayed put in India and lived out the rest of his life as a tax exile.

Although Wallace had broken with Roerich, unease about his occult connections followed him after his nomination for the vice-presidency in 1940. Republicans obtained copies of the so-called "guru letters" from the early 1930s in which Wallace had written to Nicholas Roerich as his "dear Guru" and signed himself as "G" for Sir Galahad. In the letters, Wallace told Roerich that he eagerly awaited the imminent apocalypse and the arrival of the people of North Shamballah (a Buddhist term for heaven, but used in Theosophy to refer to the place of the Ascended Masters, the aliens, etc.), who would cleanse the earth of poverty and lead to a new era of peace. Democrats contained the scandal only by threatening to reveal Republican presidential nominee Wendell Wilkie's extramarital affair with Irita Van Doren. The two parties agreed to suppress the other's scandal.

As a result of these events, party leaders and political journalists concluded that Wallace was a mystic and an occultist and unfit to be president. Unable to shake the accusations, Wallace saw his chance at the presidency evaporate in 1944 when party elders unceremoniously dumped him from the ticket. The final straw was FDR's own agreement that Wallace had become a liability, both for his occultism and for his political ineffectiveness. Wallace saw the writing on the wall, but he refused to watch his chance at real power fade away. His supporters printed fake tickets to the Democratic National Convention in the hope of rigging the vote and nominating Wallace, but party leaders caught wind of the plan and called an early adjournment. After rooting out the fake delegates, Democrats reconvened and nominated Truman. FDR died in April 1945, and Truman duly succeeded to the presidency.

Unwilling to let it go, Wallace tried to run for president in the next election, only to see the long-forgotten "Guru Letters" published in 1947, humiliating him (again) and helping to spark hostile questioning from reporters like H. L. Mencken. Truman would go on to win the nomination in 1948 and the general election as well.

What the ancient astronauts giveth, the ancient astronauts taketh away.

Notes

[1] Quoted by S. T. Joshi in *The Annotated H. P. Lovecraft* (New York: Dell, 1997), 187.

[2] H. P. Lovecraft, *The Fiction* (New York: Barnes & Noble, 2008), 726.

21. The Search for Soviet Ancient Astronauts

HAVE YOU EVER seen the pictures of the Soviet version of the space shuttle, the Buran? It looked almost like its American counterpart but was just slightly off, was used only once, and ended up on the scrapheap of history when its hangar collapsed on it, crushing it. In the same way, a lot of Soviet consumer goods were blocky, inefficient knockoffs of Western product. I bring this up because I'd like to talk about the Soviet version of the ancient astronaut theory. Like the country's consumer goods, the Soviet ancient astronaut theory was derivative, clunky, and an ersatz copy of the West. But unlike Soviet cars and clothes, the Soviet ancient astronaut theory was influential.

The communist government of the Soviet Union was staunchly atheistic, following Marx's dictum that religion was the "opiate of the masses." Soviet scholars struggled to find a way to combat religion by providing a suitably scientific-sounding explanation for ancient mysteries and beliefs. The West already had a mystical tradition, Theosophy, which had suggested that beings from other planets stood behind ancient gods and human evolution (see Chapter 2). There was also literature, known to Soviet thinkers, about ancient astronauts, most notably the famed French novella *The Xipéhuz*, about alien-like creatures in Neolithic Mesopotamia. By the 1950s, Europe had started to develop a science-fiction-inspired set of proto-ancient-astronaut texts, including the early work of the Italian Peter Kolosimo and the UFO works of George Adamski and others, which adapted Theosophy's spiritual beings from other worlds as actual extraterrestrial, biological Venusians. Could Western pseudoscience, religion, and science fiction be adapted into a suitably socialist-realistic, materialist framework? And could it be used to defeat the claims of religion?

The Soviet mathematician Matest M. Agrest (1915-2005) sparked the Soviet ancient astronaut craze nearly a decade before the theory gained widespread popularity in the West. In 1959, he proposed that Sodom and Gomorrah had been destroyed by an extraterrestrial nuclear device (which conveniently also killed Lot's wife in the presence of witnesses), and that the terrace of Baalbek in Lebanon was a launch pad for alien spacecraft. Because Agrest was a scientist, unlike earlier European and American writers, his work attained a spurious credibility, especially with Jacques Bergier and Louis Pauwels, who saw in it not the anti-religious propaganda it was but rather confirmation that H. P. Lovecraft and Charles Fort had been on to something. His work found its way into *Morning of the Magicians* (1960), through which it was disseminated to Erich von Däniken, Zecharia Sitchin, and countless others.

As the ancient astronaut theory developed as a pop culture phenomenon among New Agers in first France, then all Europe, and then America, in the Soviet Union officials wondered if it could be used as a propaganda tool for atheism. Beginning in the 1960s, Carl Sagan began working with Soviet scientists on questions of extraterrestrial life. He worked closely with I. S. Shklovskii, who in 1962 first developed the suggestion, expanded with Sagan's input in 1966 as *Intelligent Life in the Universe*, that aliens had advanced civilizations on other planets and may have been responsible for creating an "artificial" satellite for Mars, the moon Phobos. While in the United States, these questions were met, essentially, with bemusement, in the Soviet Union the suggestion that aliens existed and could be contacted was treated much more seriously, largely because of Shklovskii's credibility as a scientist. By 1964, the Soviets were fully invested in searching for extraterrestrial intelligence.

Western scholars attributed this interest in ETs and ancient astronauts to the Soviet commitment to atheism, materialism, and evolution. Soviet scholars argued that if advanced civilizations were proven to exist, and if they demonstrated aspects of socialism, then this would be another argument in favor of Marx's assertion that socialism was the inevitable product of invisible forces. Further, any proof of intelligent life in the cosmos was a *prima facie* rebuke to religion's claims of special creation, not to mention evidence in favor of materialist, godless evolution.[1]

The consequences of these official dogmas was that much of the Soviet "evidence" for ancient astronauts was highly suspect, interpreted according to communist doctrine, and in many cases outright fabrications. Even Jacques Bergier, himself no strict adherent to truth, found the Soviet works suffused with "antireligious propaganda" and poor quality evidence: "Unfortunately, they accept such evidence a little too easily, and it is not always very convincing."[2] This did not stop him, of course, from relying upon Soviet sources. Nor did it stop Erich von Däniken, Zecharia Sitchin, and sundry others from using Soviet "evidence" in their own ancient astronaut books of the 1970s.

As we shall see in the next chapter, after 1970, Soviet interest in ancient astronauts declined at exactly the time the West began to embrace the idea.

Notes

[1] See James A. Herrick, *Scientific Mythologies* (InterVarsity, 2008), 49, 67.

[2] Jacques Bergier, *Extraterrestrial Visitations from Prehistoric Times to the Present* (Chicago: Henry Regnery Company, 1973), 133.

22. Ancient Astronauts, Soviet Geopolitics, and the Spitsbergen UFO Hoax

Is this the CIA's smoking gun in ancient astronaut studies? Did the CIA know months before the publication of *Chariots of the Gods* (1968) that ancient astronauts flew through earth's prehistoric skies? This passage from a declassified CIA memo would seem to confirm that they did. The relevant paragraphs are as follows:

> Some people think that UFOs have appeared in the earth's atmosphere only during the past two decades. This is not the case. The UFO phenomenon has been observed throughout the history of mankind. There are medieval and ancient reports strikingly similar to our own.
>
> Among the earlier UFO reports, as an example, may be the well-documented observations of a "large saucer" in 1882 and a "procession of bolides" in 1913. These reports still await investigation.
>
> The most remarkable UFO phenomenon is the famous "Tungusky meteorite." In recent years Soviet scientists have established that the Tungusky explosion had every parameter of an atmospheric nuclear blast. *The USSR Academy of Sciences Reports* (Volume 172, Nos. 4 and 5, 1967), include studies by Alexei Zolotov which attempt to prove that the Tungusky body could not be a meteorite or a comet.[1]

A close reading of the document shows that it is not, in fact, confirmation that the U.S. government believed in ancient astronauts, but rather that CIA analysts were following Soviet ancient astronaut developments closely for what they had to say about potential Soviet weapons programs and technological developments.

The document is actually a CIA abstract of an article written by Soviet ufologist Feliz Ziegel in 1968 in *Soviet Life* magazine, a publication aimed at Western audience, advocating for the study of UFOs in the months when Ziegel was pressuring the Soviet government to launch an official UFO inquiry, a request the Soviet government denied. By 1970, the Soviet Academy of Physics denounced Ziegel's claims, including ancient astronauts and a nuclear blast at Tunguska, as "fables." Not only that, but the article contains little original research; its ancient astronaut claims had been floating around Soviet circles since 1959 (see Chapter 21).

The CIA made an abstract of this article as part of its longstanding effort to keep abreast of Soviet science. Out of context, it looks like CIA interest in ancient astronauts. In context, it is one of thousands of Soviet news reports and journal articles translated or abstracted on a bewildering variety of subjects. The CIA may have been interested in UFOs and ancient astronauts, but only because they could be used as leverage in the Cold War. Interestingly, the American embassy in Moscow sent Washington an unclassified airgram—a secret communication by diplomatic pouch—on February 20, 1968 following up on this *Soviet Life* article and reporting that a new article by V. Lyustiberg "debunks flying saucers completely." The author, the embassy said, "makes no attempt to square this belief with previously published Soviet articles, including that rather spectacular article primarily for U.S. consumption in Soviet Life."[2] The State Department could not have then known of the growing disapproval of UFO studies in the Soviet government or the efforts to end Zeigel's pseudoscientific investigations.

The embassy attached a copy of Lyustiberg's article and someone at the NSA carefully circled a paragraph reporting on "an abandoned silvery disc" found buried in a Norwegian coal mine on an island in Spitsbergen in 1952, "pierced and marked by micrometer impacts." It was, the article said, "sent to the Pentagon" where it disappeared. Upon receipt, the NSA marked this paragraph with the word "PLANT" in all caps, demonstrating that the U.S. government was in the business of fooling the Soviets with false UFO reports.[3] Unfortunately, the report fooled many Western ufologists, and when the story's false premises began to unravel (witnesses, for example, turned out to be fictive), the tale was put down to fabrication on the part of a news reporter.

Spitsbergen was (and is) a coal-rich Norwegian island in the Svalbard archipelago high in the Arctic.

This much is well-reported in the ufological literature, including several books by journalist Nick Redfern. He dismisses the Spitsbergen crash as a government hoax, but does no additional probing to find out why it might have occurred. He simply implies nefarious government conspiracies of no certain purpose by the "all powerful" NSA.[4]

CIA documents, however, present a plausible reason for the UFO hoax cover story, one that ufologists like Redfern would easily have found in the FOIA documents publicly available on the CIA website had they expanded their search beyond the keyword "UFO" and took the time to put together the clues scattered across a range of strategic documents. From these, the following story emerges relatively clearly:

1952 was the same year that the CIA began monitoring the Yakutsk Cosmic Ray Station, a Soviet research facility whose work remained mysterious through the 1950s.[5] (It was monitoring neutron radiation from space, but the CIA thought it might have served as cover for nuclear research.) The site is a relatively short hop across the North Pole from Spitsbergen, and Spitsbergen was the closest Western territory to Yakutsk in 1952. The U.S. expressed strategic interest in Spitsbergen from at least World War II, and declared it a strategic imperative to monitor Soviet activities in concessions the USSR claimed in the Svalbard archipelago, where the CIA feared the USSR might build a covert air or submarine base to attack Europe or the United States.[6] The USSR had demanded Norway cede Bear Island and other Svalbard archipelago territories to the Soviet Union in 1944 and 1946, a request Norway rejected. Translated Soviet material kept classified by the CIA until 2009 confirms that the Soviets

viewed Spitsbergen as an essential territory to control for unrestricted nu-
clear-armed submarine warfare against NATO.[7]

Additionally, the CIA in 1954 wrote that it needed to study the effects
of Arctic magnetism on magnetically-guided long-range missiles in order
to counter Soviet advances in understanding Arctic magnetism.[8] This was
sparked by a wave of Soviet aerial activity in the Arctic region, beginning
in 1948, of immense concern to the CIA since the North Pole is the quick-
est route to deliver nuclear weapons from Russia to North America. This
route had been thought closed to the Soviet Union until the first Soviet
polar flight in 1947, the same year that UFO hysteria began in America.

Putting it all together, the available information supports three possible conclusions: (a) America hoaxed a UFO crash as a message to the Soviets; (b) America hoaxed a UFO crash to cover up a weapons or vehicular
test aimed at the Soviet Arctic; (c) America hoaxed a UFO crash to cover
up the recovery of a Soviet missile, submarine, or aircraft. Without more
information, it is not possible to determine which actually occurred, but
none requires an extraterrestrial craft.

Therefore, CIA monitoring of Soviet UFO and ancient astronaut research was about more than interest in ETs; rather, it appears to be inti-
mately tied in to Cold War geopolitics by other means. Again, let me em-
phasize that no UFO researcher I have been able to discover has ever tried
to place the Spitsbergen UFO hoax in its geopolitical context, or even
acknowledged that Cold War tensions were playing out on the island. So
much for "proof" of the CIA's interest in ancient astronauts and buried
UFOs.

Notes

[1] Central Intelligence Agency, "Unidentified Flying Objects (Abstract)," 1968, CIA Electronic Reading Room.

[2] U.S. Department of State, "Flying Saucers Are a Myth," Airgram No. A-1221, March
22, 1968, National Security Agency FOIA Reading Room.

³ Ibid. The circle and handwritten text do not appear on other agencies' copies of the airgram, indicating they originated with the NSA.

⁴ Nick Redfern, *Body Snatchers in the Desert* (New York: Simon and Schuster, 2005), 181.

⁵ Central Intelligence Agency, Office of Research and Reports, "Recent Developments in the Soviet Arctic," October 13, 1954, CIA Electronic Reading Room.

⁶ Central Intelligence Agency, "Spitsbergen," ORE 25-50, June 26, 1950, CIA Electronic Reading Room; "Information Requested of the Norwegian Government Reference Soviet Activity on Spitzbergen," March 21, 1951, CIA Electronic Reading Room.

⁷ William E. Nelson to Director of Central Intelligence, December 19, 1975, "*Military Thought (USSR):* The Operational-Strategic Employment of Naval Forces," CIA Electronic Reading Room.

⁸ CIA, "Recent Developments."

23. Taking Aliens and Ancient Texts Literally

I F ALTERNATIVE WRITERS cannot be bothered to conduct a literature search regarding the context surrounding modern UFO claims (see Chapter 22), they fair no better in cherry-picking the texts of antiquity. The value of what ancient astronaut theorists (AATs) refer to as "ancient texts" (in reality a stew of poetry, prose, oral history, and later missionary or anthropological reports) cannot be underestimated. When they are not outright fabricating them, AATs believe that these ancient texts are a literal record of prehistoric events. According to these theorists, ancient people were something akin to stenographers, incapable of recording anything than the literal truth about what they saw and experienced, though some distortion may have occurred later in time. The theory's most prominent proponent, Erich von Däniken, explained this idea in the theory's key text, *Chariots of the Gods?*, in 1968:

> If we take things literally, much that was once fitted into the mosaic of our past with great difficulty becomes quite plausible: not only the relevant clues in ancient texts, but also the 'hard facts' which offer themselves to our critical gaze all over the globe.[1]

The key to this phrase is, of course, the "if" clause.

Similarly, Giorgio Tsoukalos, the head of the Ancient Alien Society, formerly the Archaeology, Astronautics, and SETI Research Association (AAS RA), and a talking head and "consulting producer" on *Ancient Aliens*, put it this way:

Even after the "evidence" or the "artifact" was lost, hidden, or destroyed, the memories and recollections pertaining to the object and/or the visitors associated with it, remained. Facts were preserved orally through ritual traditions of significant events which happened a long, long time ago, dating back decades, centuries, or possibly even longer. Using this inherent form of "recording," actual—at that time highly significant—events in the remote past were preserved over the course of millennia. These accounts should thus be used in the careful analysis of ancient myths and traditions containing intricate descriptions of "confrontations with technological content and background".[2]

According to the AATs, a "careful analysis" of the texts shows that the "gods" of ancient mythology are in fact accurate traditions of extraterrestrial beings whose superior technology made them seem magical and godlike. Further, descriptions of doomed cities like Sodom and Gomorrah are literal reports of nuclear explosions, and descriptions of Hindu flying chariots are first-hand accounts of alien spaceships. The publisher of von Däniken's 2002 book, *The Gods Were Astronauts*, writes in the book's publicity materials that the author entertains "the suggestion, *based on a thorough examination of ancient texts*, that alien beings employed high-tech vehicles in epic aerial battles" (emphasis added).[3]

But such speculations are supportable only if we are justified in taking "ancient texts" literally. In order to justify a literal interpretation, AATs would need to show that ancient texts are verifiably accurate and that they consistently describe true events in a recoverable and understandable way. If these two conditions are not met, we end up with a situation like Nostradamus' quatrains, where readers are actively creating their own (often contradictory) meanings from real or imagined suggestions in the text, leading to a multiplicity of interpretations.

The key issue in the ancient astronaut theory's view of ancient texts is that where the gods appear, the gods are aliens. Humans are unable to entirely comprehend these aliens and attribute to them godlike power. As von Däniken wrote in *Chariots*, the first humans "had tremendous respect for the space travellers. Because they came from somewhere absolutely unknown and then returned there again, they were the 'gods' to them."[4] Their spaceships, of course, were titular flaming "chariots."

So, what becomes of what von Däniken himself admitted was "speculation" if the ancient texts fail to support the idea that the gods came from the sky in fiery spaceships?

Let's look at some "ancient texts" and find out.

I'd like to start with Herodotus (c. 484 – c. 425 BCE), an obviously ancient author, and one that AATs have had no trouble citing when his material meets their purposes. For example, von Däniken cites Herodotus in *Chariots* and repeatedly in 1996's *Eyes of the Sphinx*. According to Herodotus, the Thracians had a god named Salmoxis (Zalmoxis), who was their main deity, their savior god, and their lawgiver. Now, according to the ancient astronaut theory, if it has any predictive value, we should expect this god to have come from the sky and to have a flying saucer. What does Herodotus say of him?

> This Salmoxis I hear from the Hellenes who dwell about the Hellespont and the Pontus, was a man, and he became a slave in Samos, and was in fact a slave of Pythagoras the son of Mnesarchos.[5]

Further, besides being unforgivably human, Salmoxis fails even the most basic test of ancient astronautics: He isn't even from the sky!

> [Salmoxis] was making for himself meanwhile a chamber under the ground; and when his chamber was finished, he disappeared from among the Thracians and went down into the underground chamber, where he continued to live for three years.[6]

That's right: Salmoxis lived *underground*. Now, of course Herodotus doesn't say he came from underground, but as a human neither did he come from the sky.

Of course this is merely one god, and an obscure one. Surely, the Greek gods, whom von Däniken claimed were extraterrestrials in his 1999 book *Odyssey of the Gods*, and whom Giorgio Tsoukalos announced on *An-*

cient Aliens lived in a flying saucer on Mt. Olympus, have better support in the "ancient texts" for their extraterrestrial *bona fides*?

Here is Cyprian, writing in 247 CE, in *On the Vanity of Idols*:

> That those are no gods whom the common people worship, is known from this: they were formerly kings, who on account of their royal memory subsequently began to be adored by their people even in death. Thence temples were founded to them; thence images were sculptured to retain the countenances of the deceased by the likeness; and men sacrificed victims, and celebrated festal days, by way of giving them honour. Thence to posterity those rites became sacred, which at first had been adopted as a consolation.[7]

But perhaps this is too recent (though it should not be since von Däniken has no trouble in *Chariots* citing Norse sagas from 1200 CE as "ancient texts" recording prehistoric traditions). Let's look at what Cicero (106-43 BCE) has to say in *De natura deorum*, where the Republican Roman orator relates "the theory that these gods, who are deified human beings, and who are the object of our most devout and universal veneration, exist not in reality but in imagination."[8]

Such a philosophy derives from the work of the fourth century BCE Greek mythographer Euhemerus whose books, unfortunately, do not survive. His ideas, however, were preserved in the works of Diodorus Siculus and Plutarch, who explains in *Isis and Osiris* that Euhemerus spread atheism "by describing all the received Gods under the style of generals, sea-captains, and kings, whom he makes to have lived in the more remote and ancient times, and to be recorded in golden characters in a certain country called Panchon..."[9]

So, we see that some "ancient texts" state that the gods were merely human beings promoted by time and ignorance to the status of gods. On what basis can we discount these texts while privileging other texts that hew closer to the ancient astronaut theory's views? The answer, of course, is that we cannot. Of course, it is possible to argue that these texts represent a later development, or that they represent later efforts to interpret earlier myths that were in turn influenced by aliens. But this brings us to a paradox.

On one hand we have actual, unambiguous ancient texts that literally state that the gods were *not* aliens but humans. And on the other hand we have texts that AATs have *interpreted* as *seeming like* they depict 1960s-era astronauts. So which do we believe: the ancients' actual words, or von Däniken's and Tsoukalos' reconstructions of what they believe some (but not all) of those words mean?

According to the rules of the ancient astronaut theory, as laid down by von Däniken and Tsoukalos above, we must assume that "ancient texts" are literal and accurate, while discounting the possibility of interpretation or subjective judgment, since according to the AATs, ancient people lacked the imagination or the ability to create fantasy wholesale. As von Däniken wrote in *Chariots*: "Even imagination needs something to start it off. How can the chronicler give descriptions that presuppose at least some idea of rockets and the knowledge that such a vehicle can ride on a ray and cause a terrifying thunder?"[10] Therefore, we must also ask what "imagination" led Euhemerus to suggest the gods were humans? What fact led to a thousand years of Greco-Roman "secret" traditions that the gods were mere human beings?

To complicate matters further, the father of "alternative" history, Ignatius Donnelly, chose to interpret the ancient texts cited above literally in his *Atlantis: The Antediluvian World* (1882) to argue that the Greek gods were in fact ancient kings of Atlantis: "The history of Atlantis is the key of the Greek mythology. There can be no question that these gods of Greece were human beings. The tendency to attach divine attributes to great earthly rulers is one deeply implanted in human nature."[11] He then went on to interpret the rest of Greek mythology *symbolically*, to argue that it was a distorted reflection of the events of the last days of Atlantis.

As the reader has likely realized, this exercise is predicated on incorrect assumptions. Ignatius Donnelly, Erich von Däniken, and Giorgio Tsoukalos have chosen to interpret some "ancient texts" literally and others symbolically, mostly according to how well these texts support their preconceived notions. As we have just seen, this ad hoc method supports diametrically opposed results with equal certainty. Any attempt to impose a blanket rule—even the ancient astronaut theorists' own rule, observed mainly in the breach, that texts should be taken at face value—inevitably produces a paradox whereby "ancient texts" confirm and deny the same "facts."

The reason for this should be obvious: "Ancient texts" are not monolithic, literal records of what happened in the past. They were written by different authors for different purposes in different times and places. Every ancient document has its own unique history, composition, biases, and (for some) even false or fictitious elements. To truly explore ancient literature is to understand these facets of these works and to analyze them according to a methodology established prior to the attempt to use the texts to justify a prefabricated theory.

The AAS RA ancient astronaut organization describes ancient texts as including:

> Myths and other legends telling about observations - including details - that can hardly be attributed to fantasy. [...] there are new, astonishing interpretations possible when the "ET factor" is included. Descriptions mostly appear as circumscriptions here, where the unknown is compared to things known in the respective era and culture using the principle of "Looks like...".[12]

But isn't this exactly what the AATs themselves are doing—cherry-picking ancient literature for random paragraphs and incidents that "look like" their childhood fantasies of Apollo-era NASA rockets and spacesuits? As I have just shown, cherry-picking the ancient texts can equally well "prove" that the gods, far from being aliens, simply never existed at all.

Of course, that particular picked cherry also has the benefit of being true.

Notes

[1] Erich von Däniken, *Chariots of the Gods? Unsolved Mysteries of the Past,* trans. Michael Heron (New York: Bantam, 1973), p. 95.

[2] Giorgio Tsoukalos, "Expansion of SETA to Planet Earth," *Legendary Times* [online], 2002.

[3] Jacket copy on Erich von Däniken, *The Gods Were Astronauts: Evidence of the True Identities of the Old 'Gods'* (Vega, 2008).

[4] Von Däniken, *Chariots,* 52.

[5] *Histories* 4.95, translated by G. C. Macaulay.

[6] *Histories* 4.95

[7] Treatise 6.1, trans. Robert Ernest Wallace in *Ante-Nicene Fathers,* vol. 5., edited by Alexander Roberts, James Donaldson, and A. Cleveland Coxe (Buffalo, NY: Christian Literature Publishing Co., 1886).

[8] *De natura deorum,* 3.53, trans. H. Rackham in *Cicero: On the Nature of the Gods,* Loeb Classical Library (Cambridge: Harvard University Press, 1972).

[9] *De Iside et Osiride* 23, trans. William Watson Goodwin.

[10] Von Däniken, *Chariots of the Gods?,* 57.

[11] Ignatius Donnelly, *Atlantis: The Antediluvian World* (New York: Harper & Bros., 1882), 285.

[12] AAS RA, "Paleo-SETI: Interdisciplinary and Popularized," *Legendary Times* [online], no date.

24. What Was the Scholomance?

I N *DRACULA*, Bram Stoker includes an intriguing allusion to a mysterious devil's school in Transylvania: The Draculas, he wrote, "had dealings with the Evil One. They learned his secrets in the Scholomance, amongst the mountains over Lake Hermanstadt, where the devil claims the tenth scholar as his due."[1] The vampire himself was one of these scholars, a diabolic genius.

This school is no mere piece of fiction, however. As has been well-documented, Stoker derived his knowledge of the Scholomance from Emily Gerard's 1885 article on "Transylvanian Superstitions":

> As I am on the subject of thunderstorms, I may as well here mention the *Scholomance,* or school supposed to exist somewhere in the heart of the mountains, and where all the secrets of nature, the language of animals, and all imaginable magic spells and charms are taught by the devil in person. Only ten scholars are admitted at a time, and when the course of learning has expired and nine of them are released to return to their homes, the tenth scholar is detained by the devil as payment, and mounted upon an *Ismeju* (dragon) he becomes henceforward the devil's aide-de-camp, and assists him in 'making the weather,' that is to say, preparing the thunderbolts.[2]

But what exactly was this Scholomance, and where did the legend come from?

Gerard's version of the story is not a professional anthropological re-port, but rather the story of an amateur traveling through the (then) Habsburg territories. By luck, a folklorist, R. C. Maclagan, produced a re-port for the journal *Folklore* in 1897 that included a more accurate version of the story then-current in Transylvania:

> Here we find that the *drac* is the devil in person, who instructs certain persons to be magicians and medicine men in a college under the earth. Of these, one in eight receives instruction during fourteen years, and on his return to earth he has the following power. By means of certain magi-cal formulæ he compels a dragon to ascend from the depths of a loch. He then throws a golden bridle with which he has been provided over his head, and rides aloft among the clouds, which he causes to freeze and thereby produces hail.[3]

Notice that now the school is under the earth, which forms one part of the solution to the puzzle of the Scholomance. There are two other parts that complete the picture. To understand this, however, it's important to remember that before Transylvania was a Christian territory, it was part of the pre-Christian Roman province of Dacia, which before the Roman con-quest was culturally affiliated with Thrace. In both regions, priests of the pagan gods retreated to the woods and secret places to learn the secrets of the gods.

The first puzzle piece is the presence of the supposed scholars of the Scholomance among the Transylvanians. These scholars learned to control the weather and ride dragons, which are strange things for the devil to teach until one realizes that Transylvania (now Romania) has an indige-nous legend of itinerant wizards who perform those same two miracles: riding a dragon and summoning storms.

Later called the Solomanari (after the supposed connection between Solomon and alchemy), the Zgriminties or Hultan were shaman-priests who claimed control over storms and could summon a *balaur* (dragon) to ride. Before Christianity, they were seen as benevolent forces able to im-plore the gods to deliver much-needed rain to fertilize the crops. Christians defamed the Solomonari as devil-worshippers, but in reality they originated as pre-Christian pagan priests. They most likely worshipped the pre-Christian god Zalmoxis or Salmoxis (also: Zalmus), whose power they are able to wield. Remarkably little is known about this god outside of Greek reports, but the ancients declared that he taught astrology[4] as well as the doctrine of immortality.[5] According to Diogenes Laertius, he was the equivalent of the harvest-god Kronos (Saturn),[6] and Hippolytus assert-ed that those who followed this god as disciples (= scholars) worshipped him in isolated, underground chapels.[7] Christians, following Biblical au-thority,[8] saw this god as a devil or demon, as with all pagan gods (e.g., St. Augustine: pagan gods are "most impure demons, who desire to be thought gods"[9]).

The earliest, and likely quite distorted, account of Zalmoxis occurs in Herodotus (followed by all later authors) in a passage that explains, I think, the origin of the Scholomance. Herodotus wrote that Zalmoxis was not really a god but a slave of Pythagoras, and that after being freed and gaining great wealth he

> prepared a banqueting-hall, where he received and feasted the chief men of the tribe and instructed them meanwhile that neither he himself nor his guests nor their descendants in succession after them would die; but that they would come to a place where they would live for ever and have all things good. While he was doing that which has been mentioned and was saying these things, he was making for himself meanwhile a chamber under the ground; and when his chamber was finished, he disappeared from among the Thracians and went down into the underground cham-ber, where he continued to live for three years: and they grieved for his loss and mourned for him as dead. Then in the fourth year he appeared to the Thracians, and in this way the things which Salmoxis said became credible to them.[10]

Herodotus says this story is how the Greeks understood the Thracian or Dacian (pre-Christian Romanian) god's story. But the likelihood is that this is a distortion of the actual Dacian religious story, which probably involved the god's death and resurrection in an underground chamber, a great hall where he taught the secrets of immortality and of life and death. The ethnocentric Greeks interpreted this as a version of their own Pythagorean philosophy, and in so doing sought to make the Dacian faith little more than a derivative of a Greek original. Modern scholars believe the myth of Zalmoxis as Pythagoras' slave derives from the Dacian and Thracian priests' forehead tattoos, which the Greeks misinterpreted as slave-traders' brands.[11]

It seems to me that the pre-Christian religious teachings of Zalmoxis are what first Greeks, then Romans, and then Christians misunderstood, the Christians slandering the old god as the Devil himself, and his underground chamber where he taught the secrets of immortality as the school of the Devil. Whether this underground cult center was entirely mythical or whether it reflects a genuine Dacian or Thracian cult center where worshippers received priestly indoctrination and training (perhaps at what Strabo calls Zalmoxis' holy mountain of Cogaeonum[12]), it is impossible now to say. But, with this information, we now have the essential elements of the Scholomance and the scholars who study there. As for the dragon, so widespread are dragon myths in Greek, Slavic, and Christian lore that I'm not sure a specific origin for the Solomonari's dragons is possible, or entirely necessary. Maclagan may well have been right in 1897 when he suggested that the dragon was a symbol for the thunderclouds the shaman-priests claimed to command.

It is rather remarkable that in its essentials this story should survive in folklore for 2,500 years, more remarkable still that our archetypical vampire Dracula more or less accidentally draws on this ancient set of beliefs in the power of pagan resurrection to fuel his own unholy un-death. And as with the pagan gods, the cross and the communion wafer destroyed Dracula. Without Stoker's conscious knowledge, *Dracula* recapitulates the process whereby the pagan scholar-priests and their god were demonized and forced to submit to the dominance of Christianity.

Notes

[1] Bram Stoker, *Dracula: A Mystery Story* (New York: W. R. Caldwell & Co., 1897), 241.

[2] Emily Gerard, "Transylvanian Superstitions," *The Nineteenth Century,* July 1885, 136.

[3] R. C. Maclagan, "Ghost Lights of the West Highlands," *Folk-Lore* 8 (1897): 238.

[4] Strabo, *Geography* 7.3.5.

[5] Plato, *Charmides* 156-158.

[6] *Lives of the Eminent Philosophers* 8.1.1.

[7] *Refutation of All Heresies* 1.2.

[8] e.g. 1 Corinthians 10:20.

[9] *City of God* 7.33 (translated by Marcus Dods), parallel to Psalm 96:5.

[10] *Histories* 4.94, translated by G. C. Macaulay.

[11] Porphyry, *Life of Pythagoras* 15; E. R. Dodds, *The Greeks and the Irrational* (Berkeley, California: University of California, 2004), 163n.44.

[12] *Geography* 7.3.5.

25. Oannes: The Best Evidence for Ancient Astronauts?

NOT LONG BEFORE his death in 2012, the ancient astronaut author Philip Coppens appeared on the *Joe Rogan Experience* podcast and discussed the three-hour online movie *Ancient Aliens Debunked* and the "very clever" ways filmmaker Chris White attempted to make criticism of *Ancient Aliens* as a TV show synonymous with debunking the ancient astronaut hypothesis as a whole. Coppens specifically told host Joe Rogan that White's biggest omission was his failure to address the Babylonian tale of Oannes (which he mistakenly claimed was known to the much earlier Sumerians; this cannot be proved). Coppens asserted that this story is the "amongst the best evidence that we might have potentially been visited by" extraterrestrials in prehistory. He further told Rogan:

> You should really try to negate this if you want to *pretend* that you have completely destroyed the ancient alien theory. You can try to attack the *Ancient Aliens* series, but as long as you don't go for the best evidence, like the Oannes story, and you do it on a scientific level, you kind of like, you argue why Carl Sagan thought this was interesting, why other scientists thought this was interesting, then you can make a documentary and *pretend* that you have completely destroyed the possibility that we were ever visited in the past by ancient aliens, but you haven't.[1]

OK. Fair point. So let's look at Oannes to see just why this Babylonian fish-man is not an ancient astronaut.

The story of Oannes is told only by Berossus (also spelled Berosus or Berosos), a late Babylonian priest who related the tale along with a cosmology in his *Babylonian History*, which does not survive. Summaries were made by Apollodorus, Abydenus, and Alexander Polyhistor, but of course none of these survive either. Extracts from these Greek summaries were recorded in Late Antiquity by Eusebius of Caesaria and in the Middle Ages by George Syncellus, whose books are the sole surviving record of Berossus' work. We know Berossus existed because he is mentioned by other writers, such as Pliny, whose works survive. (Unrelated fragments of Berossus' astronomical works were also preserved by Seneca.)

But this isn't the end of the story. The Greek fragments of Berossus are known to modern readers in the form given them in the early 1800s by I. P. Cory, whose *Ancient Fragments* (1826; 2nd ed. 1832) freely ran together material from Eusebius and Syncellus while excising the presumed contributions of the Greek-speaking authors to produce relatively linear narratives. These fragments were further adapted in 1976 by ancient astronaut author Robert Temple, who published them in the appendix to his *Sirius Mystery* from Richard Hodge's 1876 revision of Cory's *Fragments*. This is the form of Berossus' work ancient astronaut hypothesizers know.

Now, Berossus is generally an accurate writer, but the form of his work that comes down to us does not perfectly match cuneiform records where such records exist. For example, the Greek summarizers make Berossus state that during the Creation, Belus (Marduk) "cut off his own head, upon which the other gods mixed the blood, as it gushed out, with the earth; and from thence men were formed."[2] However, the Babylonian creation epic, the *Enuma Elish*, differs on this detail in the cuneiform text. Marduk decrees that the god Kingu must be cleaved with an ax and his blood used by Ea to create man.[3] Now, had the work of Berossus—a priest of Marduk—come down to us perfectly, it is very unlikely we should see such a profound mischaracterization of a sacred act of the chief god himself. As a result of such mistakes, we simply cannot be certain that the Oannes passage is uncorrupted.

Nevertheless, reading the fragments of Berossus as they currently stand gives us no confidence that they describe an extraterrestrial. In fact, Berossus says nothing about outer space at all:

> At Babylon there was (in these times) a great resort of people of various nations, who inhabited Chaldæa, and lived in a lawless manner like the beasts of the field. In the first year there appeared, from that part of the Erythræan sea which borders upon Babylonia, an animal destitute of reason, by name Oannes, whose whole body (according to the account of Apollodorus) was that of a fish; that under the fish's head he had another head, with feet also below, similar to those of a man, subjoined to the fish's tail. His voice too, and language, was articulate and human; and a representation of him is preserved even to this day.
>
> This Being was accustomed to pass the day among men; but took no food at that season; and he gave them an insight into letters and sciences, and arts of every kind. He taught them to construct cities, to found temples, to compile laws, and explained to them the principles of geometrical knowledge. He made them distinguish the seeds of the earth, and shewed them how to collect the fruits; in short, he instructed them in every thing which could tend to soften manners and humanize their lives. From that time, nothing material has been added by way of improvement to his instructions. And when the sun had set, this Being Oannes, retired again into the sea, and passed the night in the deep; for he was amphibious.
>
> After this there appeared other animals like Oannes, of which Berossus proposes to give an account when he comes to the history of the kings.[4]

Such legends prompted Carl Sagan to write in the 1960s that "stories like the Oannes legend, and representations especially of the earliest civilizations on Earth, deserve much more critical studies than have been performed heretofore, with the possibility of direct contact with an extraterrestrial civilization as one of many possible alternative explanations."[5] Sagan later discounted this when he learned more about myths and legends and why they are unreliable.

Note that *contra* Coppens, Berossus clearly states that this event happened at Babylon (not Sumer), which was only founded in 1894 BCE, many centuries after the arts and sciences the creature claimed to bring with him were already in use at Sumer, Eridu, and Ur. (You can claim Berossus is wrong here, but if so, why trust anything else?) Note, too, that Oannes is described as a fish-man (and depicted in "literal" ancient art as a man in a giant fish suit) who lives in and returns to the sea. This is *not* outer space, and the only reason anyone ever thought it had anything to do with space is because at one particular moment in history—the 1960s and '70s, when Sagan and Temple wrote—spacecraft routinely "splashed down" in the ocean, thus leading to an erroneous—and artificial— assumption of a connection between space and water.

But the story is hardly unique. In the Book of Enoch, the Fallen Angels do exactly as Oannes and his brethren did:

And all the others together with them took unto themselves wives, and each chose for himself one, and they began to go in unto them and to de- file themselves with them, and they taught them charms and enchant- ments, and the cutting of roots, and made them acquainted with plants. And they became pregnant, and they bare great giants, whose height was three thousand ells: Who consumed all the acquisitions of men. And when men could no longer sustain them, the giants turned against them and de- voured mankind. And they began to sin against birds, and beasts, and rep- tiles, and fish, and to devour one another's flesh, and drink the blood. Then the earth laid accusation against the lawless ones.

And Azâzêl taught men to make swords, and knives, and shields, and breastplates, and made known to them the metals of the earth and the art of working them, and bracelets, and ornaments, and the use of antimony, and the beautifying of the eyelids, and all kinds of costly stones, and all colouring tinctures. And there arose much godlessness, and they commit- ted fornication, and they were led astray, and became corrupt in all their ways. Semjâzâ taught enchantments, and root-cuttings, Armârôs the re- solving of enchantments, Barâqîjâl, (taught) astrology, Kôkabêl the con- stellations, Ezêqêêl the knowledge of the clouds, Araqiêl the signs of the earth, Shamsiêl the signs of the sun, and Sariêl the course of the moon. And as men perished, they cried, and their cry went up to heaven . . .[6]

The Hebrews got the better end of the deal, apparently, since Azâzêl gave them makeup and jewelry in addition to boring things like seeds and math.

Nor is Enoch the only parallel. Osiris, in his role as civilizer of Egypt, did exactly the same thing, as recorded in Plutarch, *On Isis and Osiris*:

> One of the first acts related of Osiris in his reign was to deliver the Egyptians from their destitute and brutish manner of living. This he did by showing them the fruits of cultivation, by giving them laws, and by teaching them to honour the gods. Later he travelled over the whole earth civilizing it without the slightest need of arms, but most of the peoples he won over to his way by the charm of his persuasive discourse combined with song and all manner of music. Hence the Greeks came to identify him with Dionysus.[7]

Now, you can be like Atlantis theorizers and assume that these are all independent stories of civilizing agents coming from a lost civilization (Graham Hancock does) or an ancient astronaut hypothesizer proclaiming them all aliens. (That the same evidence is found in both claims does little to boost our confidence in the correctness of either.) But I think it should be fairly obvious that this is a widespread cultural myth of the "civilizing hero" to whom the various accomplishments of society are retroactively attributed. There are dozens upon dozens of such heroes worldwide.

Now, if we might like some facts about Oannes—which, of course, spoil the fun—we can begin by noting that Oannes isn't his real name. This is a Greek rendering of *Uanna*, a name found in the cuneiform Library of Ashurbanipal as an alternate name for the better-known hero Adapa, whose oldest reference dates from 1335 BCE at Amarna in Egypt, in cuneiform materials supplied to Akhenaton. This figure was held to be the (human) son of Ea (Sumerian: Enki), the man who brought civilization to Eridu and who broke the wings of the wind when it overturned his boat. He later was tricked out of immortality but took his place among the Seven Sages. "Ea," the tablets state, "anointed Adapa ... to fish for his temple in Eridu."[8]

The word used for "sage" comes from the Sumerian for "Great Water," thus associating Adapa-Oannes with the sea, as Berossus seems to have confusedly remembered, an association strengthened by the memory that Eridu had been located at the head of the Persian Gulf, where Oannes supposedly operated. In the *Erra and Ishum*, the Seven Sages are banished to the underground sea, the Apsu, the home of Adapa's father Ea, because they angered the gods (cf. Fallen Angels). From this watery abyss, whose entrance was believed to be beneath Ea's temple at Eridu, they became described as "pure puradu-fish," a type of carp still held sacred in the region, thus yielding the literalized description of Oannes as a hybrid fish-man, when hero and symbol became identified. (This is like the way Jesus is sometimes depicted as the Lamb of God.) In short, Berossus' description (as related by the Greeks) is a very late, somewhat confused synthesis of the earlier myths of a human hero who was banished to the underground sea (which of course does not actually exist), took a fish as his symbol, and returned from the sea to teach wisdom. It's worth noting that Adapa is paired in myth with Tammuz, another who ended up in the underworld (this time the realm of the dead) and returned.

Since we can trace in historical texts and iconography the evolution of Adapa from human figure in the ancient Library of Ashurbanipal (as well as at Akhenaton's city of Amarna) to fish-man much, much later in Berossus, and from banished sage to risen denizen of the waters, we have no warrant for assuming the final, jumbled Greek summaries of Berossus are in any way historical. If the Babylonians failed to tell Akhenaton that Adapa was an alien from space in 1335 BCE, or their own king in the 600s BCE, why should we trust a demonstrably corrupt Greek summary of a text written centuries later?

This is the "best evidence" of ancient astronauts?

Notes

[1] *The Joe Rogan Experience*, episode 280 [online], November 5, 2012.

[2] Berossus quoted in Alexander Polyhistor, preserved in Syncellus, *Chronicon* 28 and Eusebius, *Chronicon* 7, translated by I. P. Cory and Richard Hodges, *Cory's Ancient Fragments* (London: Reeves & Turner, 1876), 60.

[3] *Enuma Elish* 6.19-27.

[4] Berossus, in Cory and Hodges, *Ancient Fragments*, 56-58.

[5] I. S. Shklovskiï and Carl Sagan, *Intelligent Life in the Universe* (San Francisco: Holden-Day, 1966), 461.

[6] 1 Enoch 7:1-8:4, translated by R. H. Charles.

[7] Plutarch, *De Iside et Osiride* 13.1, translated by Frank Cole Babbitt.

[8] Tel-al-Amarna Tablet A, British Museum, translated in Victor H. Matthews and Don C. Benjamin, *Old Testament Parallels: Laws and Stories from the Near East*, 3rd ed. (Mahwah, New Jersey: Paulist Press, 2006), 44.

26. Was Oannes John the Baptist or a Sleeping King?

RUMMAGING THROUGH the 1969 New Age alternative history classic *Hamlet's Mill*, I ran into a weird little claim that I had forgotten about since I first read the book many years ago. The book's authors, Giorgio de Santillana and Hertha von Dechend, endorse the claim of Robert Eisler (1921), citing Arthur Drews (1910) and Charles François Dupuis (1795), that John the Baptist was originally the Oannes of Babylonian myth[1] (see previous chapter). This story is a giant mess, and I can only sketch the outline of the problems involved in this silly identification.

The problem comes from the fact that "Oannes" is a transliteration in Latin characters of a Greek transliteration of an uncertain original. In the Greek texts, the names Oannes and Iannes appear, suggesting a similarity to Ioannes, the Greek form of Yohanan, the Hebrew name of John the Baptist. Both figures have something to do with water and fishes, so they must therefore be the same. De Santillana and von Dechend ignore the subtle distinction Eisler tried to make: He merely claimed that Oannes myths paved the way for acceptance of the Baptist in Mesopotamia, not that they two were the same man.[2] They do so because their concern is that Oannes is the principle representative and originator of the myth of the Sleeping King, exemplified by Arthur and Frederick Barbarossa, asleep in their mountains awaiting the time when they are needed again. We shall return there anon.

Eisler saw fish symbolism everywhere and assumed a connection between Christianity and pagan fish cults. He also claimed that Jesus' statement that the Baptist came "eating no bread and drinking no wine"[3] shows dependence on Berossus' statement that Oannes "took no food" during daylight hours when he was above sea level.[4] Eisler elides both of these statements to make them say that neither figure ever "ate nor drank," though this is clearly not the meaning of either. (John eats locusts and honey in the book of Mark, for example.[5]) Eisler also leaves out the fact that abstaining from certain earthly food or drink is a mark of holiness in the Bible. John the Baptist is forbidden wine by divine decree because it was forbidden to all Nazarites, a mark of special holiness.[6] But also: God forbids fermented liquids in the Tent of Meeting.[7] Similarly, while in the presence of God on Sinai, Moses "ate no food and drank no water,"[8] just as Saul abstained from food and drink in the presence of Jesus on the road to Damascus.[9] Are all they Oannes, too?

By contrast, Oannes partook of no human food because he was not a human any longer. But to understand this means exploding one more misconception. Eisler and de Santillana and von Dechend assume wrongly that Oannes is a corruption of "Ea-Hani," making Oannes an avatar of the water god Ea (the Sumerian Enki). This was somewhat possible to support when all that was known of him was Berossus, but in light of the cuneiform inscriptions of Nineveh and Tel-al-Amarna, it is insupportable. These inscriptions confirm that Oannes is a Greek transliteration of Uan, an alternate name for Adapa. Adapa is one of the Seven Sages, who was offered the food of the gods but, on bad advice, declined it, losing immortality. (See previous chapter.) When Berossus says Oannes ate no human food, he is referencing a somewhat corrupt tradition about Adapa and the gods' food. (Or, more likely, the Greek summarizers misunderstood whatever Berossus really said—as evidenced from discrepancies between the Greek summaries of Berossus and the *Enuma Elish*, as discussed in Chapter 25.)

Now, as a point toward the Baptist comparison, it is true that John the Baptist was called a fisher of men in southern Mesopotamia, and Adapa was known as he who "fish[ed] for his [Ea's] temple at Eridu."[10] Adapa was believed to have been banished by the gods to the underground sea for hubris, but to have returned from time to time to teach wisdom. In this, he may well have been seen in late Antiquity as an analogue to John the Baptist, much the way the similarity in name and iconography between Elijah and Helios led to the saint with the fiery chariot taking over for the god with his fiery chariot in some local cults.

But Eisler is wrong to claim Berossus knows six reincarnations of Oannes. He seems here to be referencing Berossus' statement that several beings like Oannes rose from the sea "after him." These would be the Seven Sages, I suppose, though elsewhere he calls them seven of the first ten kings of Babylon. There is no indication that they are reincarnations, or that their lives were successive rather than overlapping.

De Santillana and von Dechend see in Eisler's mistakes the prototype of the Sleeping King. They follow him in mistaking Oannes for Ea, and identify Ea with the planet Saturn, which they then identify with the god Kronos (the Roman Saturn). However, Ea was not associated with the planet Saturn but with Mercury, according to the Sumerian tablets (though this was not consistent through time). In the *Enuma Elish* Ea casts a spell on the god Abzu to put him to sleep,[11] but this is hardly the same as being the sleeping god himself.

By contrast, the Sleeping King story is very much an Indo-European story, found from the Celtic fringe straight through Europe to Greece. (A very few, very late stories from the Americas use the same motif, but these are post-Conquest in origin and derive from European sources.) There are dozens upon dozens of these sleeping gods/kings in their mountains, of whom Charlemagne and Frederick Barbarossa are among the latest. The best-known version of the story is that of King Arthur, who was taken to the Isle of Avalon, where according to a Welsh legend, he and his knights sleep in a cave awaiting the time when they will rise again to defend Britain during a great conflagration. But this is hardly the only version of the story, or even the first.

In Denmark, the hero Holgar Danske sleeps beside his knights in a tomb beneath Kronberg Castle. Both Charlemagne and Frederick Barbarossa (or sometimes Frederick II) are believed to be entombed within mountains (Odensburg and Kyffhäuser, respectively) waiting to rise up and reclaim their thrones, as are the Saxon King Harold, the Duke of Monmouth, Byzantine Emperor Constantine XI, and Portugal's King Sebastian. (Some of these are entombed in caves rather than mountains.) In most cases, the sleeper is a powerful man with a long white beard.

An interesting sidelight to this story comes from Serbia, where the hero Marko is believed to be asleep in a cave high atop a mountain, awaiting the moment he is needed. A large number of Europeans gathered at the foot of Mount Rtanj (also called Šiljak after its highest peak), believing that an extraterrestrial-built pyramid was concealed within the mountain and would save them from the predicted disaster of the 2012 Maya apocalypse (which, of course, never happened).

The suggestion that the mountain is hollow may derive from the fact that for many years a large coal mine operated on the mountain, at an elevation of 800 meters. (It might still, for all I know.) But the mountain has always been important in its region since it is the only tall peak in its area and has a seemingly (but not really) unnaturally regular pyramidal shape. Traditionally, it was considered the "navel of the world," around which the axis of the world spins. In the aftermath of World War I, Romanian nationalists traveled the region in gaudy robes preaching that the mountain was sacred, claiming it was the focus of divine portents, and offering prophecies of doom if it did not become part of Romania.[12]

But an older layer of legend also claimed that the peak once held the tower of a powerful wizard, as tall as the mountain itself, within which a fabulous treasure lay concealed. Due in part to the peak's propensity for being struck by lightning, legend also says it is surrounded by spirit lights. These, in turn, gave rise to the modern myth that it was a base for UFOs, thus yielding the alien pyramid story when all these tales merged into a newer, sillier one.

The idea that a mountain is the right location for a hidden treasure is an old one in Indo-European lore, going back to the idea of the Sleeping King beneath the mountain as well as the myth of the dragon, the serpentine monster that supposedly guards such treasures. Consider, as mentioned above, the stories of Beowulf or Sigurd, or, more to the point, the fact that the Serbian hero Prince Marko is one of the Sleeping Kings. This Marko was a historical figure, but his folklore counterpart incorporated older myths and legends from pre-Christian times. Thus, the Marko of folklore was a giant who did not die but either was sealed up in a cave atop a mountain or lived in a vast house concealed in a pit under the earth. It isn't hard to see the alien pyramid within Mt. Rtanj as a variant of a supernatural underground palace like that of Marko (not to mention that of neighboring deity Zalmoxis, as discussed in Chapter 25), which allows those within to live on past the point of natural death.

Many scholars believe all of these myths trace their source back to Odin, the Norse (and also Germanic) god of war who was the first to slumber within a sacred mountain (note that one such mountain is Odensburg, "Odin's Mountain"). Odin shares the long white beard of the dead heroes, and many scholars also believe that the knights routinely entombed with the hero originate in the dead warriors who rested in Odin's Valhalla awaiting the violent end of the world, Ragnorak, when they would be needed for the final battle against the forces of evil.

That this story is ancient can be seen in Plutarch, who reports a myth from the Celtic fringe of the Roman Empire in two sections of his *Moralia.* Here Cronus, the father of the gods, can be read as Odin:

...in this part of the world there is one island where Cronus is confined, guarded while he sleeps by Briareus; for his sleep has been devised as a bondage for him, and round about him are many demigods as attendants and servants.[13]

There are three other islands equidistant from Ogygia and from one another, in the general direction of the sun's summer setting. The natives have a story that in one of these Cronus has been confined by Zeus, but that he, having a son for gaoler, is left sovereign lord of those islands and of the sea, which they call the Gulf of Cronus.[14]

This ancient myth is the model for the sleeping god stories, whether they be, like Cronus and Arthur, on an island, or like Charlemagne and Frederick, in a mountain. The difference is probably due to geography—islands being less plentiful than mountains in Europe's interior.

De Santillana and von Dechend discuss Plutarch's report of Kronos' imprisonment on Ogygia and ask us to read it as cosmology, but it is just another variation on the Sleeping King motif. The fact that Plutarch's longer discussion of the myth in the *Moralia* (*De Faciae* 27) is very much a morality tale about what makes one Greek does not inspire confidence that it hides a cosmological core. The shorter of the two discussions (*De Defectu Oraculorum* 18), is attributed to British holy men—Celts, possibly Druids—and suggests that a separate Celtic version was then in existence and that some syncretism between Celtic and Graeco-Roman versions had already occurred by Plutarch's day.

If this is true, then Plutarch's use of the planet Saturn is a Greco-Roman layering onto the myth of Hellenistic astrology (which, incidentally, did know of precession), not necessarily an original characteristic—especially since it isn't found in any other Indo-European version of the story, and, no, not even in the unrelated story of Oannes.

Notes

[1] Giorgio de Santillana and Hertha von Dechend, *Hamlet's Mill: An Essay Investigating the Origins of Human Knowledge and Its Transmission through Myth* (Boston: Nonpareil, 1998), Appendix 33.

[2] Robert Eisler, *Orpheus—The Fisher: Comparative Studies in Orphic and Early Christian Cult Symbolism* (London: J. M. Watkins, 1921), 151-155.

[3] Luke 7:33

[4] Berossus quoted in Alexander Polyhistor, preserved in Syncellus, *Chronicon* 28 and Eusebius, *Chronicon* 7, trans. I. P. Cory and Richard Hodges, *Cory's Ancient Fragments* (London: Reeves & Turner, 1876), 57.

[5] Mark 1:6

[6] Luke 1:15 with Numbers 6:3

[7] Leviticus 10:9

[8] Deuteronomy 9:9

[9] Acts 9:9

[10] Tel-al-Amarna Tablet A, British Museum, translated in Victor H. Matthews and Don C. Benjamin, *Old Testament Parallels: Laws and Stories from the Near East*, 3rd ed. (Mahwah, New Jersey: Paulist Press, 2006), 44.

[11] *Enuma Elish* 1.63ff.

[12] T. R. Georgevitch, *The Truth Concerning the Rumanes in Serba* (Paris: Imprimiere Graphique, 1919), 22-23. Many Serbians have claimed that science fiction writer Arthur C. Clarke declared Rtanj the "navel of the world." As Georgevitch's text demonstrates, the mountain was so known by the locals long before Clarke (allegedly) mentioned it.

[13] *De Defectu Oraculorum* 18, translated by Frank Cole Babbitt.

[14] *De Faciae* 27, translated by A. O. Prickard.

27. Was the Golden Fleece an Airplane?

H AVE YOU HEARD about Erich von Däniken's claim that the Golden Ram of Greek mythology, the flying creature who rescued Phrixus and Helle from their murderous stepmother and whose fur later became the Golden Fleece, was an airplane? Von Däniken makes the claim in *Odyssey of the Gods* (1999):

> The greatest ship of the time [the Argo] is supposed to have been built, and sons of gods and kings to have freely offered their services, in the quest of a ridiculous bit of fur? [...] No, definitely not, for the Golden Fleece was a very particular skin with astonishing properties. It could fly! [...] So the Golden Fleece was some kind of flying machine that had once belonged the god Hermes. [...] Sometime or other, many millennia ago, an alien crew landed upon earth. Our forefathers[' ...] simple minds must have regarded the aliens as 'gods'--although we all know there aren't any gods.[1]

Would it surprise you that von Däniken was copying an earlier writer? Of course it doesn't. In this case, he's copying Robert Charroux, who made the same claim almost thirty years earlier:

> An important detail is that the *golden fleece* was that of a flying ram, traditionally identified with a *flying machine* used by Initiators. This particular relic, which no doubt was the wreck of an airship, was to be located in Georgia.[2]

More interesting is the fact that Charroux wasn't the first to suggest this, either. An Afrocentrist named Drusilla Dunjee Houston asserted the Fleece was an airplane in 1926 and claimed the Ethiopians built it!

[We will discuss the] "Wonderful Ethiopians," who produced fadeless colors that have held their hues for thousands of years, who drilled through solid rock and were masters of many other lost arts and who many scientists believe must have understood electricity, who made metal figures that could move and speak and may have invented flying machines, for the "flying horse Pegasus" and the "ram of the golden fleece" may not have been mere fairy tales. [...] We seek for the place and the race that could have given the world the art of welding iron. The trail reveals that the land of the "Golden Fleece" and the garden of the "Golden Apples of Hesperides" were but centers of the ancient race, that as Cushite Ethiopians had extended themselves over the world.[3]

Now this is all well and good, but it rests on the assumption that the Golden Ram actually *flew*. But that is only one variant of the story. In the oldest known versions of the story, the ram is *swimming*, not flying. The swimming ram appears on the oldest Greek vases to depict the tale, from the fifth century BCE, predating our written sources. (A few older versions are known, but they are in too poor a condition to determine flight.) The literary warrant for flight dates back perhaps to the second century BCE and Callimachus, though the oldest extant text is that of Apollodorus, which, in its entirety states that "borne through the sky by the ram they [Phrixus and Helle] crossed land and sea."[4] Eratosthenes, by contrast, talks of a swimming ram.[5] (Apollodorus' version is the basis for modern myth manuals, which is where ancient astronaut writers get their information, not from primary sources.)

Since ancient astronaut writers counsel us to take ancient texts literally, we have a problem: the Ram both flew *and* swam according to the ancient texts, which, of course, cannot err. Worse, the ancients weren't entirely comfortable with this whole "Ram" thing, either. Palaephatus, a euhemerist, said that "Ram" was merely the name of a *person* who built a ship to haul Phrixus and Helle away, and "Fleece" was the name of a golden statue in the ship's cargo![6] Diodorus instead states that the "Flying Ram" was really a ship whose prow was carved in the likeness of a ram,[7] which Tacitus also considered a likely explanation.[8] Diodorus further preserves an alternate version whereby the Golden Fleece is rather grimly supposed to be the gilded skin flayed from the corpse of Phrixus' executed tutor, a man named Mr. Ram (Greek: Krios, Latinized as Crius—an actual ancient first name):

> And much like to this story, is what they say concerning Phryxus: for they say that he sailed in a ship, upon whose fore-deck was carved the head of a ram, and that Helle by leaning too much forward over the sides of the ship to vomit, fell over-board into the sea.
>
> Others say, that about the time that Phryxus with his schoolmaster was taken by Æetes, the Scythian king, the father-in-law of Æetes, came to Colchis, and fell in love with the boy, and upon that account he was bestowed by Æetes upon the Scythian, who loved him as his own child, and adopted him as his heir and successor to the kingdom. But that the school-master whose name was *Crius,* was sacrificed to the gods, and his skin, according to the custom, was fastened to the walls of the temple.[9]

Well, that's quite the quandary for ancient astronaut writers. I'm glad I don't have to try to explain why we should accept one sentence from one writer against all the other writers' texts and all the artists' vases depicting a *swimming* ram.

Notes

[1] Erich von Däniken, *The Odyssey of the Gods: The Alien History of Ancient Greece,* translated by Matthew Barton (Shaftsbury: Element Books, 2000), 5, 27.

[2] Robert Charroux, *The Mysterious Unknown,* translated by Olga Sieveking (London: Neville Spearman, 1972), 210.

[3] Drusilla Dunjee Houston, *Wonderful Ethiopians of the Cushite Empire* (Oklahoma City: Universal Publishing, 1926), 4-6.

[4] *Library* 1.9.1, translated by James George Frazer.

[5] Pseudo-Eratosthenes, *Catasterismi* 19.

[6] *On Incredible Tales*, Myth 15.

[7] *Library of History* 4.47

[8] *Annals* 4.34.4

[9] *Library of History* 4.47, translated by G. Booth.

28. Were Bible Characters Worshiped as Gods?

I T'S NO SECRET that I'm not a fan of ancient astronaut writer Robert Temple, who argued that flying space frogs from Sirius taught the Sumerians astronomy (see Chapter 42). But I do have to thank him for something. One of his articles[1] called my attention to a passage in the fourth-century bishop Epiphanius' *Panarion* that I would not otherwise have seen. In it, Epiphanius describes heretics who worship Biblical figures as gods:

> The profundities and glories of the sacred scriptures, which are beyond human understanding, have confused many. The natives of Petra in Arabia, which is called Rokom and Edom, were in awe of Moses because of his miracles, and at one time they made an image of him, and mistakenly undertook to worship it. They had no true cause for this, but in their ignorance their error drew an imaginary inference from something real. And in Sebasteia, which was once called Samaria, they have declared Jephthah's daughter a goddess, and still hold a festival in her honor every year. Similarly, these people have heard the glorious, wise words of the scripture and changed them to stupidity. With overinflated pride they have abandoned the way of the truth, and will be shown to have fabricated stories of their own invention.[2]

Temple, characteristically, takes the ancient text at face value, but there is more to the story than a bunch of crazy pagans going around worshiping Bible characters.

The second half of Epiphanius' passage (unquoted by Temple) suggests the truth behind Epiphanius' denunciation. In Judges 11, Jephthah makes a vow to god to sacrifice his daughter to God if God will help him defeat his enemies. He grants the girl two months to run through the meadows mourning her virginity before dealing the fatal blow. Commentators have for centuries noted that this story has clear parallels to Agamemnon's sacrifice of Iphigenia to Artemis, as well as the meadow through which the virgin Kore plays before her rape by Hades. In later myth, Iphigenia "was not killed but, by the will of Artemis, became Hecate," the underworld goddess, according to Pausanias.[3] In fact, Thomas Römer argued in 1998 that the redactor of Judges had indeed written the Biblical tale to conform to its Greek antecedents.[4]

The implication is clear: The Samarians did not mistake Jepthah's daughter for a goddess; they had a ceremony similar to the mystery rites of Persephone or adolescent coming of age rites of Iphigenia which were, either for religious or political reasons, given a Jewish gloss through identification with the story in Judges. (This was a fairly common practice; after Christianization, for example, several pagan gods were co-opted as unofficial Christian saints in rural Greece.[5])

At Petra, the inhabitants worshiped Arabian gods and goddesses down to the coming of Christianity in the fourth century, and they also deified their kings and worshipped them as gods. So, when the inhabitants of Petra "worshiped" an "image" of Moses long before Epiphanius wrote, they weren't confused about the true nature of Moses as Robert Temple would have it; instead they were offering to the Jews—then the dominant power in the region—the highest honor their civilization could bestow, worshiping one of their "kings" alongside their own. This was not unprecedented; the Romans welcomed such foreign gods as Cybele and Isis into their pantheon, and the Roman emperor Severus Alexander was said to have placed a statue of Jesus among the deified emperors in his collection of household gods.[6]

Notes

[1] Robert Temple, "Who Was Moses?", *New Dawn*, Winter 2009, 51-56.

[2] Epiphanius, *Panarion* 4.1.9-11, translated by Frank Williams, *The Panarion of Epiphanius of Salamis* (Leiden: Brill, 1987), 78.

[3] *Description of Greece* 1.43.1, translated by H. G. Evelyn-White.

[4] Thomas Römer, "Why Would the Deuteronomists Tell about the Sacrifice of Jephthah's Daughter?" *JSOT* 77 (1998): 27–38; but for an opposing view, see David Janzen, "Why the Deuteronomist Told about the Sacrifice of Jephthah's Daughter," *JSOT* 29/3 (2005): 339-357. Janzen, however, agrees that the sacrifice is meant to parallel non-Jewish, foreign practices.

[5] For example, the sun god Helios is masked behind the official Saint Elias, who took over his shrines, while the goddess Artemis became an unofficial Christian saint, as the still-venerated folk saint Artemis, and again as the (male) St. Atremidos, in both cases protectors of children, as was the old goddess. (The gender swap was in response to intense Madonna-veneration and thus the need to avoid competing with the Mother of God.) Dionysus the wine god became St. Dionysios, patron of wine. (See "The Greek Islanders," *The Quarterly Review,* July 1886, 217.)

[6] *Scriptores Historiae Augustae*, "Severus Alexander," 29

29. Who Were the Nephilim?

NDREW COLLINS, who believes in "sentient" "light beings" composed of plasma that can be contacted by buying his books, wrote a tome about the Nephilim in 1998.[1] He claimed that these Biblical beings were in fact a "shamanic elite" from the last Ice Age who sparked the Neolithic Revolution and reigned as a parasitic ruling class until the end of the Bronze Age. These same Nephilim are also found in Zecharia Sitchin's work as space aliens. This is quite a bit to read into a single line from Genesis, the only[2] Biblical description of these creatures:

> There were giants [*nephilim*] in the earth in those days; and also after that, when the sons of God came in unto the daughters of men, and they bare children to them, the same became mighty men which were of old, men of renown.[3]

Scholars have differed on the origin and meaning of the specific word *nephilim*. Some claim that it means "fallen" and refers to fallen angels; Biblical scholar Michael S. Heiser has made a persuasive case that the King James translators had it right in following the Greek text in assigning the meaning of "giants." He identifies the Hebrew term as a loan word for giants taken from the Aramaic.[4] But in *Chariots of the Gods*, Erich von Däniken, reading the passage in Genesis, immediately recognized aliens:

> "Giants" haunt the pages of almost all ancient books. So they must have existed. What sort of creatures were they, these "giants"? Were they our

forefathers, who built the gigantic buildings and effortlessly manhandled the monoliths, or were they technically skilled space travelers from another star? One thing is certain. The Bible speaks of "giants" and describes them as "sons of God," and these "sons of God" breed with the daughters of men and multiply.[5]

The passage in Genesis (chapter 6, verses 1-4) and later tradition actually differentiate between the "sons of God" and the giants, who were their offspring. In the earliest interpretations, the "sons of God" were identified with angels, though later commentators came to favor a more earthly interpretation in which the "sons" became "sons of Seth" (i.e. the righteous), who mated with the daughters of Cain (i.e. the sinful). Shimon bar Yochai is said to have cursed any attempt at an interpretation of Genesis 6:4 other than this in the first century CE.[6] The later Book of Enoch and Book of Jubilees favor the fallen angel version, explicitly identifying the "sons of God" with angels who descended from heaven and taught men such forbidden arts as metallurgy and cosmetology (yes, I mean makeup[7]). According to these texts, the angels rebelled against God because they were overcome with sexual desire for human females.

I'm going to admit here that what follows is mostly speculation, though I hope based on fact. I find Genesis 6:4 interesting, but I think it belongs in the broader context of early Near Eastern myth. Literally, the phrase translated as "sons of God"[8] says in Hebrew "sons of the gods" (banê hā'ĕlōhîm) in the plural. This has been rationalized as something akin to the Royal We, but many have suggested it is a remnant of a pre-Judaic polytheistic pantheon. We know than in other Near Eastern cultures, the gods had sons and these sons were considered superhuman beings. The most famous is Gilgamesh, two-thirds god and one-third man, the hero who built the high walls of Uruk. Another is Humbaba, the terrifying, radiant giant who was the child of Hanbi and the ward of the sun god. The Greeks, too, imagined that the race of heroes that preceded their own— mostly the sons of the gods—were of gigantic stature, which they "confirmed" by claiming the bones of prehistoric elephants to be the remains of the giant heroes.

But here is where it gets interesting. By 100 BCE, the writers of the Jewish apocryphal text called the Book of Giants—a sort of sequel to the Book of Enoch—included both Gilgamesh[9] and Humbaba[10] as two of the antediluvian giants. This in and of itself is not conclusive, since it is centuries after Genesis, but it suggests that there was a tradition that the giants of Genesis reflected a Jewish interpretation of the widespread Near Eastern claim that the giants of old were the sons of the pagan gods.[11] Since we know that other widespread Near Eastern myths had Biblical versions, including the Near Eastern Flood myth and the battle between the storm god and the chaos monster, it seems to me that the origins of Genesis 6:4 are to be found in Near Eastern hero stories that would have been the common folk culture of the region.

I'm not the only one to see such a connection; unfortunately, though, most of the alternative writers who see the same connection claim that Gilgamesh is one of the Nephilim and therefore is an alien hybrid! It comes down to the key assumption one makes in thinking about ancient myth: are these stories to be taken as literature, or as fact? Until some skeletons of these giants show up—and no, the elephant bones don't count—it is terribly dangerous to take literally stories that have been told and retold in countless forms across time and space.

Bonus: Alternative theorists like to take ancient texts literally, but for those paying attention, this poses a problem. In the *Epic of Gilgamesh*, Gilgamesh lives *after* the Flood, but in the Book of Giants, he lives *before* the Flood. Clearly, both ancient texts can't be right, and if one is wrong, this calls into question the practice of using ancient texts uncritically as literal reports of mythic events.

Notes

[1] Andrew Collins, *From the Ashes of Angels: The Forbidden Legacy of a Fallen Race* (Bear & Company, 1998).

[2] They appear again in Numbers 13:3, but in a different context.

[3] Genesis 6:4, KJV.

[4] Michael S. Heiser, "The Meaning of the Word *Nephilim*: Fact vs. Fantasy," *MichaelSHeiser.com* [online], no date.

[5] Erich von Däniken, *Chariots of the Gods? Unsolved Mysteries of the Past,* trans. Michael Heron (New York: Bantam, 1973), 35.

[6] Jacob Neusner, *Judaism and Christianity in the First Century,* vol. 3 of Origins of Judaism (Garland Publishing, 1990), 36.

[7] 1 Enoch 8:1-2: "And Azâzêl taught men to make swords, and knives, and shields, and breastplates, and made known to them the metals of the earth and the art of working them, and bracelets, and ornaments, and the use of antimony, and the beautifying of the eyelids, and all kinds of costly stones, and all colouring tinctures. And there arose much godlessness, and they committed fornication, and they were led astray, and became corrupt in all their ways." (translated by R. H. Charles.)

[8] Genesis 6:2.

[9] *Dead Sea Scrolls* 4Q530 2 ii 1–3 and 4Q531 22

[10] Dead Sea Scrolls QG11, under the name Hobabiš

[11] See Matthew Goff, "Gilgamesh the Giant: The Qumran Book of Giants' Appropriation of Gilgamesh Motifs," *Dead Sea Discoveries* 16, no. 2 (2009): 221-253.

30. Did Aliens Design the Pyramids?

IN RESPONSE TO a tweet questioning whether human beings were responsible for "the pyramids," by which I presume the author was referring to the pyramids of Egypt, ancient astronaut proponent Giorgio Tsoukalos issued a tweet in late 2012 asserting that while humans were responsible for their construction, the "ancients" said that they received help from aliens in so doing. Tsoukalos made a similar claim about the "ancients" attributing the design of the pyramid to the "Guardians of the Sky" back in 2011. In that tweet, Tsoukalos cited as his source an Arabic text from the fourteenth century, the *Al-Khitat* of Al-Maqrizi—at 4,000 years remove from the pyramids' construction!

Because I'm not willing to take claims at face value, I tracked down a French edition of Al-Maqrizi in 2012 and translated all the references to the pyramids in the book, since Tsoukalos provided no specific reference. Al-Maqrizi says that the Arabs had many traditions about the pyramids (which he quotes at great length), but no one knows who actually built them. Since Al-Maqrizi knows nothing of the builders, whom Tsoukalos concedes were the pharaohs of old, how can we trust that he somehow preserved a perfect tradition of the *aliens* who assisted them? Al-Maqrizi offered more than a dozen different explanations, drawn from various authors. But none of them featured "Guardians of the Sky." I finally found, though, the source for Tsoukalos' claim of supernatural interference in the building of the pyramids.

Among Al-Maqrizi's discussions is the following, which Maqrizi borrows from the early medieval poet Said al-Lagawi:

Said al-Lagawi, in his book *The Biography of Peoples,* reported that all the sciences known before the Flood were first taught by Hermes, who lived in Upper Egypt. This Hermes was the first to ponder celestial bodies and the movement of the stars. He was the first to build temples to worship God. He occupied himself with science and medicine, and he wrote well-measured poems for his contemporaries about things terrestrial and celestial. It is also said that he was the first to predict the Flood and anticipate that a celestial cataclysm would befall the earth in the form of fire or water, so, fearing the destruction of science and the disappearance of industrial processes, he built the pyramids and temples of Upper Egypt. Within these he included representations of the trades and tools, including engraved explanations of science, in order to pass them on to those who came after him, lest he see them disappear from the world. This Hermes is the same as Edris.[1]

Lest there be any confusion, note: Hermes is not the Greek god but is here identified with Edris (Idris), the Islamic prophet, who is otherwise identified with Enoch, and is in any case human, not extraterrestrial. There are no aliens here, only claims for really good astrology. But, as it so happens, I actually found the passage Tsoukalos has been talking about, no thanks to him! Here it is in all its ancient astronaut glory:

Master Ibrahim bin Wasif Shah said that King 'Adim (or 'Ad), son of Naqtarim, was a violent and proud prince, tall in stature. It was he who ordered the rocks cut to make the pyramids, as had been done by the ancients. In his time there lived two angels cast out of heaven, and who lived in the Aftarah well; these two angels taught magic to the Egyptians, and it is said that 'Adim, the son of El-Budchir, learned most of their sciences, after which the two angels went to Babel. Egyptians, especially the Copts, assure us that these were actually two demons named Mahla and Bahala, not two angels, and that the two are at Babel in a well, where witches meet, and they will remain there until the Day of Judgment.[2]

Ibrahim bin Wasif Shah lived c. 1000 CE, and the quotation comes from his book, *A Summary of Marvels,* though there is a question whether the book, which Maqrizi quotes and which still exists, was actually written by him. But do note: In the passage, 'Ad built the pyramids, but the text doesn't say the "angels" had anything to do with it. They taught *science,* sure, but it says nothing about helping out with the pyramids.

I think it should be fairly obvious that this is merely the story of the Watchers from the Book of Enoch filtered down through Arabian folklore, especially the story of Harut and Marut, the angels of the Qur'an who encountered the sorcerers of Babylon.[3] In Islamic folklore, these angels ask to become human, commit sins as humans, and are punished by Allah. Many commentators on the Qur'an believe the story is an Islamic interpretation of an earlier Christian tale about the Fallen Angels.[4] The same tale is also found in the Jewish Midrash, where the two sinning angels are hung up by their feet in Babylon.[5] Note that the *Al-Khitat* passage even uses the Hebrew form of the name 'Ad, "'Adim." The story of the "fallen" angels, the teaching of science, and the confinement underground, are all identical to the account in Enoch. Since we already know that the Arabs associated the pyramids with Idris, who was thought to be Enoch, this is a very logical connection. So, this means that some 3,500 years after the pyramids were built, some people with pre-existing Enochian mythology attributed the pyramids to that myth cycle. I fail to see the aliens at work here. That said, in his *Menippus,* Lucian describes an underground watery cave in the marshes near Babylon where the Babylonian mages would go to consult with the chthonic gods,[6] so there actually is something to this witches' well, and perhaps this is the origin point for conflating the fallen angels with the underground sorcerers to produce two demons in a well.

However, the 'Ad mentioned here is the king of the Adites, whose son Shaddad built Iram of the Pillars, and whose people were punished by God for their sins, as given in the Qu'ran[7] and *Arabian Nights.*[8] These fellows were also said to be giants, sinful, etc. They're the Watchers from Enoch, which is quite plain. Fans of H. P. Lovecraft will remember "Irem, the City of Pillars" from Lovecraft's "The Nameless City" (1921), where the ancient

Arabian city is mentioned in connection with a fabulous race of lizard people, and again in the "Call of Cthulhu" (1926), where it is a cult center for the Old Ones. The city is described in the Qur'an:

> Hast thou not considered how thy Lord dealt with Ad, *the people of* Irem, adorned with lofty buildings, the like whereof hath not been erected in the land; and with Thamud, who hewed the rocks in the valley *into houses*; and with Pharaoh, the contriver of the stakes: who had behaved insolently in the earth, and multiplied corruption therein? Wherefore thy Lord poured on them various kinds of chastisement.... [9]

Later legends, embellishing on this story, suggest Allah buried the city in the sands of the Arabian desert after "a loud cry assaulted us from a tract of the distant horizon," as reported in a poetic fragment recorded in the *Arabian Nights*.[10] (How this was remembered when the city and all in and around it perished, I can't fathom to guess: the poem in question is allegedly spoken by the dead king of the city and recorded by his son!) I was amused, therefore, to read in Bob Curran's *Lost Lands, Forgotten Realms* (2011), a supposedly nonfictional examination of lost civilizations, the following passage about Iram and its alleged connection to the Arabian demons, the djinn:

> Some traditions say that Irem was built by the djinn themselves before the time of Adam, and was later inhabited by men. This tradition stems from the name "Irem of the Pillars"—the ancient Arabic word for "pillar" corresponding to another meaning, namely "Old One." The name, therefore, was a city of the Old Ones (that is, the djinn).[11]

Philip Gardiner's *Secret Societies* (2007) also repeats the same alleged facts and accepts Lovecraft's *Necronomicon* as real, and embodying real traditions of Iram! By contrast, Jacques Bergier, who did more than anyone to try to make Lovecraft "real" (see Chapters 2 and 3) failed in his *Extraterrestrial Visitations* (1970) even to understand that Iram was a genuine Arabic myth and instead claimed that Lovecraft originated the story, though drawing, he thought, on secret pre-Islamic traditions.[12]

Would it surprise you to learn that the "tradition" of a pre-human Iram is not a mythological one but rather a "tradition" invented by Lovecraft and the writers of the Cthulhu Mythos, and the "magickal" practitioners of Lovecraftian magick? Asenath Mason, in the *Necronomicon Gnosis* (2007) claims that "pillar" is "code" for "Old One," not an actual translation,[13] but Curran has gone beyond the Mythos (and Mythos-magickal) writers to invent a fake Arabic translation!

The actual Arabic as given in the Qur'an is somewhat ambiguous. It may mean "Iram of the Pillars," or it could also mean "the people of Iram, who were very tall, like pillars." The "legend" that it predates Adam appears to be a conflation of the Lovecraft's imaginary Cthulhu cult (probably via the common misreading of the Nameless City as being Iram itself) and a misreading of a line in the *Arabian Nights*, in which a visitor to Iram found within it no "created being of the sons of Adam."[14] The *Nights*, however, make clear that a human king named Shaddad built it. I can find no support for the claim that angels or djinn built the city outside of Lovecraftian or magickal texts.

Notes

[1] *Al-Khitat* 1.9, my translation.

[2] Ibid., 1.10, my translation.

[3] Qur'an 2:102-103.

[4] For example, Jude 1:6: "And the angels who did not keep their positions of authority but abandoned their proper dwelling—these he has kept in darkness, bound with everlasting chains for judgment on the great Day."

[5] Ali, Abdullah Yousf, *The Meaning of the Holy Quran*, eleventh edition (Amana Publications, 2006), note at 2:104, p. 45.

[6] Lucian *Menippus* 2, 6–10, 21–2

[7] Qur'an 89:6-13.

[8] *The Thousand and One Nights*, vol. II, translated by Edward William Lane (London: Charles Knight, 1840), 342-346.

[9] Qur'an 89:6-13, translated by George Sale.

[10] *The Thousand and One Nights,* vol. II, 346.

[11] Bob Curran, *Lost Lands, Forgotten Realms: Sunken Continents, Vanished Cities, and the Kingdoms that History Misplaced* (Pompton Plains, New Jersey: New Page, 2011), eBook edition.

[12] Jacques Bergier, *Extraterrestrial Visitations from Prehistoric Times to the Present* (Chicago: Henry Regnery Company, 1973), 86.

[13] Asenath Mason, *Necronomicon Gnosis: A Practical Introduction* (Edition Roter Drache, 2007), 64.

[14] *The Thousand and One Nights*, vol. II, 343.

31. The Pyramids and the Flood

As I discussed in Chapter 30, the *Al-Khitat* of Al-Maqrizi, written around 1400 CE, is obviously not "Ancient Egyptian" as ancient astronaut celebrity Giorgio Tsoukalos has implied, but the fact that the book hasn't been translated into English (to my knowledge) lets Tsoukalos get away with making any claim he likes for it. However, after I translated all of the pyramid references in the *Al-Khitat*, a much more fascinating story about Near Eastern myths of the pyramids and Great Flood emerged, a tale the offers a fascinating glimpse into the continuity of tradition across millenniums.

Al-Maqrizi says explicitly that the Arabs know nothing solid about ancient Egypt, only mutually contradictory myths and legends with no foundation. "There is no agreement on the time of their construction, the names of those who have raised them, or the cause of their erection. Many conflicting and unfounded legends have been told of them."[1] This is not a good sign, but it does eliminate Al-Maqrizi as a suspect in the creation of Tsoukalos' alien-intervention myth. So, if not Al-Maqrizi, then who? Maqrizi quotes at great length the work of Ibrahim ibn Wasif Shah (d. 1203), who tells of the wonders of the pyramids. This material is scattered across the *Al-Khitat*, primarily in chapters 10 and 40, and it makes following the story somewhat complex.

Ibn Wasif Shah begins by discussing the legendary King 'Adim (or 'Ad), the leader of the Adites, the Arabian desert people who in the Qur'an are punished by God for their sins.[2] According to Ibn Wasif Shah, King 'Adim ordered the rocks cut for the Two Pyramids—these would be the pyramids of Dashur—but he did not actually construct them himself. The chronology is unclear, but around this same time two demons or Fallen Angels appeared to him and taught him science before being cast into a well in Babylon to await judgment. These "angels cast out of heaven" must be the "Guardians of the Sky" Tsoukalos is referring to, but there is no explicit discussion of the angels having anything to do with cutting the rocks for the pyramids. This much Maqrizi relates in chapter 10.

In chapter 24, Maqrizi takes up the story again with Saurid (or Sourid), the figure most closely associated in Islamic lore with the building of the pyramids at Giza. Saurid has a dream in which he sees a meteor shower and some bad astrological omens predicting the Great Flood of Near Eastern myth (Qu'ranic version, of course) and therefore builds the two largest pyramids, filling them with treasures and covering them in silk. (The story is also given in almost identical words by Murtadi and Ibn 'Abd al-Hakam.) We are then told that the Copts hold that Shaddad ibn 'Ad, the son of King 'Ad, built the pyramids at Dashur with the stones cut and left behind by King 'Ad. Apparently—and I am not clear on this— Saurid is descended in some way from Shaddad.

Ibn Wasif Shah explicitly connects these events to the wickedness preceding the Flood, recounted most explicitly in Genesis and the Enochian literature but also known in Islamic lore. He has Saurid's chief priest recount a dream in which angels descend from heaven to punish mankind for wickedness and sin and declare that any who wish to be saved must go to the Ark to be rescued from the imminent Flood. Saurid then builds the pyramids to preserve science and knowledge, presumably that given by the Fallen Angels, when the Flood comes. This is a widespread Arab myth.

Now since we know that the Arabs also had a tradition that pyramids were built by Idris, whom they identified with Hermes, and Hermes with Enoch, the Hebrew prophet, it is no stretch to see a parallel here with Enoch's "heavenly tablets"[3] on which are engraved the secrets of the forthcoming flood, as well as the "books of my forefathers" from Jubilees[4] that discuss secret knowledge. This makes much more sense as the mythic wellspring for Ibn Wasif Shah's claim that the Giza pyramids were engraved with technological treatises and their interior chambers filled with scientific books than any facts. As we all know, (a) the Giza pyramids do not feature hieroglyphic inscriptions and (b) those pyramids that do have them are not scientific treatises on antediluvian scientific knowledge—let alone Ibn Wasif Shah's astronomical tables and "the list of events of past eras under their [the stars'] influence, and when they must be examined to know the future of everything about Egypt until the end of time."[5] Since Ibn Wasif Shah was wrong about the interior design of the pyramids, the purpose and content of the hieroglyphics, and pretty much everything else, we have no reason to believe him about Fallen Angels either.

Erich von Däniken, in *History Is Wrong*, claims that Idris and Saurid were identical based on Maqrizi's chapter 33, but in actuality Maqrizi in that passage merely asserts that Idris, Enoch, Saurid, and Shaddad were *all* proposed by various peoples as the builders of the pyramids—they were not identical with each other. Now here's the kicker: In *Odyssey of the Gods* (1999) von Däniken mistakenly calls Maqrizi's work, which he paraphrases, cites, and partially quotes, "ancient Egyptian texts"[6]—this must be where Tsoukalos got his mistaken idea! It's even the same wording!

So, in sum, the tale told my Ibn Wasif Shah in al-Maqrizi's *Al-Khitat* is very much in keeping with the Near Easter flood myth dating back to the Sumerians. In all the versions, human become sinful, in part due to corruption from sinful gods, demigods, or angels, leading to the high god(s) sending a flood to cleanse the earth. It is interesting that these fallen creatures all do the same thing. Compare Oannes of Babylonian myth, the Watchers of Enoch, and the angels who visited 'Ad:

OANNES

This Being was accustomed to pass the day among men; but took no food at that season; and he gave them an insight into letters and sciences, and arts of every kind. He taught them to construct cities, to found temples, to compile laws, and explained to them the principles of geometrical knowledge. He made them distinguish the seeds of the earth, and shewed them how to collect the fruits; in short, he instructed them in every thing which could tend to soften manners and humanize their lives.[7]

THE WATCHERS

And Azâzêl taught men to make swords, and knives, and shields, and breastplates, and made known to them the metals of the earth and the art of working them, and bracelets, and ornaments, and the use of antimony, and the beautifying of the eyelids, and all kinds of costly stones, and all colouring tinctures. ... Semjâzâ taught enchantments, and root-cuttings, Armârôs the resolving of enchantments, Barâqîjâl, (taught) astrology, Kôkabêl the constellations, Ezêqêêl the knowledge of the clouds, Araqiêl the signs of the earth, Shamsiêl the signs of the sun, and Sariêl the course of the moon.[8]

THE ANGELS OF 'AD

In his time there lived two angels cast out of heaven, and who lived in the Aftarah well; these two angels taught magic to the Egyptians, and it is said that 'Adim, the son of El-Budchir, learned most of their sciences, after which the two angels went to Babel.[9]

In each case, too, the beings are thrust back to the depths. Oannes (as Uan, or Adapa) is punished for revealing his knowledge by being confined to the underground Apsu sea. The Watchers are thrust into a pit in the deserts of Mesopotamia. The Angels of 'Ad are buried in a well at Babylon. In 1 Enoch and in Ibn Wasif Shah the transmission of knowledge from heaven to humanity is the primal sin that enrages God and unleashes the Flood. (In the earliest Flood myth, in the *Epic of Gilgamesh*, the source of the corruption is not named.)

The substantive identity of these stories should serve to prove that the Arabs merely translated to Egypt myths once told of Mesopotamia, as indicated by the fact that the stories supposedly originate with 'Ad of Iram, a legendary king in Arabia, not Egypt. This agrees very well with what we know of pre-Islamic Arabian myths, where the Tower of Babel was once believed to have been built by the Fallen Angels (probably derived from the Babylonian belief in the *Enuma Elish* that the Babylonian temple of Esagil was built by angry Annunaki[10]) and to have a relationship of some sort with the eventual revelation of astrology and science by Abraham.[11] Too, it agrees with the Judeo-Christian legend recorded by Flavius Josephus of Seth's children (the antediluvian men of old, elsewhere called the giants[12]) inscribing all knowledge on pillars before the Flood:

> They also were the inventors of that peculiar sort of wisdom which is concerned with the heavenly bodies, and their order. And that their inventions might not be lost before they were sufficiently known, upon Adam's prediction that the world was to be destroyed at one time by the force of fire, and at another time by the violence and quantity of water, they made two pillars, the one of brick, the other of stone: they inscribed their discoveries on them both, that in case the pillar of brick should be destroyed by the flood, the pillar of stone might remain, and exhibit those discoveries to mankind; and also inform them that there was another pillar of brick erected by them. Now this remains in the land of Siriad to this day.[13]

Note that the "fire" and "water" exactly parallel Saurid's dream, and Siriad (= the land of Sirius) has traditionally been identified with Egypt, where Sirius was used to mark the calendar. I think we're starting to get the picture. It's the same story, but in a much older and less folktale form. I find all these connections fascinating—especially the way the story remained remarkably consistent across time and across cultures—and could go on for many more pages, but let's stop there for now. I think this is sufficient to cast doubt on any claim that the *Al-Khitat* records an alien architect at Giza. In the next chapter, we'll look at what else this ancient legend can tell us about alternative history's pyramid claims.

Notes

[1] *Al-Khitat,* chapter 40. All *Al-Khitat* translations in this chapter are my own.

[2] 89:6-13

[3] 1 Enoch 106:19

[4] 21:10

[5] *Al-Khitat,* chapter 40.

[6] Erich von Däniken, *The Odyssey of the Gods: The Alien History of Ancient Greece,* trans. Matthew Barton (Shaftsbury: Element Books, 2000), 74.

[7] Berossus quoted in Alexander Polyhistor, preserved in Syncellus, *Chronicon* 28 and Eusebius, *Chronicon* 7, translated by I. P. Cory and Richard Hodges, *Cory's Ancient Fragments* (London: Reeves & Turner, 1876), 57.

[8] 1 Enoch 8:1-2, translated by R. H. Charles.

[9] *Al-Khitat,* chapter 10.

[10] 6.53-63

[11] Eupolemus, qtd. in Eusebius, *Praep. Evan.* 9

[12] Rabbinical opinion differed on whether the giants were angels (the sons of God in a literal sense) or the offspring of Seth's godly line (figuratively the godly sons). See Chapter 29. Josephus here follows the latter view.

[13] Flavius Josephus, *Antiquities of the Jews* 1.2.3, translated by William Whiston.

32. The Strange Case of Proclus and the Pyramid

ONE CLAIM ALTERNATIVE historians have made from the eighteenth century down to today is that the Greek Neoplatonist philosopher Proclus supposedly wrote in his commentary on Plato's *Timaeus* that the Great Pyramid of Egypt had a flat top from which the priests of Egypt observed the stars and recorded the rising and setting of Sirius. This claim apparently first appeared in John Greaves's *Pyramidographia* (1646), in which he writes: "Upon this flat [top], if we assent to the opinion of *Proclus*, it may be supposed that the *Aegyptian* Priests made their observations in Astronomy; and that from hence, or near this place they discovered, by the rising of Sirius the [Sothic cycle]."[1] His source, he said, was Book One of Proclus' commentary on *Timaeus*, but nothing more specific.

The claim was then picked up by many (if not most) writers on the pyramids down to Richard Anthony Proctor, who used this single line of Proclus to argue for the Great Pyramid's astronomical function in several nineteenth century books. He did not, however, provide a reference for Proclus. This has not stopped modern writers from John Anthony West to Alan Alford to Robert Bauval to Graham Hancock from quoting or citing Proctor's assertion, derived apparently from Greaves, that Proclus had declared the pyramid an observatory. All of these writers use this assertion in their works, and none quotes Proclus directly—only Proctor. I have never read in any later writer the specific words of Proclus on this subject.

I have tried in vain to track down the exact words of Proclus, and I have not been able to do so. I have reviewed both a nineteenth century and a 2007 translation of Proclus' commentary on *Timaeus*, and there does not appear to be any reference to the Egyptian pyramids in it. Nor did I find a reference to Sirius, or even much about astronomy. Instead, the earliest version of the claim appears in Robert Greaves's *Pyramidographia*, and all later versions are dependent upon this source, directly or indirectly. At first I thought that Greaves had simply made up a fake quotation, but a careful review of Greaves's passage helps us to see the most logical explanation for what happened. Here's Greaves's text:

> [The Great Pyramid] ends not in a point, as mathematical pyramids do, but in a little flat or square. [...] By my measure it is thirteen feet, and 280 of 1000 parts of the *English* foot. Upon this flat [top], if we assent to the opinion of *Proclus*, it may be supposed that the *Aegyptian* Priests made their observations in Astronomy; and that from hence, or near this place they discovered, by the rising of Sirius the [Sothic cycle]. [...] That the priests might near these Pyramids make their observations, I no way question [...] But that these pyramids were designed for observatories [...] is no way to be credited upon the single authority of *Proclus*.[2]

His source for this is given as Proclus' commentary on Plato's *Timaeus* at Book One, chapter 1. It seems to me that Greaves must have been heavily interpreting one of Proclus' sentences, which otherwise had nothing to do with the Great Pyramid, since no mention of the pyramid appears in Book One. This is what Proclus actually said in the cited passage:

> For extending to the Egyptian priests the most ancient transactions of the Greeks, he [Solon] leads them to the narration of their antiquities; *of which the Egyptians participate in a remarkable degree, as they survey without impediment the celestial bodies, through the purity of the air, and preserve ancient memorials, in consequence of not being destroyed either by water or fire.*[3]
> (emphasis in original)

I am not expert enough in ancient Greek to read Proclus in the original, so I cannot confirm the original meaning of the word scholars have translated variously as "antiquities" (as in things) or "antiquity" (as in time). If the Greek is the former, Greaves may well have read this as a direct reference to the pyramids, which the priests would therefore seem, by the grammar of the sentence, to use in making the observations of the second half. Then, a bit later, Proclus writes that "the history is from pillars, in which things paradoxical and worthy of admiration, whether in actions or inventions, are inscribed."[4]

Greaves wrote that he believed that obelisks, pillars tapering to a pyramid-shaped peak, were "but lesser models of the Pyramids,"[5] and he recalled the tradition (see Chapter 31) that "all sciences are inscribed" in the Pyramids,[6] though his own firsthand observations contradicted the point. Since Greaves discounted the claim he ascribes to Proclus that the Egyptians used the pyramids as observatories, it may well be that he was reading into Proclus' two passages a discussion of the Pyramids in light of the other traditions about the pyramids with which Greaves disagreed. The later information in Greaves about the Sothic cycle is Greaves's own inference and is not derived from Proclus.

From Greaves's account, Richard Anthony Proctor in his posthumously-published *Old and New Astronomy* (1892) grossly exaggerated Greaves's discussion of the *currently existing* small square platform at the top of the pyramid into something completely different:

> ...we are told by Proclus that the priests observed from the summit of the pyramid, when that structure terminated at the top in a platform. [...] Unquestionably, Proclus must have been referring to a tradition relating to a time when the grand gallery of the Great Pyramid opened out on a large square platform, where priests could be stationed in order to observe and record observations...[7]

This was a claim Proctor had been flogging since 1883, in an earlier book on the pyramidology called, oddly enough, *The Great Pyramid*, though never in so great of detail.[8] In neither book, however, did Proctor cite a source for Proclus, because there is no warrant for the claim outside of Greaves, an author Proctor explicitly cites elsewhere as a source.[9]

These claims then reappear wholesale in later alternative history books. Robert Schoch, for example, repeats it, with credit to Proctor, in *Pyramid Quest* (2005), without any effort to cite Proclus directly. From there he attempts to divine Egyptian astronomical techniques based on this speculative notion. John Anthony West does the same in *The Traveler's Key to Ancient Egypt* (1985; rev. ed. 1995), though West completely misunderstands the distinction between the (assumed) Proclus and Proctor's own ideas: Proclus, he said, "mentioned that the Great Pyramid had served as an observatory *before* it had been completed."[10] Needless to say, Proctor's claim entered the work of popular pyramid theorizers Robert Bauval and Adrian Gilbert, neither of whom sought Proclus' original text but who, in *The Orion Mystery* (1994) pretended as though the line attributed to Proclus by Proctor had an existence outside of Proctor, and even claimed—with no citation of any kind—that Proclus had declared the pyramid "part of a machine, whose function is beyond us"![11]

Other authors also repeated Proctor's speculation with varying allegiance to fact. In *Starseekers* (1980) Colin Wilson recited the claims with attribution to Proctor, but by the time of *From Atlantis to the Sphinx* (2004), he wrote that "it had been stated as fact" by Proclus that "the Pyramid was used as an observatory while it was under construction."[12] He then says Proctor merely repeated Proclus' original claim, using nearly the same words as Bauval and Gilbert. An Italian book, *The Pyramids of Giza and the Sphinx* (2006), dispenses with Proctor altogether and attributes the claim that the Grand Gallery (not the platform) was an observatory solely to Proclus, who she says inspired "a number of eighteenth century astronomers"[13]—wrong on all counts since Greaves wrote in the seventeenth century and Proctor the nineteenth. Proclus is again claimed as the originating source in Alan Alford's *Pyramid of Secrets* (2003), though all of his citations are indirect—to Proctor, Bauval, and other alternative writers.

But where did the claim originate? My reading of Al-Maqrizi's medieval compilation of Arab history and lore, the *Al-Khitat*, provided the accidental evidence that finally let me come up with a reasonable explanation for what happened—and which demonstrates a rather striking continuity of tradition across a thousand years or more.

Al-Maqrizi, writing c. 1400 CE, claimed to have found a manuscript in which an earlier writer wrote down some verses recited by the Qadi Fakhr Al-Din Abd al-Wahab Al-Masrime centuries earlier. These verses lay out all the then-common pyramid theories, many identical to those proposed by Piazzi Smyth hundreds of years later, including the claim that the pyramid represents the planets, or the cosmos, or something similar. In the poem, the poet asks who built the pyramid and why:

> Did he build them for his treasures and his corpse,
>> As a tomb to protect them from the Flood?
> Or are these observatories for the planets,
>> Selected by learned observers because of the excellence of the place?
> Or are they the description of planetary calculations,
>> Such as those once done by the Persians and the Greeks?[14]

And there we have it: proof that there was an ancient, or at least medieval, tradition that the pyramids had been celestial observatories. And here is how it connects back to Proclus: Proclus wrote in his commentary on Plato's *Timaeus* that the Egyptians "survey without impediment the celestial bodies, through the purity of the air, and preserve ancient memorials, in consequence of not being destroyed either by water or fire." He also claims—and this is crucial—that the Egyptian history could be found on "pillars, in which things paradoxical and worthy of admiration, whether in actions or inventions, are inscribed." Now, combine this with the Jewish myth recorded by Flavius Josephus in *Antiquities of the Jews*, speaking of the children of Seth, the descendants of Adam before the Flood:

> They also were the inventors of that peculiar sort of wisdom which is concerned with the heavenly bodies, and their order. And that their inventions might not be lost before they were sufficiently known, upon Adam's prediction that the world was to be destroyed at one time by the

force of fire, and at another time by the violence and quantity of water, they made two pillars, the one of brick, the other of stone: they inscribed their discoveries on them both, that in case the pillar of brick should be destroyed by the flood, the pillar of stone might remain, and exhibit those discoveries to mankind; and also inform them that there was another pillar of brick erected by them. Now this remains in the land of Siriad to this day.[15]

Some believe that Josephus mistakenly conflated Seth, the son of Adam, with Sesostris, the Egyptian pharaoh, while others think it was Set, the Egyptian god-hero. Siriad refers to Egypt in its guise as the "Land of Sirius," the star venerated most in Egypt.

Can you see the connection? The tradition of destruction by both fire and water persists from at least Josephus to Proclus, from the first century CE to the fifth, with the idea that the great pillar of stone was inscribed with scientific knowledge and had some relationship to Sirius and the stars. The original Greek manuscript of Josephus is long gone (though an eleventh-century edition remains), so some have speculated that the Latin word *columna* (pillar) in the oldest extant Latin text might have been translating the Greek word for pyramid rather than specifically a standing column. This is, of course, speculation.

At any rate, Josephus' work was translated into Arabic and was well known to the Arabs before and after the coming of Islam. From these sources, we can then very clearly see the origin of the famous Arab story of how the pyramids were built. Note in this version of the Arab story that both the Flood and the rather unusual (and non-canonical) scourge of fire are found, just as in Josephus:

We have seen what the stars predicted. We saw a disaster descend from the sky and come up out of the earth. When we were sure what this event would be, we sought more information and we found that the waters would cover the earth, destroying its animals and plants. Being quite sure of the event, we told our king, Saurid ben Sahluq: He built a tomb for himself and others for his family. [...] He raised a house (?) in the Delta and in the Saïd and engraved on their walls the details of science, astronomy and prognostication, the stars, alchemy, art, medicine, and all the useful or harmful things. These were briefly explained and easy to understand for those who know our writing and language. [...] Then we looked at what would happen after this disaster. The world would have to bear calamities, and we discovered that the planets presage a new scourge descending from the sky that would be the opposite of the first. This scourge of fire would burn the four corners of the earth. [...][16]

Several versions of this story exist, differing in the details. Several versions suggest that the scientific inscriptions were written in or on the pyramids themselves. The version given above is the only one attributed to a non-Arab or non-Coptic source. Al-Maqrizi quotes an earlier writer, el-Galil Abu Abd Allah Mohammed Ben Salamat el Qodai, as claiming this text derives from an Egyptian manuscript translated into either Greek or Latin in the time of the Roman emperor Philip the Arab (244-249 CE)—a suspiciously convenient Arab emperor.

We know from Pliny that "most" Romans believed the pyramids to simply be the make-work project of megalomaniacs,[17] so the observatory-Flood tradition must derive from a non-Greco-Roman source, probably originating in a Jewish interpretation of Isaiah 19:19 in which there will be a monument (a "pillar," or a *matstseba*) on the border of Egypt as a reference to the Great Pyramid of Egypt. What better way to turn the tables on one's oppressors than to claim their greatest work as the Lord's own? And if it was a work of God, it must therefore predate the Flood, from a time before Egypt had fallen into idolatry.

Neither Herodotus nor Diodorus Siculus mentions scientific knowledge being written on the pyramid's surface.[18] Both claim only that a few inscriptions mark the cost of the foodstuffs used to feed the builders (1,600 talents for radishes, onions, and garlic), and no inscriptions have been found on the remaining casing stones of the Giza pyramids. Thus the "scientific" inscriptions (allegedly carved and inlaid in blue stone no less!) must derive from the Jewish myth, probably when the oldest form of the legend, as given above, became confused and the inscriptions observed on the temples of Egypt (which were often painted blue) were mistakenly attributed to the pyramids as well. Arranging the various legends from simplest (and most likely earliest) to most elaborate finds that the writing was attributed to the temples in the simplest legends, but in the most complex and elaborate was added to the pyramids too, like in this one where the priests wrote "on every surface of the pyramids, the ceilings, foundations, and walls, all the sciences familiar to the Egyptians."[19] (It should also be noted that sixth dynasty pyramids had interior hieroglyphic inscriptions, but not the Giza pyramids.) It is probably telling that the stories told of the blue inscriptions of scientific knowledge on the Great Pyramid's casing seem to all date from after the removal of the casing stones to build the mosques and walls of Cairo.

Even the name of the king most frequently associated with the pyramids, Surid (or Sourid or Saurid), may be a corruption of Sesostris, the (apocryphally) legendary pharaoh, or Suphis, a Greek transliteration of Khufu as given in Manetho,[20] otherwise called Cheops by Herodotus. (Possibly Suphis → Suphid → Surid.) This would be particularly interesting since a legend in Manetho recorded by the Christian writer Julius Africanus and preserved in Syncellus and Eusebius in slightly different versions told that Suphis raised the Great Pyramid, held the pagan gods in contempt, and wrote a sacred book, thus making him a good candidate for monotheistic veneration. In Africanus' version:

> Suphis reigned 63 years. He built the largest pyramid which Herodotus says was constructed by Cheops. He was arrogant towards the gods, and wrote the sacred book; which is regarded by the Egyptians as a work of great importance.[21]

Later Christian and Islamic writers took this to mean that Suphis suppressed idolatry or otherwise promoted monotheism, though this is not the apparently meaning of the text.

This must be the origin of the idea that the pyramid builder had secret knowledge. Now, for the Jews the prophet Enoch lived before the Flood and was believed to have also, like Saurid, received a dream vision from God that included the coming Flood *and* the final punishment of nonbelievers "full of fire and flaming, and full of pillars of fire."[22] Given that he also wrote his book (the Book of Enoch, which was not actually ancient but believed to be) to preserve knowledge of astrology, the Jewish tradition thus seems to have influenced the fictive history of Egypt under another name, especially since the Arabs connected the dots and identified Saurid with Edris (Idris), who was also identified with Enoch.

It therefore seems probable that the tradition of Enoch's vision of Flood and fire, of astronomy and secret knowledge, wed to Manetho's observations on Khufu's sacred book and contempt for the pagan gods, read in light of the Jewish tradition of the pre-Flood pillars, gave rise to Arab pyramid myths. This is a remarkable—and to my knowledge unexplored—continuity of tradition from Antiquity to the late Middle Ages.

When John Greaves wrote his *Pyramidographia* in the sixteenth century, he must have had the Arab texts in mind when he was discussing Proclus, giving accidental rise to the story that the pyramids were observation platforms for Sirius. But that is the least interesting thing about the whole scenario. Once again, though, we find that alternative authors, in dealing only with the surface of stories at their most literal level, have missed the most interesting and informative connections among ancient and medieval peoples.

Notes

[1] John Greaves, *Pyramidographia*, in *Miscellaneous Works of Mr. John Greaves, Professor of Astronomy in the University of Oxford*, vol. 1 (London: 1737), 99-100.

[2] Ibid., 98-100.

[3] Proclus, comment on *Timaeus* 22a; translated by Thomas Taylor in *The Commentaries of Proclus on the* Timaeus *of Plato*, vol. 1 (London: 1820), 84.

[4] Proclus, comment on *Timaeus* 22b; *op. cit.*, 86.

[5] Greaves, *Pyramidographia*, 87.

[6] Ibid., 125.

[7] Richard A. Proctor and A. Cowper Raynard, *Old and New Astronomy* (London: Longman, Green and Co., 1892), 23.

[8] "Proclus informs us that the pyramid terminated at the top in a platform, on which the priests made their celestial observations." (Richard A. Proctor, *The Great Pyramid: Observatory, Tomb, and Temple* [London: Chatto & Windus, 1883], 319.)

[9] Proctor, *The Great Pyramid*, 143-147.

[10] John Anthony West, *The Traveler's Key to Ancient Egypt: A Guide to the Sacred Places of Ancient Egypt*, new edition (Wheaton, Illinois: Theosophical Publishing House, 1985), 91.

[11] "... the Grand Gallery looks like part of a machine, whose function is beyond us. This is not a recent observation; the Neoplatonist Proclus draws our attention to this in his fourth century commentary on Plato's Timaeus." The authors' endnote on this passage merely describes the content of the *Timaeus*. They provide no source for their assertion, though it is obviously Proctor, whose work they discuss immediately following Proclus in the same paragraph. (Robert Bauval and Adrian Gilbert, *The Orion Mystery: Unlocking the Secrets of the Pyramids* [New York: Three Rivers Press, 1994], 43.)

[12] Colin Wilson, *From Atlantis to the Sphinx: Recovering the Lost Wisdom of the Ancient World* (Boston: Weiser, 2004), 63. His unstated source is obviously Proctor, whose 1883 *Great Pyramid* is discussed but one sentence later.

[13] *The Pyramids of Giza and the Sphinx*, English edition, edited by Giovanna Magi (Florence: Casa Editrice Bonechi, 2006), 12.

[14] Al-Maqrizi, *Al-Khitat*, chapter 40; my translation.

[15] Josephus, *Antiquities* 1.2.3, translated by William Whiston.

[16] Al-Maqrizi, *Al-Khitat*, chapter 40; my translation.

[17] *Natural History* 36.16.

[18] Herodotus, *Histories* 2.124-134; Diodorus Siculus, *Library of History* 1.63-64.

[19] Ibrahim ibn Wasif Shah, quoted in Al-Maqrizi, *Al-Khitat*, chapter 40; my translation.

[20] Manetho, Book 2, as preserved in Syncellus, *Chron.*, 54-59; Eusebius, *Chron.* 45-47.

[21] Africanus, as preserved in Syncellus; translated in I. P. Cory, *Ancient Fragments*, second edition (London: William Pickering, 1832), 102. The 1876 Hodges edition of *Ancient Fragments* mistranslates the passage and incorrectly asserts that Suphis was "translated to the gods" like Enoch.

[22] 1 Enoch 90:20-27, translated by R. H. Charles.

33. Scholars' Three-Century Mistake about Myth

INTELLECTUAL LAZINESS, scholarly shortcuts, and outright fabrications aren't unique to alternative historians and ancient astronaut speculators. But whoever takes the shortcuts, the result is almost always the same: mistakes are perpetuated, are accepted as truth, and corrupt the historical record. This chapter offers an object lesson in what happens when scholars rely on secondary sources and repeat earlier writers' work uncritically. This sidelight into Greek mythology was a gigantic pain to untangle thanks to more than three centuries of scholars copying each other. My thanks go to the great Hellenist M. L. West for his assistance in tracking down the origins of this weird little mistake.

In modern manuals of mythology, it is common to list the "original" name of the Greek hero Jason, of Argonautic fame, as Diomedes. It appears as such in the Oxford University Press's *Dictionary of Ancient Deities* (2000), Robert Graves's *The Greek Myths* (1950), and even the monumental *Dictionary of Greek and Roman Biography and Mythology* (1849), the most complete account of Greco-Roman sources ever assembled. Scholars such as F. Max Müller, the Abbé Banier, and countless others have accepted the identification and built theories upon it.

But what bothered me is that I couldn't find any evidence of Jason ever being called Diomedes in the ancient Greek and Roman literature. Not once. And that's where things got complicated.

The scholarly sources all cite the ancient scholia (notes) made on the poet Pindar's Fourth Pythian Ode, the oldest poem to tell the story of Jason. Specifically, they cite the scholion at verse 211 (old system), commenting on Jason's claim in the poem that the centaur Chiron, his teacher, called him by the name Jason. At verse 211 the scholiast wrote that Chiron gave Jason his name, but the scholiast does not specify any former name. Neither does the scholiast who repeated the exact same information in the scholia to Apollonius of Rhodes' Jason epic the *Argonautica* at 1.554. So where did the name Diomedes come from?

It comes from a scholarly mistake.

In 1567, the Renaissance humanist Natali Conti (Natales Comes) published his monumental Latin-language compilation of Greco-Roman mythology, called *Mythologiae*, which quickly became the standard manual of myth, called a mythography, of the Renaissance and the basis for nearly all modern mythographies via its use in the Abbé Antoine Banier's influential 1711 mythography, *Mythologie et la fable expliqués par l'histoire*. In the first edition, Conti reported the Pindar/Apollonius scholia correctly: "When Jason had become a man and had learned from Chiron the healing art, he was called Jason."[1] But in the expanded edition of 1581, something had changed: "When Jason had become a man and had learned from Chiron the healing art, he was called Jason, having first been called Dolomedes."[2]

The Classical scholar Winifred Warren Wilson noted in 1910 that Conti had amended his original line to add information from the Apollonius scholia at 3.26, but he made a mistake. He misread the Greek word δολόμηδες ("crafty") as a proper name and affixed it to Jason despite the scholion having nothing to do with him.[3]

So far, so good. But how did Dolomedes become Diomedes?

Well, as it turns out, most modern mythographers derive their work, ultimately, from the Abbé Banier, who produced the first scholarly mythography in 1711. According to Wilson, when Banier developed his mythography, he was using a flawed copy of Natali Conti, which contained numerous typographical misprints. Banier used the Lyons edition of

1653, based on the Geneva edition of 1651, in which "Diomedes" is misprinted for "Dolomedes." This typographical error became Banier's authoritative assertion that Chiron taught Jason "the Sciences, which he himself professed, especially Medicine, and gave him for that Reason the name of *Jason*, instead of *Diomedes*, which he had before."[4]

And with the exception of Winifred Warren Wilson and me, for three hundred years almost no one bothered to check the original sources and blindly accepted as fact Banier's assertion, based on a typographical misprint of Conti's original error. If a legitimate scholar said it, it had to be true. Right?

Notes

[1] *Mythologiae Librem Decem* 6.8 (Venice, 1568); my translation.

[2] *Mythologiae Librem Decem* 6.8 (Venice, 1581); my translation.

[3] Winifred Warren Wilson, "Jason as 'Dolomedes,'" *The Classical Review* 24 (1910): 180.

[4] Abbé Banier, *The Mythology and Fables of the Ancients, Explain'd from History*, vol. 4 (London: 1740), 9, note (a).

34. Afrocentrism, Ancient Astronauts, and the Black Sea Africans

AFROCENTRISTIC THEORISTS and ancient astronaut theorists don't agree on much, but one thing they share is a common belief that ancient texts can be used without any confirming evidence to generate radical revisions of ancient history. In Herodotus we find an accounted of the mythical Egyptian pharaoh Sesostris, whom the Greek historian claims conquered lands as far north as modern Georgia.[1] Archaeology has failed to find any evidence of this, and most historians think the story is a corruption and exaggeration of events from the reigns of Ramesses II, Seti I, and possibly Senusret II. Later, Diodorus Siculus and Strabo magnified this pharaoh still further, making him the conqueror of the entire world. Needless to say, there is no evidence whatsoever of Egyptians in France, or England, or Spain.

Herodotus also says that the Colchians, the people of modern Georgia, are the descendants of Sesostris' army and of a colony founded on the Black Sea. His evidence was primarily the shared rites of circumcision, along with some nebulous claims that the people were "black," which in those days was a conventional way of saying they were located close to the east, where the sun rose and therefore "burned" them. The same word for "black" was also used to describe Greece's own olive-skinned people.

For the people of Colchis are evidently Egyptian, and this I perceived for myself before I heard it from others. So when I had come to consider the matter I asked them both; and the Colchians had remembrance of the Egyptians more than the Egyptians of the Colchians; but the Egyptians said they believed that the Colchians were a portion of the army of Sesostris. That this was so I conjectured myself not only because they are dark-skinned and have curly hair (this of itself amounts to nothing, for there are other races which are so), but also still more because the Colchians, Egyptians, and Ethiopians alone of all the races of men have practised circumcision from the first. [The Colchians] alone work flax in the same fashion as the Egyptians, and the two nations are like one another in their whole manner of living and also in their language...[2]

Based on this, Robert Temple, the ancient astronaut writer, argued in *The Sirius Mystery* (1976) that Colchis was an actual Egyptian colony and that it was through this colony that the sacred truth that flying space frogs from Sirius had given humanity civilization was passed from Egypt to Greece, and thus from the Greeks to the Dogon of Africa.

At least Temple stopped there.

Afrocentric theorist R. A. Jairazbhoy proposed in a 1988 article that not only was Colchis an Egyptian colony but because the Egyptians were racially identical with sub-Saharan West Africans (the ancestors of most African-Americans), Colchis was therefore a Black colony, and in fact all of the Greek myths associated with it were nothing more than Greeks misinterpreting Black Egypt's African pomp and splendor.[3] Strangely, there almost seemed to be confirming evidence of this. There is an actual population of African descendants living in Georgia. In 1988 Afrocentrist John G. Jackson explained why these people prove that Africa had conquered the classical world and gave it civilization:

This area has been called the 'Black Soviet' because there are so many Black people living down there. Of course they tell you in the history books that these people are the descendants of slaves that the Russians imported in the Middle Ages. But if this territory was settled by the Egyptians in ancient times, then these people are probably their descendants.[4]

But this isn't really true. The most sympathetic researchers looking for "so many Black people" found a population of no more than thirty people, and that was in 1959—three decades before Jackson and Jairazbhoy claimed widespread African populations on the Black Sea.[5]

For these thirty people to have been the remains of Sesostris' army requires us to assume, as several scholars have noted, that the Egyptians brought an army composed of both Black men *and* women, that they inbred for three thousand years, never took any non-Black people for spouses, and somehow maintained a reproductively viable population in the face of isolation and discrimination. The Africans of Colchis knew the truth and tried to tell the Afrocentrists, who refused to listen. Ethnographers and archaeologists listened, and through their work we know the truth: They are the last descendants of Ottoman-era slaves from when the territory was part of Turkey.[6]

This is a far cry from imaginary Egyptian armies and flying space frogs, but it has the virtue of being true.

Notes

[1] *Histories* 2.102-111.

[2] *Histories* 2.104-105, translated by G. C. Macaulay.

[3] R. A. Jairazbhoy, "Egyptian Civilization in Colchis on the Black Sea," in *African Presence in Early Asia,* eds. Runoko Rashidi and Ivan Van Sertima (New Brunswick: Transaction, 1988), 61-64.

[4] Quoted in James E. Brunson and Runoko Rashidi, "Sitting at the Feet of a Forerunner: An April 1987 Meeting and Interview with John G. Jackson," in *African Presence in Early Asia,* eds. Runoko Rashidi and Ivan Van Sertima (New Brunswick: Transaction, 1988), 198.

[5] Patrick T. English, "Cushites, Colchians, and Khazars," *Journal of Near Eastern Studies* 18, no. 1 (1959): 49-53.

[6] Martin W. Lewis and Kären Wigen, *The Myth of Continents: A Critique of Metageography* (Berkeley: University of California, 1997), 257n.66.

35. Afrocentrism and the Aztec Calendar

I F YOU READ a "fact" in an alternative history book, you can be fairly certain of one thing: It won't be true. In *They Came before Columbus* (1976) the Afrocentrist writer Ivan Van Sertima, for whom evidence exists solely as grist for polemic, claimed that the ancient Mexican and Egyptian calendars were substantively similar because a scholar, the Abbé Hervas, had written that

> The Mexican year began upon the 26th of February, a day celebrated in the era of Nabonassar, which was fixed by the Egyptians 747 years before the Christian era; for the beginning of their month *Toth*, corresponded with the meridian of the same day. If those priests fixed also upon this day as an epoch, because it was celebrated in Egypt, we have there the Mexican Calendar agreeing with the Egyptian. But independent of this, it is certain, that the Mexican Calendar conformed greatly with the Egyptian.[1]

Van Sertima declines to note that the Abbé Hervas lived in the eighteenth century, and his discussion was a private letter sent to the cleric Francesco Saverio Clavigero (also known as Francisco Javier Clavijero Echegaray) and published in 1780 in *The History of Mexico*.[2] He acknowledges this obliquely in the end notes (citing the 1804 edition), but does not mention the fact in the body text.[3] Van Sertima then manages to misunderstand Hervas despite having two hundred years of advances to draw upon. He seems to think that the Egyptian calendar "began" on February

26, 747 BCE but does not seem to understand what is meant by this. Van Sertima seems to think that time began anew on that date for the Egyptians (though he acknowledges that their calendar is older than this), but this is not true. Hervas recognized that "Nabonassar" (i.e. Nabu-nasir), a king of Babylon, had reformed the Babylonian calendar, creating intercalary months to marry lunar and solar calendars and establishing an eighteen year cycle.

However, Hervas takes the Hellenistic astronomer Ptolemy at his word in the *Almagest* that this established a universal *Anno Nabonassari*,[4] but in fact the only reason Nabu-nasir's name is remembered is because Ptolemy and other Hellenistic astronomers used his calendar to calculate the motion of the stars. This, in turn, occurred because it is only with the ascension of Nabu-nasir that complete and careful astronomical and calendar records began to be kept at Babylon, which Ptolemy drew upon. There is no evidence of an *Anno Nabonassari* until Ptolemy introduced it.

Nor was this the only "era" used by Ptolemy; he also said that the calendar began anew with Philippus Aridaeus, Caesar Augustus, Hadrian, and Antoninus Pius. He did not mean that the calendar *literally* started to mark time for each of these men; rather, this was how Ptolemy was referencing dates to try to reduce confusion created by the traditional (eastern) practice of counting years by the name of the monarch—i.e., "the third year of Cleopatra VII," etc.—by grouping years together in larger eras. Nabu-nasir came first because he had the oldest usable records. Besides, it would have been strange for Egypt to have used a Babylonian king to define their calendar for all time.[5] (In 747 BCE, Egypt was in the Third Intermediate Period, with control divided among native rules and the Nubians, from the south.) Such facts are beyond Ivan Van Sertima, who cares nothing for what Ptolemy actually said so long as someone, somewhere said something he could use for Afrocentric polemic.

Since the Mayan calendar, which marks time from August 11, 3114 BCE, was not deciphered and correlated to the Gregorian calendar until the twentieth century, Hervas must have been talking about the Aztec calendar, which was already understood in the eighteenth century. This calendar, though, was nothing like the Egyptian. The Egyptian calendar had twelve months of thirty days plus five intercalary days. The Aztec calendar had eighteen months of twenty days plus five intercalary days. The coincidence of five intercalary days—something Hervas emphasizes and Van Sertima quotes gleefully[6]—stems entirely from the impossibility of dividing the 365 days of the solar year into even units, not from any magical ancestral calendar. It is simple math, derived from the coincidental remainder when dividing 365 evenly by either eighteen months (as in Mexico) or twelve months (as in Egypt). In both cases, five days are left over.

Nor is the beginning of the calendar cycle well-fixed. The earliest recorders differed in their descriptions. Diego Durán, a Dominican friar, held that the new year began on March 1, while Bernardino de Sahagún, a Franciscan priest, held that the new year began on February 2. At any rate, the celebration of the New Year, even if it were February 26, is hardly the same thing as Ptolemy suggesting that a new era began on one specific February 26 in 747 BCE. The Egyptian New Year began on August 29, at least in the late period. Because they had no concept of the leap day, the calendar gradually shifted across the seasons.

Van Sertima, ignoring all of this, then completely misunderstands Hervas, writing that "Egyptian influence may be traced to…the time Mexicans began to count the years…."[7] Hervas never says that the Mexican calendar *began for all time* on February 26, and in fact stated that the *new year* began that day.[8] Van Sertima confuses the New Year's date with the foundation date of the calendar.

Read Hervas's subsequent sentence carefully: "If those [i.e. Aztec] priests fixed also upon this day as an epoch, because it was celebrated in Egypt, we have there the Mexican Calendar agreeing with the Egyptian."[9] The "if" clause is important. It is telling us that Hervas is asking us to assume that *if* the Mexicans adopted the Egyptian calendar's "epoch," *then* the Mexican calendar is also the Egyptian calendar. This is circular reasoning made possible because Hervas adopted the widespread (and fictive) belief that "the Mexicans [i.e. Aztec] had their Calendar from the Toltecas (originating from Asia)…."[10] Hervas believed the Toltecs were originally from Asia and had contact with the Egyptians, and that contact occurred at a relatively early date, c. 800 BCE. (Later research would prove that the Toltec actually flourished much later—from 800 to 1000 CE—and were indigenous Americans whose last Asian ancestors were at least ten thousand years in the past.)

This fictive history of the Toltec, in turn, was made possible by the religious belief that the first Americans were descendants of one of Noah's sons, probably Shem, a people who migrated to the Americas sometime after 2356 BCE, the calculated year of the Flood based on creation in 4004 BCE. According to theories popular in the eighteenth century, these people were probably some of the Lost Tribes of Israel, who therefore did not reach the Americas until after the Assyrian conquest of Israel in 720 BCE, when they disappear from the Biblical record. This is the deep background for why Hervas felt that the Toltec must have brought the post-747 BCE Nabonassar calendar with them, since it would have been in universal use, or so he thought, in the Near East of the age.

But Van Sertima cares nothing for this, or for the longstanding controversy about the peopling of the Americas that it forms a small sidelight upon. Hervas was a man of his time, but that time had long passed by 1976, and Ivan Van Sertima—a graduate student at Rutgers that year—should have known that centuries-old sources cannot be used uncritically, and that hoary old claims do not automatically pass a "rigorous test" in his words simply by being old.[11] Hervas's claims do not match modern discoveries, and Van Sertima displayed his monumental hubris in pretending that two centuries of subsequent research and findings could be ignored because a letter in an appendix to an old book could help him make a case for Afrocentrism when the facts, as known to science, could not.

Notes

[1] Translated in Francesco Saverio Clavigero, *The History of Mexico*, vol. 1, translated by Charles Cullen (London: 1787), 466.

[2] Ivan Van Sertima, *They Came before Columbus: The African Presence in Ancient America* (New York: Random House Paperbacks, 2003), 173-174.

[3] Ibid., 181n.99.

[4] *Almagest* 3.7.

[5] Olaf Pedersen and Alexander Jones, *A Survey of the Almagest* (New York: Springer, 2010), 126-128.

[6] Van Sertima, *They Came before Columbus*, 174 (= Clavigero, *History of Mexico*, 466).

[7] Van Sertima, *They Came before Columbus*, 174.

[8] "The Mexican year began upon the 26th of February..." (Clavigero, *History of Mexico*, 466 [= Van Sertima, *They Came before Columbus*, 173]).

[9] Clavigero, *History of Mexico*, 466 (= Van Sertima, *They Came Before Columbus*, 173).

[10] Clavigero, *History of Mexico*, 466, unquoted by Van Sertima.

[11] Van Sertima, *They Came before Columbus*, 175.

36. Egyptian Dog Chariots in Mexico?

I DON'T THINK THAT Ivan Van Sertima actually knew how to read. At least that's the impression I get every time I try to trace back one of his Afrocentrist claims from *They Came before Columbus* (1976) back to its source. Van Sertima wrote his book when he was a graduate student at Rutgers, and it says little for that institution's educative training that one of their bestselling graduates simply could not understand what he read in articles and books.

In discussing the alleged "connections" between the Nubian people of the Sudan and the Olmecs of Mexico, Van Sertima makes a rather bizarre argument that, frankly, is difficult to follow. The background is that the Nubians (more properly the Kushites of the Kingdom of Kush of 800 BCE to 350 CE—"Nubians" being the people who replaced them) adopted and modified Egyptian culture, building their own pyramids and making statues of the Egyptian gods.

With that established, we can now look at Van Sertima's tortured argument. He first identifies that importance of dogs in ancient Egypt, claiming they were mummified by the pharaohs. (This is true, but dogs were not universally part of the pharaoh's funerary package; dogs were more likely to be buried in mass animal tombs, excepting perhaps beloved pets.) He then pivots and says that the "Nubians," whom he confuses with Kushites, "were fascinated by horses"[1] and buried *horses* in Kushite royal tombs along with full chariots:

Yet in spite of this departure from the Egyptian type of burial, the coexistence of the two cultures was preserved by a symbolic Nubian homage to the dog. The Egyptian dog-headed god, Anubis, graces the Nubian funerary offering tables.[2]

Anubis had the head of a *jackal*, not a domestic dog.

This is where things get weird:

In this very period the Olmecs began to sculpt little clay dogs attached to wheels or to tiny chariots with wheels. In this peculiar blend of dog and chariot lies virtually their only use of the wheel. [...] How they struck upon this ritual association (dog/wheeled chariot) is an intriguing question.[3]

It would be, especially since Van Sertima just told us that the "Nubians" (Kushites) buried *horses* and not dogs. Van Sertima intends us to believe that the Olmec were visited by the Kushites during the high point of their culture, 800 BCE to 350 CE, bringing with them the post-747 BCE calendar discussed in our previous chapter. This is *just* chronologically possible since the Olmec flourished between 2500 BCE and 400 BCE. But does Van Sertima's source support his claim?

Van Sertima relies entirely upon one academic journal article for this claim: Gordon F. Ekholm's 1946 *American Antiquity* article "Wheeled Toys in Mexico."[4] It does not say what Van Sertima says it says.

In his article, Ekholm describes a series of toys found in Mexico, dating from primarily from the last few centuries before the Spanish conquest, which he called "period V," dating to around 1200 CE. He does not provide dates for all the pieces, but those he does date are *not* Olmec. Ekholm describes these toys as "wheeled vehicles," by which he meant that they could be pulled on a string, like children's toys today. Van Sertima mistakes this phrase for confirmation that the toys were intended as a "peculiar blend of dog and chariot." This is not what was meant by "vehicle." Instead, Ekholm describes a particular animal toy with wheels that had been found in 1880 and labeled by its discoverer, the French archaeologist Claude-Joseph-Désiré Charnay, as a "chariot." Well, that's how Ekholm summarized it. In the original, Charnay calls it a "cart" and discusses how the word "chariot" was used differently in post-Conquest Mexico. But Charnay was describing the resemblance of the low-slung, flat animal with wheels to a cart with an animal face. Charnay thought it might represent an Aztec wagon or cart.[5] Examining the illustration Charnay provided of the cart in his volume makes plain that this is an animal with wheels, not as Van Sertima mistakenly believes from Charnay's wording as conveyed by Ekholm a "little clay dogs attached ... to tiny chariots with wheels." Nor is it of Olmec extraction; it was found near Mexico City and dates from either late Toltec or early Aztec times (around 1200 CE), *as Ekholm clearly explained.*[6]

The final piece, the only one that Van Sertima could reasonably have associated with the Olmec, was described as coming from Oaxaca, near the Olmec heartland. However, Ekholm explains in no uncertain terms that he believed the toy "must have been made in Spanish times" since it depicted a horse with a saddle, something unknown in pre-Columbian Mexico.[7] Saddles were only invented anywhere on earth around 700 BCE and were not in widespread use in the Old World until the Olmec had vanished. He also said it was of the Zapotec (Monte Alban) style, not Olmec.[8]

The earliest example identified Ekholm placed in the Teotihuacan Period (100 BCE-700 CE), again not Olmec. He did write that such toys might be "the result of contact with or influence from some Old World culture," which Van Sertima gleefully seized upon, ignoring the subsequent statement that such a possibility was "quite unlikely."[9]

Ekholm does not identify the wheeled animals as dogs. He cites others as identifying some as peccaries and armadillos, and suggesting the above-mentioned animal was a horse. Charnay's illustration perhaps resembles a dog, but there is no way to be sure. The figures are stylized. Some, especially those found after he wrote, undoubtedly were dogs,[10] but Ekholm doesn't say so and Van Sertima never went in search of those sources.

In sum, Ivan Van Sertima either purposely misrepresented Ekholm's article for profit, or he was simply incapable of understanding the material that he read. Given the polemical nature of Van Sertima's book, the former would seem the more prudent conclusion, but given his admitted ignorance of the Olmec in later years, I suspect the latter.

Van Sertima's *They Came before Columbus* was not given a full academic review until the twenty-first century, and so far as I know, its claims have never been systematically evaluated. It's painful to see that entire careers can be built on misunderstandings, fabrications, and lies just because no one ever bothered to check the sources.

Notes

[1] Ivan Van Sertima, *They Came before Columbus: The African Presence in Ancient America* (New York: Random House Paperbacks, 2003), 161-162.

[2] Ibid., 162.

[3] Ibid.

[4] Gordon F. Ekholm, "Wheeled Toys in Mexico," *American Antiquity* 11 (1946): 222-228. Van Serima misspells Ekholm's name in his sole reference, *They Came before Columbus,* 179n55.

[5] Désiré Charnay, *Ancient Cities of the New World*, translated by J. Gonino and Helen S. Conant (New York: Harper & Brothers, 1887), 174-176.

[6] Ekholm, "Wheeled Toys," 223.

[7] Ibid., 224.

[8] Ibid.

[9] Ibid., 225.

[10] See, for example, Robert H. Lister, "Additional Evidence of Wheeled Toys in Mexico," *American Antiquity* 12 (1947), 184-185.

37. The Pineapple of Pompeii

WHILE I'M ON the subject of alleged Old World incursions in to the ancient New World, let's pause to consider the an alleged case of the reverse. The Afrocentrist scholar Ivan Van Sertima discussed in his *They Came before Columbus* (1976) his belief that Native American travelers reached Roman-era Europe in 62 BCE, based on a text by Pliny discussing "Indians" from India, not America[1] (see Chapter 47), and in so doing, he adds a weird little detail that he believed Native Americans brought pineapples with them while traveling from North America to Germany:

> These Americans came to early to have been the carriers of the maize grain to the Old World, but they might have brought the pineapple. Their visit occurred in 62 B.C. About a hundred years later (79 A.D.) a catastrophe struck the Roman city of Pompeii. Excavating under the volcanic dust archaeologists turned up a mural that depicted this plant, completely unknown in the Old World.[2]

Imagine that: A few Native Americans in a bark canoe following the Gulf Stream somehow brought a pineapple from lower South America all the way up to the North American coast and then across the Atlantic— keeping it fresh, no less—before turning it over to the Romans, who dispatched it not to the capital but to a resort town where its image was faithfully preserved, though only in an obscure corner of a single mural, for 140 years. It makes perfect sense.

Van Sertima then claims that Domenico Casella, a botanist whom he identifies as a scholar of Pompeii, recognized the mural as a pineapple, as did plant taxonomist E. D. Merrill. Casella, in turn, proposed in a 1950 study published in *Pompeiana* that images on the murals of Pompeii depict three tropical fruits: the pineapple, the mango, and the custard-apple.[3] The latter two are images of highly stylized fruits that no other scholar has been able to identify—as tropical or anything else. They are too doubtful to assign a meaning, let alone to propose absent any supporting proof that they represent a fruit unseen anywhere else in ancient Europe.[4] The "pineapple" is a more interesting case. The image, found at the "House of the Ephebe," depicts what nearly most scholars are sure is the cone of the umbrella pine.

Those who disagreed early on that the image was that of a pine cone were usually scholars who were not native to Italy and therefore based their opinions solely on Casella's text rather than knowledge of Italian botany. One of these was anthropologist George Carter, who accepted Casella's argument without question, and to it attached a number of other diffusionist claims about American products in the Old World.[5] Carter was well-known as a diffusionist and proponent of the theory that humans had lived in America for more than 100,000 years—nearly 10 times the scholarly consensus. His work has not stood up to skeptical inquiry. E. D. Merrill, a botanist, certainly was qualified to speak about plants, though he was not an expert in Roman art or Old World archaeology. His judgment was based entirely on the degree to which he felt the image depicted on the mural resembled the pineapple.[6]

Despite these supporters, archaeologists and art historians immediately criticized Casella's claims, and in the 1950s a lively exchange played out across the academic journals. Ivan Van Sertima either knew nothing of this or cared nothing about it, or the emerging scholarly consensus that the Roman image depicts an umbrella pine cone. Instead, he draws on the tradition represented by coverage of the pineapple claim in *The Interamerican* (1967) and *The New Diffusionist* (1973) of simply repeating controversial academic papers without a fair presentation of the broader intellectual argument surrounding them. We should credit him, however, for resisting the temptation to pluralize the pineapple, as is done by less cautious alternative authors like Gunnar Thompson who frequently write of the many "pineapples" depicted in Pompeian murals, thus transforming Casella's tentative identification of a single image into a wide-ranging crop of pineapples.

The similarity of pineapple and pine cone has a linguistic echo. The very word "pineapple" was coined in early modern England to describe the cones of pine trees, the "apple" (or fruit) of the "pine." It was only when European explorers found the American pineapple (native to South America) and saw the visual similarity that they applied the name to the American fruit, causing the new meaning to supersede the old. The older meaning, however, clung on in places, which is why Marc Monnier's 1886 book on the *Wonders of Pompeii* could describe an image at Herculaneum as depicting a serpent "eating a pineapple,"[7] a description drawn from a half a century of earlier descriptions all referencing the "pine-apple" or "pineapple" on the sign, meaning a pinecone. Similarly, Asclepius (the god of healing) was said in pre-1900 manuals of mythology to be associated with "the pineapple," which later writers were forced to clarify meant a "pinecone" due to confusion caused by the American fruit and their similar appearance.

Notes

[1] Pliny the Elder, *Natural History* 2.67, discussing "certain Indians ... sailing from India."

[2] Ivan Van Sertima, *They Came before Columbus: The African Presence in Ancient America* (New York: Random House Paperbacks, 2003), 255.

[3] Domenico Casella, "La frutta nelle pitture pompeiane," *Pompeiana: Raccolta di Studi per il II Centenario degli Scavi di Pompei*, ed. Amadeo Maiuri (Napoli, G. Macchiaroli, 1950), 355-86.

[4] Wilhelmina Feemster Jashemski, Frederick G. Meyer, and Massimo Ricciardi, "Plants: Evidence from Wall Paintings, Mosaics, Sculpture, Plant Remains, Graffiti, Inscriptions, and Ancient Authors," in *The Natural History of Pompeii,* eds. Wilhelmina Feemster Jashemski and Frederick G. Meyer (Cambridge: Cambridge University Press, 2002), 81.

[5] George Carter, "Before Columbus," *The Book of Mormon: The Keystone Scripture,* ed. Paul R. Cheesman (Provo, Utah: BYU Religious Studies Center, 1988), 151-163; accessed online at BYU Religious Studies Center.

[6] E. D. Merrill, "The Botany of Cook's Voyages and Its Unexpected Significance in Relation to Anthropology, Biogeography and History," *Chronica Botanica* 14, nos. 5/6 (1954), 367.

[7] Marc Monnier, *The Wonders of Pompeii,* English trans., Wonders of Art and Architecture (New York: Charles Scribner's Sons, 1886), 75.

38. A Dinosaur in the Congo?

HE ZEAL OF AFROCENTRISTS to find Africans around the world was quite obviously a response to the imperialist-colonialist zeal to disinherit indigenous peoples from their own history and to link native peoples the world over with the primitive and the wild. The alleged dinosaur living in the Congo Basin, *mokèlé-mbèmbé*, has appeared widely in popular culture, thanks in large part to early twentieth century writers who reported Congolese folklore about the creature and saw in it a reflection of the most primeval times of earth's history. The earliest report for the supposed monster is almost universally claimed to be a passage in a 1776 book by the Abbé Liévin-Bonaventure Proyart (1743-1808), a French cleric and writer later executed for writing the wrong thing about Louis XVI during the reign of Napoleon. Proyart served as a missionary in the Congo Basin in the 1760s, and in an early chapter of his book on the region, *Histoire de Loango, Kakongo, et autres royaumes d'Afrique* (1776), he describes the animals of west and central Africa using reports compiled by fellow missionaries in the area.

He devotes only two sentences to the monster later cryptozoology authors have claimed as a dinosaur. This creature is frequently said to be a sauropod on the order of Apatosaurus (Brontosaurus). These authors tend to selectively quote only a part of the first sentence, mostly because the second sentence makes plain that the "monster" is in no wise the equivalent of a dinosaur. They also tend to all abridge the exact same translation, first provided, so far as I can tell, in the journal *Cryptozoology* in 1982.

(Seriously, does anyone in alternative studies actually review primary sources? I mean, if I can do it, it can't be *that* hard...)

Roy P. MacKal's *A Living Dinosaur: The Search for Mokele-Mbembe* (1987) at least provided the correct measurements and a full, if not absolutely faithful, quotation.[1] By contrast, Michael Newton's account in *Hidden Animals* (2009) is dependent upon MacKal (an acknowledged source) but garbles the discussion and claims Proyart described "tribal stories of a beast known as *mokele-mbembe*...,"[2] which he certainly did not do. Since this passage is almost never given in full and sometimes given incorrectly, allow me provide my own translation to clarify things:

> The Missionaries have observed, passing along a forest, the trail of an animal they have not seen but which must be monstrous: the marks of his claws were noted upon the earth, and these composed a footprint of about three feet in circumference. By observing the disposition of his footsteps, it was recognized that he was not running in his passage, and he carried his legs at the distance of seven to eight feet apart.[3]

This monster, as you can see, is not terribly large by the standards of dinosaurs. Note, for example that my own footprint has a circumference of two feet (with sides of 11 inches, 4 inches, 7 inches, and 2 inches), and at 5'10" I am hardly a monstrously-sized human. By contrast, an Apatosaurus had a footprint measuring approximately ten feet in circumference (three feet by two feet in dimension), though other dinosaurs were obviously much smaller. MacKal recognized this, though minimizing the implications. He quotes a modern Franco-Belgian scientist, Bernard Heuvelmans, as suggesting the measurements are somewhat akin to the rhinoceros, though he argues that it cannot be one because rhinoceroses lack claws.[4]

The trouble seems to be that modern writers are confusing circumference for length (they are not the same), and they have taken Proyart's adjective *monstrueux* as an indication that he was referring to a "monster." However, while *monstrueux* carries the implication of "horrific" or "monstrous" today, in the eighteenth century, the word carried instead the connotation of "prodigious," or very large, according to French dictionaries published in that era; it is modern people who added terror to the older sense.[5] Proyart and his sources did not express any great terror at the creature, whose description he sandwiches between passages on the elephant and the lion, and the context of the passage clearly implies that he considered the creature simply one of many animals of similar bulk. A rhinoceros, for comparison, has a footprint averaging seven inches (18 cm) in diameter, according to zoologists, but which can easily top eleven inches (28 cm). This yields a circumference (using π times diameter) of two feet (56.5 cm) for an average rhino and our required three feet (91 cm) for the eleven-inch rhino foot. The rhinoceros also has a head-and-body length averaging around twelve feet (3.7 m), with a body length of about eight feet (2.4 m), meaning its legs are seven to eight feet (2.1-2.4 m) apart.

The greatest objection to identifying Proyart's monster as a rhinoceros is that the rhinoceros does not have claws. Its footprint, however, takes the appearance of three enormous, sometimes pointed, claw marks, which are actually its toes but appear distorted when smeared through mud. A hippopotamus is also a close fit, with a footprint that similarly resembles that described by Proyart, with what look like "claw" marks but are actually the toes. Keeping in mind that Proyart did not witness the tracks firsthand, this would seem to be a reasonable description of a rhinoceros or hippopotamus track.

A second objection to identifying Proyart's print as a hippopotamus or rhinoceros is the claim that such creatures do not currently live in the area of the Congo now home to the legend of *mokèlé-mbèmbé*. Proyart did not provide a location for his missionary friends' sighting of the prints, so this objection cannot be sustained. There is no way to localize Proyart's description to the same territory where the (current) *mokèlé-mbèmbé* myth is centered. Both the rhinoceros and the hippopotamus had ranges that included areas visited by missionaries when Proyart was active in Africa. The hippopotamus range included the Congo, and the rhinoceros the areas to the north. (Sadly, both have declined markedly since then and are no longer found in their historic ranges.) Most damning of all is the fact that

Proyart does not describe either the hippopotamus or the rhinoceros in his book, meaning that he was probably not aware that the hippopotamus lived in sub-Saharan Africa. The rhinoceros, then known primarily from Asian species, would also have been beyond his knowledge in 1776. Since Proyart describes the monster in a passage listing elephants and lions, this would imply that the creature was probably not in the rainforest, perhaps making the rhinoceros the more likely animal.

At any rate, given the measurements provided by Proyart and the secondhand nature of the report, it is not possible to infer the existence of a dinosaur from his description of relatively small footprints.

Notes

[1] Roy P. MacKal, *A Living Dinosaur: The Search for Mokele-Mbembe* (Leiden: E. J. Brill, 1987), 2. MacKal paraphrases the second sentence somewhat for clarity, but his translation does not change the essential meaning.

[2] Michael Newton, *Hidden Animals: A Field Guide to Batsquatch, Chupacabra, and Other Elusive Creatures* (Santa Barbara: ABC-CLIO, 2009), 44.

[3] *Les Missionnaires ont observé, en passant le long d'une forêt, la piste d'un animal qu'ils n'ont pas vu; mais qui doit être monstrueux: les traces de ses griffes s'appercevoient fur la terre, & y formoient une empreinte d'environ trois pieds de circonférence. En observant la disposition de ses pas, on a reconnu qu'il ne couroit pas dans cet endroit de son passage, & qu'il portoit ses pattes à la distance de sept à huit pieds les unes des autres.* (Liévin-Bonaventure Proyart, *Histoire de Loango, Kakongo, et autres royaumes d'Afrique* [Paris, 1776], 38-39).

[4] MacKal, *A Living Dinosaur*, 4-5.

[5] Similarly, Dr. Johnson in his *Dictionary* of 1755 defined "monstrous" as being "unnatural, shocking." Both the English and French words were drawing on the older Latin sense of *monstrum*, referencing an unnatural birth, a sign from God.

39. The Secret Prehistory of El Chupacabra

O NE OF THE MOST POPULAR cryptozoological creatures, behind perhaps only Bigfoot and the Loch Ness monster, is El Chupacabra, the Latin American goat sucker, so named from the creature's alleged habit of sucking the blood of goats and other livestock. The first modern report of the chupacabra occurred in Puerto Rico in 1995, when Madelyne Tolentino claimed to see a lizard-like creature that skeptic Benjamin Radford has persuasively argued was in fact derived from a memory of the imaginary extraterrestrial in the 1995 movie *Species*.[1] Around the same time, there was a rash of animal deaths, leading some to connect Tolentino's sighting to the dead animals, giving birth to the modern legend.

The origin of the name "chupacabra" (literally: goat sucker) is attributed in some popular sources to Silverio Pérez, a Puerto Rican comedian, who used the word to describe the animal Tolentino claimed to see and to link that sighting with a rash of unexplained animal deaths on the island. However, while he may have been the first to use the word to describe the alleged creature, he was not the originator of the term. In fact, the chupacabra name derives from 2,300 years of European and American traditions about nocturnal creatures that prey on livestock.

And it all started with a small, completely harmless little bird.

The first chupacabra was not a monster, nor was it a vampire. Originally, the goatsucker was so named not because the creature sucked blood like a vampire but because it sucked milk directly from the teat. The legend originates in a story told about the European nightjar (genus Caprimulgus), a smallish, nocturnal, and insectivorous bird that inexplicably developed a bad reputation, earning it the name "goatsucker." The first author to record this story is Aristotle, in his *History of Animals*, written around 350 BCE:

> The goatsucker, as it is called, is a mountain bird, larger than the blackbird, and less than the cuckoo. It lays two, or not more than three eggs, and is slothful in its disposition. It flies against the goats and sucks them, whence its name (ægothelas, the goat-sucker). They say that when the udder has been sucked that it gives no more milk, and that the goat becomes blind. This bird is not quick sighted by day, but sees well at night.[2]

It has been suggested that the origin of this myth was the observation of nightjars flying through goat pastures in the twilight hours, darting as they are wont to do between the legs of cows and goats. This same story is repeated in Pliny the Elder's *Natural History* of 77-79 CE:

> "Caprimulgus" is the name of a bird, which is to all appearance a large blackbird; it thieves by night, as it cannot see during the day. It enters the folds of the shepherds, and makes straight for the udder of the she-goat, to suck the milk. Through the injury thus inflicted the udder shrivels away, and the goat that has been thus deprived of its milk, is afflicted with incipient blindness.[3]

It would not surprise me if the same natural forces responsible for reports of "cattle mutilation"—namely the tendency of soft tissues like udders to decay first—gave rise to Pliny's report of the decayed udder when the nightjar was seen flying about eating the insects attracted to rotting goat corpses. But this must remain speculation. In his *Tracking the Chupacabra*, Benjamin Radford claims "no serious researcher" would link the goatsucker of Aristotle (and thus of Pliny) with that of Puerto Rico,[4] but as we shall see, his judgment is too hasty and closes off a profitable line of inquiry into the prehistory of the chupacabra.

Pliny's word *caprimulgus*, which became the genus name for the night-jar, is a direct Latin translation of Aristotle's Greek *aegothelas*, both meaning goat-sucker. Thus, the nightjar is known as the "goatsucker" in most European languages. In Italian, it is the *succiapre*. In (early) Spanish *chotacabra*, and in Portuguese, *chupacabra*.[5] The name, in its now-obsolete Spanish form *chotacabra*, was in common use in Spanish America (including Puerto Rico) from at least the nineteenth century (and probably many centuries earlier), changing to *chupacabra* in the twentieth century when the older Spanish verb *chotar* (to suck) became obsolete and gave way to the newer synonym *chupar*.

It was the authority of Pliny and Aristotle that perpetuated this mistaken bit of folklore about the nightjar, in spite of a failure to observe any actual goat sucking by the bird, which is actually insectivorous. In Pliny, though, we see the beginning of El Chupacabra's vampire-like reputation, for in this passage not only is the goat rendered blind but also she has part of her body destroyed. In popular superstition, this bird seems to have become confused with a myth about the screech-owl, namely that it attacks infants and suckling animals, mutilating them to obtain blood. Ovid reports the popular misconception about owls in his *Fasti*, written around and after 8 CE:

> There are greedy birds, not those that cheated Phineus' maw of its repast [i.e., Harpies], though from those they are descended. Big is their head, goggle their eyes, their beaks are formed for rapine, their feathers blotched with grey, their claws fitted with hooks. They fly by night and attack nurseless children, and defile their bodies, snatched from their cradles. They are said to rend the flesh of sucklings with their beaks, and their throats are full of the blood which they have drunk. Screech-owl is their name, but the reason of the name is that they are wont to screech horribly by night.[6]

The similarities between the birds—their nocturnal habits, their alleged attacks connected to nursing animals, and their terrible screeches—led to the confusion. In later European folklore, many other birds, real and imagined, became confused or conflated with the ancient goatsucker, and the association with mutilation and blood continued. During the Middle Ages, the nightjar was believed to kill the goats it sucked. In medieval England, the nightjar became associated with the evil spirit Puck, himself associated with the devil. A close association with vampires emerged when Europeans discovered the vampire bat in the Amazon and lumped the goatsucker in with folklore's other fluid-drinking nightmare animals—especially since both vampire bats and goatsuckers were seen together at twilight. The relationship between the goatsucker and the myth of (human) vampires was recognized as early as the 1820s.[7]

This essential unity of folklore and myth is hidden in the English-speaking world, where the common name "nightjar" began to supersede that of the goatsucker among scholars after 1630, so named from the noise (or "jar") the bird makes at night. Thus, many modern Anglophone commentators fail to recognize that when the Spanish and the Portuguese began colonizing the New World in the fifteenth and sixteenth centuries, they brought their myths and superstitions of the goatsucker with them. These they must have applied to the American birds of the same genus, recognized from early on as similar species.

The nightjar is native to Puerto Rico, and I have been able to find printed references to the bird on the island as "chotacabra" dating back to at least 1948 (when the Puerto Rico Dept. of Agriculture so described it), but certainly it had been so known much earlier. The bird was once common on Puerto Rico, but its numbers declined and in the twentieth century it was even thought extinct. Today it is extremely endangered, with perhaps fewer than 1,500 left in the wild. In the Americas, interestingly, we know that the nightjar already had a sinister reputation before the Spanish conquest, at least in parts of South America. Among the Makusi in South America, for example, the nighttime cry of the goatsucker (the bird) was believed to be the shriek of evil spirits.[8] According to Claude Lévi-Strauss, the goatsucker was simply the "bird of death" in Central and South America, and myths of its evil nature were widespread throughout the Americas.[9] For example, among the Maya, they were the guardian birds of the underworld.

Thus, it is not entirely conjectural to suggest that the Native and later Hispanic peoples of the Caribbean came to adopt the negative folkloric association of the goatsucker in all its vampiric glory from Spanish and Portuguese influences (probably in adopting a European language and European animal names) and combined them with indigenous ideas of the goatsucker as an evil demon. These two strands of goatsucker lore neatly encapsulate everything the modern chupacabra represents: a demonic creature that sucks the blood from animals.

We know that the term "chotacabra(s)" was in popular usage in Puerto Rico and was well-understood because the Spanish translation of Oliver Wendell Holmes' *A Mortal Antipathy* (1885) translates character Maurice Kirkwood's pseudonym "Sachem" or "Night-Hawk" as "El Chotacabras," and this translation appears as early as 1951 in the journal *Asomante* published by the University of Puerto Rico. The term also appears in Spanish dictionaries in use in the region in the nineteenth century.

In 1995, a myth to explain unexplained animal deaths and sightings of strange creatures could have taken many forms. Indeed, before the creature acquired a name, it was described as everything from a bird to a Bigfoot to a (human) vampire, and its victims were everything from chickens to horses to cows—but only rarely goats. Many early attacks were specifically attributed to monstrous *birds*, including a wave of sightings in 1975. Among the victims in 1995 were eight sheep, three roosters, and a teddy bear. During August 1995, 150 farm animals and pets were allegedly killed, with dozens of additional animals said to have been killed in November, among which were a few goats. Following Tolentino's sighting, the chupacabra name was attached to the conjectured monster by Silverio Pérez before the end of the year.

It was the application of the specific name of "goatsucker" that helped to define the direction the story of the chupacabra would take. The bird for which it was named was rare; most modern Puerto Ricans would never have seen one. It does not take much conjecture to suggest that the myths associated with the bird could therefore be transferred from the now-rare and mostly forgotten avian to a cryptid that people believed really existed.

When Pérez applied the term "goatsucker" to the monster, he must have been reusing (consciously or not) the term for the legendary bird, for the monster's victims were not all (or even primarily) goats, and absent an underlying familiarity with the ancient history of the goatsucker legend, the name simply makes no sense and would not have stuck. (The change from the obsolete form *chotacabra* to the modern form *chupacabra*, reflecting changes in colloquial Spanish, masked the connection, leading to recent claims that the word did not exist prior to 1995.) Perhaps significantly, Tolentino's 1995 sighting of the creature later labeled chupacabra, and the sighting that gave rise to the modern myth, included the detail, later dropped, that the monster had *feathers*. Only later would it become the doglike terror of modern myth.

Whether intentional or not, once the myth of the vampire monster gained that specific moniker, it began to appropriate the Old World and New World associations of its namesake—the demonic, evil nature of indigenous American mythology and the vampiric, mutilating reputation of its Old World version. Even if this association was not a conscious creation, two millennia of history associated with the name and concept of the goatsucker seems to have influenced the development of the myth, not just in Puerto Rico but elsewhere as the tale spread outward, into Mexico, and eventually to the mainland United States. It is therefore safe to say that without Aristotle's goatsucker, Puerto Rico's simply would not have taken its current form.

Notes

[1] Benjamin Radford, *Tracking the Chupacabra: The Vampire Beast in Fact, Fiction, and Folklore* (University of New Mexico Press, 2011).

[2] *History of Animals* 21.2, translated by Richard Cresswell.

[3] *Natural History* 10.56, translated by John Bostock and H. T. Riley.

[4] Radford, *Tracking the Chupacabra*, 4.

[5] Otto Springer, review of *Arv. Tidskrift for nordisk folkminnesforskning*, *Journal of American Folklore* 60 (1947): 431.

[6] *Fasti* 6.131ff., translated by James George Frazer.

[7] Referring to the vampire bat: "At sundown the vampires, bats, and goatsuckers dart from their lonely retreat, and skim along the trees on the river's bank." So said Charles Waterton in his 1825 travelogue *Wanderings in South America, the North-West of the United States, and the Antilles in the Years 1812, 1816, 1820, and 1824* (London: B. Fellowes, 1836), 11. The vampire (bat) Waterton refers to derived its name from the preexisting Slavic myth of the (human) vampire; thus, the supernatural vampire, the vampire bat, and the nightjar were all seen as similar bloodsucking nocturnal creatures. Waterton also compares the goatsucker's plumage to that of the owl, reinforcing their frequent association.

[8] L.D. Arnett, "The Soul," *American Journal of Psychology* 15, no. 2 (1904): 145.

[9] Claude Lévi-Strauss, *The Jealous Potter*, trans. Bénédicte Chorier (Chicago: University of Chicago Press, 1988), chapter 3. Lévi-Strauss also notes that the Spanish for goatsucker was *chotacabra*.

40. Investigating Graham Hancock's 7,000-Year-Old Mexican Pyramid

O NE OF THE MOST memorable factoids in Graham Hancock's *Finger-prints of the Gods* (1995) is his claim that a circular pyramid just south of Mexico City is more than 7,000 years old, and probably 8,500 years old.[1] It certainly made an impression on me when I read the book back in 1996, and I always wanted to know more. It was a challenge though. The pyramid is named Cuicuilco, but Hancock won't tell you that for reasons that will become clear later. According to Hancock, archaeologist Byron S. Cummings excavated the pyramid in the 1920s and discovered that it was buried beneath a layer of lava that geologists of the era dated to between 7,000 and 8,500 years ago. The pyramid, Cummings claimed, was the "oldest temple" in the Americas since any structure beneath the lava flow must be older than the eruption that buried it.

If true, this would be the best hard evidence ever found for Hancock's imaginary lost civilization, which he believes spread around the world at the end of the last ice age. So, it was somewhat surprising to me when I first read *Fingerprints* that Hancock declined the opportunity to further investigate this hard evidence in order to provide proof positive of his lost civilization. Why did he stick with soft claims about myths and stellar alignments when the geologic proof was staring him the face? How could science have missed a 7,000-year-old lava flow that spread, according to Hancock, over more than sixty square miles?

In fact, Cuicuilco *is* the oldest pyramid in Mexico. But it dates back to 900 BCE, not 7,000 or more years ago. So, Hancock is partly right. But here's the kicker: The lava that covered the pyramid came from an eruption that occurred between 300 and 400 CE. When Byron S. Cummings excavated in the 1920s, he did not have access to modern dating techniques. His outdated estimate (discussed below) cannot be relied upon in light of modern, more accurate dating. This same volcanic flow buried the nearby Copilco site, which radiocarbon dates place in the Preclassic period—about 5,000 years too late for Hancock's faulty estimate.

Hancock claims Cuicuilco has been "ignored by historians and archaeologists, who do not believe that any civilization capable of building a pyramid could have existed in Mexico at such an early date."[2] This site was so completely ignored, in fact, that archaeologist only excavated at the site in the 1920s, 1955, and most of the 1990s. All of these archaeological investigations must therefore have been part of a vast conspiracy to hide evidence of a lost civilization, or else Hancock is wrong. As it turns out, Hancock's claims about the pyramid were second- or third-hand. His source was Charles Hapgood's notorious *Maps of the Ancient Sea-Kings* (1966), a work of colossal pseudoscience. Hapgood carefully noted that the geologists who investigated the site estimated the age of the site by estimating how long it would take for the sediment atop it to gradually pile up. But Hapgood notes that this method is flawed and that early radiocarbon dates returned an age of 709 BCE to 414 CE, numbers Hancock fails to note in order to preserve the mystery.[3] Given that Hancock's own source understood the importance of the radiocarbon evidence, it is unconscionable that Hancock simply wished it away. Journalist that he was, Hancock should have understood the need to report the facts *at least* as fairly as Hapgood.

Hapgood attempted to rebut the radiocarbon dates with Cummings' 1920s reports about earlier culture layers dating back 2,000 years (c. 50 BCE) and 6,500 years (c. 4450 BCE), but modern research has shown that the site was first occupied around 1200 BCE with the first phase of building around 800 BCE. These occupations match Cummings' culture layers.

The discrepancy in dating is due to Cummings' use of highly inaccurate sediment deposit rate estimates to guess dates. Modern radiocarbon dates are much more exact.

It seems Hancock left out the name of the pyramid so it would be harder to look up the information that contradicts his claims about it. There is one last thing Hancock didn't tell his readers: Cuicuilco is open to the public. Anyone can go and visit and see for him- or herself the "evidence" for the 8,500-year-old pyramid. If there really was a conspiracy to suppress this site's true history, running tours to the place seems like a weird way of doing it.

Notes

[1] Graham Hancock, *Fingerprints of the Gods* (New York: Crown, 1996), 115.

[2] Ibid.

[3] Charles Hapgood, *Maps of the Ancient Sea-Kings* (Stele, Illinois: Adventures Unlimited Press, 1997), 199-200.

41. Atlantis, the Bible, and High Technology

I N MARCH 2011, the National Geographic Channel screened an hour-long documentary chronicling the efforts of Hartford University archaeologist Richard Freund to find the lost city of Atlantis. According to Freund, his research indicated Atlantis was located near Cadiz in southern Spain, and the city was destroyed by a tsunami. He also claimed to have found the actual archaeological remains of the lost city. The program, titled *Finding Atlantis*, presented a few intriguing finds and then spun those discoveries into a web of pseudoscience masquerading as science.[1] Nevertheless, the documentary created a media sensation due to the imprimatur of the National Geographic Society and the unfortunate timing of the program, airing just days after a tsunami devastated much of northern Japan following a 9.0 magnitude earthquake. Reporters were quick to accept the Atlantis claims and to draw parallels between the lost city and events in Japan. An article in *Newsweek* by Simon Winchester, the bestselling British author, uncritically proclaimed the find genuine and ranked Atlantis beside Pompeii on the list of great lost cities.[2]

Freund's claim was the latest in a long line of attempts to find a reality for the lost continent outside the imagination of its creator, the Greek philosopher Plato (c. 428-348 BCE), who invented the continent as an allegorical way of criticizing the civilization of contemporary Athens. No evidence for Atlantis has been found in any ancient material (writings, inscriptions, pottery, etc.) prior to Plato's dialogues the *Timaeus* and the

Critias (c. 360 BCE). This chapter will discuss what would be needed to prove the existence of Atlantis, and then it will evaluate Prof. Freund's claims, followed by a discussion of two other improbably claims about ancient Greek mythology. First, this chapter will review an attempt to link the Atlantis story and Greek myth to a fringe belief that the planet Venus nearly destroyed earth in prehistory, and then it will examine a scholarly publication claiming that Homer's epic poems prove the existence of advanced robotics and hydrofoil naval technology in the Mycenaean age.

Proving Atlantis

To begin thinking critically about the media circus surrounding Robert Freund's claim that Atlantis had been found in Spain, let's first consider how one would prove that a new discovery was "really" Atlantis. It isn't as simple as finding an ancient site and then trying to match it to Plato's description, no matter how loosely one interprets Plato's texts (composed c. 360 BCE).

A major hurdle is proposing a plausible method of transmission whereby knowledge of a given site can be retained and communicated through the centuries. How would Plato have known the details of whatever archaeological remains you've dug up? In his dialogues, Plato claims that his knowledge of Atlantis derives from an ancient Athenian statesman named Solon, who lived three centuries earlier and who got his information in turn from the Egyptians. If we take this at face value, we would need to prove a relationship between Egypt and the unnamed site prior to the age of Solon (638-538 BCE) *and* Egyptian knowledge of the site's layout, politics, internal organization, and destruction. We would *also* need to prove how and where Solon's information was retained and communicated for roughly three centuries between him and Plato. Needless to say, there is not a single scrap of evidence—no statue, no vase painting, no inscription, no papyrus fragment, no wall painting—nothing that indicates Egyptian or Greek knowledge of anything like Atlantis prior to 360 BCE.

Contrast this with an actual documented instance of historical memory. In the *Iliad* (c. eighth century BCE), Homer records the story of

Troy, long believed to have been a legendary city as mythical as Atlantis. But Homer included bits of genuine Bronze Age information, including references to a helmet made of boar's tusks[3] that was used only in the Mycenaean Age (prior to 1200 BCE), which indicated a core of genuine history underneath layers of myth. (Plato's Atlantis story contains no Bronze Age or earlier details.) The Greeks, however, lived among the ruins of the Mycenaean Age but knew so little of that time that they assumed the ruins were the work of giants called Cyclopes[4] and they thought the men of that era demigods. These same people who believed giants built their ancestors' homes somehow retained street-level knowledge of Atlantis but not their own cities?

Homer's geographic information (indirectly) led the German explorer Heinrich Schliemann to a site in Turkey where he found a city that has been identified as the site of Troy.[5] However, Homer's information was not perfectly accurate, but rather highly distorted, the result of imperfect transmission across centuries, contaminated with error and more recent information.

But this is not all the ancient evidence. Homer was not alone in mentioning Troy—an entire series of myths and epics (known as the Epic Cycle) by many hands recorded parts of its story, as did vase paintings. We also have Bronze Age Hittite records (c. 1250 BCE) recording interactions with Wilusa (another name for Ilion, or Troy) as well as hostility between Wilusa and a group called the Ahhiyawa, identified as the Achaeans (Greeks) of Homer's *Iliad*. The Hittite records confirm that a ruler named Alaksandu once reigned in Troy, just as in Homer the son of Troy's king is Alexander (also called Paris). Alaksandu worshipped the god Apaliunas, identified as Apollo, the god who protected Troy and Paris-Alexander in the *Iliad*. These identifications, while somewhat controversial, are accepted by the majority of scholars as indicating Hittite knowledge of Troy.

In this case, we have contemporary records, an archaeological site, and later Greek recollections of genuine Bronze Age material. These many strands work together to tell us that the site Schliemann found in Turkey is the place known as Troy. What do we have to support claims for Atlantis? We have Plato's (fictional) dialogues, and nothing else. The Egyptians, who recorded interactions with ancient peoples ranging from the Minoans and the Mycenaeans to envoys from the Near East, are silent about Atlanteans. The Greeks included Atlantis in no myths, legends, or epics. Nearly every ancient city that was genuinely prominent in the Bronze Age has myths associated with it, even if that city ceased to exist in later ages, as Martin Nilsson explained in his classic *The Mycenaean Origins of Greek Mythology* back in 1932. But somehow Atlantis got left out. Even many ancient authors themselves were fairly certain Plato made it all up.

In absence of any evidence outside of Plato for Greek knowledge of Atlantis, and in the absence of any plausible way for the Greeks (or even the Egyptians) to have known about the destruction of Atlantis, or proof that they did, we must conclude that Atlantis was what Plato meant it to be: a fictional double for Athens.

Atlantis in Spain?

With this information, what can we say about claims that Atlantis was found in Spain?

Richard Freund, who previously appeared in a 2004 *Nova* special where he identified artifacts found in Israel as part of the legendary Temple treasure lost after the Roman invasion of Jerusalem, argued that a site on the southern coast of Spain near the city of Cadiz is Plato's Atlantis as well as the biblical city of Tarshish, a trading center mentioned briefly in the books of Chronicles, Kings, and elsewhere. The theory itself is not new. E. M. Whishaw proposed the theory in a 1928 book, *Atlantis in Andalusia*, including an identification of Plato's city with the ancient port of Tartessos and thus the biblical city of Tarshish. Tartessos was an ancient civilization of the first millennium BCE widely discussed in antiquity and whose cultural area is known archaeologically as spreading throughout southern Spain. Richard Freund merely adopted the Spanish Atlantis theory wholesale, but unlike Whishaw, backed it up with an allegedly new archeological discovery. Freund claimed that the Spanish site near Cadiz conforms to Plato's description of Atlantis because geophysical scans indicate that the city stood on an island surrounded by water, as Plato described. Nevertheless, epistemological and logical problems remain.

Plato, however, said Atlantis was "larger than Libya and Asia together" (the buried island Freund advocates is nowhere near that large), and composed of several concentric rings with artificial canals connecting the rings of land in a riparian system (again, the Spanish site has not been proven to match). Finally, Plato claimed that the island was destroyed by an earthquake 9,000 years before Plato's time (c. 9,400 BCE). Again, the Spanish site does not match. Initial radiocarbon dates place it anywhere from 5,000 to 2,400 years old.

Nevertheless, Freund argued that the circular shape of the site and the fact that it was possibly destroyed by a tsunami proved that the site was the legendary Atlantis, and he repeatedly emphasized how close the match was—close if you agree to change the facts that Plato wrote to "more plausible" versions. Doing so, of course, means that Freund is free to reconstruct an imaginary Atlantis of his own devising, one which is very different from Plato's but which he can imaginatively recreate to match anything he happened to find on the ground.

Especially ludicrous is his attempt to explain a carving of a warrior holding a sword and a shield as a soldier "guarding" an aerial map of Atlantis, claiming the circular shield with its pattern of concentric circles, so very similar to other ancient shields, was really a 2,000-year-old remembered tradition of the layout of Atlantis! This in an age that did *not* make any other aerial maps! Earlier, Freund and his team were giddy with excitement after finding geometric-shaped rocks that they thought were the walls of Atlantis. They were completely natural in formation, but still Freund counted them as "evidence" on the grounds that Atlanteans "might" have built walls with them anyway—underwater, apparently, since they formed beneath the ocean.

There is no doubt, of course, that there is a real archaeological site buried in southern Spain. What it is exactly, we just don't know. However, let us give Freund the benefit of the doubt and agree that everything he claims about its age and layout are true. What does this tell us? Nothing, actually. Freund can propose no method by which this fallen city is somehow remembered in street-level detail from Spain to Egypt to Greece over the course of thousands upon thousands of years without leaving a single trace in the records of Egypt or Greece or anywhere else. Not a single inscription, or papyrus, or statue, or vase painting. Nothing at all from 5,000 BCE until 360 BCE when Plato wrote the *Timaeus* and the *Critias*, the first ever mention of Atlantis. By this standard, we must take the Cyclopes, the *Odyssey*, the Underworld, and the Golden Fleece as true people and events, too, since they are amply better documented in the ancient record. Or, alternately, we must seek out Thomas More's Utopia.

Most disturbing, I think, was Freund's attempt to argue that Atlantis was really the biblical city of Tarshish. This is the entirety of what is known of Tarshish: "every three years once came the ships of Tarshish bringing gold, and silver, ivory, and apes, and peacocks."[6] Obviously, Freund said, this is Atlantis because both Tarshish and Atlantis dealt in "metals," the only ancient cities, he said, to do so. This is patently false, since other ancient sites, like Colchis on the Black Sea, were famous for their metalworking. Incidentally, southern Spain boasts neither apes (native to sub-Saharan Africa), nor peacocks (native to India and parts of sub-Saharan Africa), nor ivory (Africa again). This kind of Bible-mongering serves little purpose except to try to rope in Atlantis as confirmation of the Bible's literal truth—something Freund inadvertently emphasized when using biblical terminology such as the "holy of holies" to describe decidedly non-Hebrew sites. It is no coincidence that Richard Freund's specialty is biblical archaeology and Judaic studies, not Classical, Bronze Age, or Neolithic archaeology.

But let us grant him his point and pretend that Atlantis is Tarshish. If this is true, then we have a contradiction. Tarshish traded with the Israelites during the reign of Solomon, traditionally around the tenth century BCE. This is thousands of years after Plato's Atlantis sunk beneath the waves (9400 BCE), and at least a thousand years off from the proposed dates when the Spanish site was destroyed (possibly c. 2000 BCE). Never mind that the books of Chronicles and Kings were likely composed no earlier than 560 BCE, at which time Tarshish must still have been an active port—one still in operation when Jonah tried to sail there in the Book of Jonah (composed c. 500 BCE).[7] So Tarshish and Atlantis, like Schrödinger's cat, both exist and do not exist, are active and destroyed, simultaneously. The only way to make the two into one is to change Plato, and once you change Plato you are no longer looking for "Atlantis" but are instead naming whatever you find in honor of Plato's fictional allegory.

Apparently Freund dropped into an active Spanish archaeological investigation into an actual ancient city, ongoing since 2005, and has hijacked it to generate publicity for his research into the connection between Solomon and Atlantis to prove the Bible true. Here is what the Spanish anthropologist Juan Villarias-Robles told the *Telegraph* newspaper about Freund:

> Richard Freund was a newcomer to our project and appeared to be involved in his own very controversial issue concerning King Solomon's search for ivory and gold in Tartessos, the well documented settlement in the Donaña area established in the first millennium BC. He became involved in what we were doing and provided funding for probes through his connections with National Geographic and Associated Producers. He left and the film company told us the documentary would be finished in April or May. But we did not hear from him and are very surprised it has appeared so soon and makes such fanciful claims.[8]

But Freund was not the only one making fanciful claims about Atlantis and ancient Greece in early 2011, or even the only one to use such claims to further an agenda to prove the Bible true. Two books released within weeks of each other in early 2011 both tried to make the case for a lost, advanced civilization lurking behind the stately façade of ancient Greece.

Atlantis and Catastrophism

On February 25, 2011, Washington, D.C.'s conservative daily, *The Washington Times*, devoted an unusual amount of space to a work of pseudoscience from Algora Publishing, a small press that distributes a number of books on "alternative" archaeology. The paper is not known for its coverage of archaeology, nor as a champion of small press literature. This was a highly unusual review. Fox News columnist Martin Sieff guest-wrote a lengthy review of Emmett Sweeney's newly-published *Atlantis: The Evidence from Science* (2010), praising the book for its evenhanded exploration of the science supporting claims that Atlantis really existed.[9] This review, however, seemed to reflect a hidden anti-science, perhaps even creationist, agenda.

Sweeney is the author of a number of volumes defending the work of Immanuel Velikovsky, the twentieth century writer who claimed that the planet Venus was really a comet that swung by earth in prehistory, influencing the course of civilization when it parted the Red Sea, destroyed Minoan civilization, and what-have-you. According to Velikovsky and Sweeney, earth's history has been grossly distorted by historians and must be set right. Velikovsky, whom Sweeney follows, claimed that the Dark Age between the Mycenaean era and Archaic Greece (the period from 1200 BCE to 800 BCE) did not exist and was the creation of close-minded scholars. By happy coincidence, if one accepts Velikovsky's claims, the historical chronology given in the Bible could be reconciled with Egyptian king lists and records, thus proving that the Bible was literally true.

None of this was discussed in Sieff's *Washington Times* review, which instead attempted to give legitimacy to Sweeney's catastrophism by giving a foothold to his work on Atlantis. At no time did Sieff discuss a troubling conflict of interest: Sieff was a founding member of the pro-Velikovsky group, the Society for Interdisciplinary Studies, a former editor of its magazine, and an active proponent of catastrophism. He wrote more than two dozen articles in support of catastrophism, some as late as the 1990s.[10] By hiding Sweeney's connection to Velikovsky, as well as his own, Sieff played the part of the disinterested journalist, legitimizing an ideological agenda in the guise of journalism.

Sieff even went beyond Sweeney to argue that a "sophisticated global, seafaring civilization certainly existed in the geological conditions before the last ice age."[11] He based this claim on the work of Charles Hapgood, a professor who misread ancient maps in the mid-twentieth century and imagined that they showed Antarctica, not officially discovered until 1818. These maps were supposedly so accurate only a sophisticated global culture could have made them; however, repeated debunkings over the past fifty years demonstrated conclusively that Hapgood was wrong, a fact even Hapgood seemed to acknowledge before his death.[12]

That Sieff relies on discredited and false evidence to support a radical rewriting of ancient history is no surprise; everyone who supports "alternative" archaeology does so at some point. What is extremely surprising is that the *Washington Times* ran this bit of rank pseudoscience. Here, it seems that a hidden agenda was at work. As noted above, acceptance of Atlantis was seen as a stepping stone to legitimizing Velikovskian theories, or at the very least, delegitimizing secular archaeology. Once the accepted, secular story of cultural evolution has been questioned, creationist theories become that much easier to put on par with actual science.

Given that the *Washington Times* is a known outlet for conservative attacks on science, as well as for the views of its owner, the Unification Church founded by the Rev. Sun Myung Moon, the entire affair seems to be of a piece—covertly attempting to subvert science in the name of dogma—catastrophist, religious, or otherwise.

Ancient Greece and Advanced Technology

A much more serious and supposedly scholarly claim about ancient Greece and its exotic mysteries came this time from modern Greece itself. Greek mechanical engineer S. A. Paipetis's *The Unknown Technology in Homer* (2005) was translated into English and released in 2010. The book purported to be a mechanical engineer's evaluation of extraordinary and precocious technological knowledge embedded in Homer's *Iliad* and *Odyssey*, two of the foundational texts of the Western, tradition composed sometime around the eight century BCE. According to the author, this anomalous knowledge demonstrates that the Mycenaeans, the ancient people of whom Homer's poems sang, had advanced modern technology c. 1600-1200 BCE.[13] The volume was published under the aegis of the academic publisher Springer's *History of Mechanism and Machine Science* series, making it a somewhat higher grade of pseudoscience pretending toward legitimacy, but pseudoscience nonetheless.

The first third of the book is an incoherent set of digressions, most of which have no bearing on the subject of ancient technology. Instead, we are treated to works of Renaissance and modern art and discussions of the Greek-revival-style vacation house built by the Austro-Hungarian empress Elisabeth, whose nickname is embarrassingly mistranslated as "Sissy" instead of "Sisi." What does the existence of a nineteenth century vacation house have to do with Mycenaean technology? Unfortunately, this tendency toward digression and irrelevancy mars an already short book (two hundred pages) with more than fifty pages of padding. Worse still, the translation from the author's original (modern) Greek to English is stilted and awkward, with innumerable mistakes of grammar and spelling that are by turn humorous or obfuscating.

The author demonstrates a clear ignorance of the ancient material he purports to analyze. In Chapter 11, he follows a long-disproved idea that the so-called *Orphic Argonautica* (c. 450 CE) predated the *Odyssey* (c. 700 BCE).[14] Earlier, the author assumes that the river Acheron in Epirus is the actual river Acheron flowing through Hades and to which Odysseus sails.[15] While later Greeks identified the two, the location of the physical Acheron in western Greece hardly matches the description of the infernal Acheron flowing at the ends of the Ocean. His discussions of Greek mythology are everywhere tinged with a non-specialist's over-simplification and ignorance of contemporary work in the field, especially complications and controversies that would undermine his simple thesis.

Relying on long-outdated studies of Greek myth and history (including the early twentieth-century work of Arthur Evans and the Depression-era studies of Martin Nilsson, largely to the exclusion of any modern work), Paipetis builds a house of cards whereby the presumption that the Mycenaeans had advanced technology leads him to interpret mythological events as technological descriptions, thus "proving" the existence of the technology. One example can stand for them all. In discussing Odysseus' passage between Scylla and Charybdis, the author assumes that the description records a Greek discourse on the physics of vortexes. Thus, Homer's phrase (in Paipetis's translation) "drive ship by as fast as you can"[16] should, in the author's words, be interpreted to mean "move fast, to account [for] speed loss due to friction and remain in course instead of diving to the bottom."[17] This he compares to the "gravitational sling" used by NASA to launch spacecraft out of the solar system by utilizing Jupiter's gravitational force. However, the "friction" is the author's own interpolation (it's not in the original), a scientific term hardly necessary for the Greeks to understand the concept of going fast to escape from a whirlpool.

The author also believes that Homer's descriptions of the automata built by the smith-god Hephaestus[18] represent descriptions of real robots with artificial intelligence. However, it has long been known that the ancients had mechanical or clockwork animals. The Byzantine emperors were particularly famous for their mechanical lions and birds. A poetic exaggeration of these real-life marvels is likely all that lies behind Hephaestus's "robots," with no naïvely literal reading of the *Odyssey* or speculation about ancient electricity necessary. (The author backtracks some and does state that electricity and computing technology are not "known to be" available to run the robots.[19])

The author's claim that an invisible net used by the god Hephaestus in the *Odyssey* to capture Ares and Aphrodite[20] is evidence of manmade Kevlar or a related material is simply ridiculous:

> Such materials are rather modern technological achievements, e.g., glass and carbon fibres, or even organic fibres such as Kevlar. If such materials were available in Homer's era, undoubtedly that civilization was marked by this highly developed technology.[21]

His identification of the boats belonging to a people called the Phaecians as "probably a high speed jet hydrofoil" is laughable.[22] Homer sang that the Phaecians' boats had no pilots but sailed according to projected thoughts.[23] There is no reason to imagine magical boats as a thousand-year memory of Mycenaean-era technology if the only evidence for their existence is Homer's own poem, a poem filled with all sorts of magic that no appeal to technology could ever sufficiently explain.

That this study was published by Springer (albeit in the mechanics rather than classics arena) has given it a false legitimacy that may deceive the unwary into assuming that this is a scholarly work on Greek history. Instead, it is a work of rank speculation masquerading as science, using false analogies and wishful thinking to recreate a lost world that never was. In our next chapter, we will look at another work of pseudoscience that since the 1970s has used the trappings of academic scholarship to give a false legitimacy to claims that Greek mythology records encounters with extraterrestrial beings.

Notes

[1] *Finding Atlantis*, National Geographic Channel (March 13, 2011).

[2] Simon Winchester, "Swallowed by the Sea," *Newsweek*, April 4, 2011 and *The Daily Beast* [online], March 20, 2011.

[3] *Iliad* 10:260-5. See note 6 on p. 63 for text.

[4] "The wall, which is the only part of the ruins still remaining, is a work of the Cyclopes made of unwrought stones, each stone being so big that a pair of mules could not move the smallest from its place to the slightest degree." (Pausanias, *Description of Greece*, 2.25.8, translated by W. H. S. Jones and H. A. Omerod.)

[5] It was actually a Scot named Charles Maclaren who used Homer and other Greek authors to propose a location for Troy. Schliemann claimed credit for the method when another man, Frank Calvert, made a discovery he attributed to Troy and let Schliemann in on the dig. Schliemann was nothing if not good at self-promotion.

[6] 2 Chronicles 9:21 (= 1 Kings 10:22).

[7] Jonah 1:3.

[8] Edward Owen, "Lost City of Atlantis 'Buried in Spanish Wetlands,'" *The Telegraph* [online], March 14, 2011.

[9] Martin Sieff, "Book Review: 'Atlantis,'" *The Washington Times* [online], February 25, 2011.

[10] "Martin Sieff," *The Velikovsky Encyclopedia* [online], April 11, 2009.

[11] Sieff, "Book Review."

[12] Ronald H. Fritze, *Invented Knowledge: False History, Fake Science and Pseudo-religions* (London: Reaktion Books, 2009), 193-201.

[13] S. A. Paipetis, *The Unknown Technology in Homer*, History of Mechanism and Machine Science, Vol. 9 (Dordecht: Springer, 2010).

[14] Ibid., 83.

[15] Ibid., 46.

[16] The author is oddly translating ungrammatically a phrase from Odyssey 12.109, which he misidentifies as 7.103-106, in which Circe advises Odysseus, in standard translation, to "drive thy ship past quickly."

[17] Ibid., 88.

[18] Odyssey 7.91ff.

[19] Paipetis, *The Unknown Technology in Homer*, 111.

[20] *Odyssey* 8.266-366.

[21] Paipetis, *The Unknown Technology in Homer*, 104.

[22] Ibid., 117.

[23] *Odyssey* 7.555-563, 13.76-92.

42. Golden Fleeced

ROBERT TEMPLE'S *The Sirius Mystery* (1976) is one of the most important works in the ancient astronaut genre. It has been fairly well-established that Temple's thesis about extraterrestrial visitation has little basis in fact. Temple had claimed that an African tribe called the Dogon had sophisticated knowledge of the invisible companion to the star Sirius, known to modern astronomers as Sirius B, and that this knowledge derived from amphibious aliens that descended to earth in ancient Sumeria thousands of years ago and were worshipped as gods. Their possession of esoteric knowledge of deep space unknown in the West until the nineteenth century is taken as proof of extraterrestrial contact.

Though anthropologists failed to find a genuine Sirius B tradition among the Dogon outside what they had gleaned from recent contact with Europeans,[1] and skeptics refuted Temple's extraterrestrial conclusions, *The Sirius Mystery* continues to serve as a standard reference work in the New Age and alternative archaeology movements. In recent years alone, works such as Christopher Penczak's *Ascension Magick* (2007), R. M. Decker's *35 Minutes to Mars* (2004), and Stephen S. Mehler's *The Land of Osiris* (2002) utilize Temple's book to a greater or lesser extent to support their alternative and New Age claims.[2] The internet, too, is a hotbed of Temple-derived Sirius theories. And, of course, Temple continues to publish books of alternative archaeology, including *The Sphinx Mystery* (2009).[3] Therefore, renewed study of *The Sirius Mystery* is no moot point but an inquiry into an active and important touchstone for the alternative movement.

It is not my intention to review the case against Temple's space-faring fish-men and their watery revelations. Such work has already been done, exhaustively, and, to most skeptics' minds, conclusively.[4] Instead, I would like to explore Robert Temple's misuse of Greek mythology, specifically the myth of Jason and the Argonauts, to refute frequently repeated claims that, even if one doubts his most outrageous conclusions, Temple is "scholarly, careful, and scientifically honest."[5] Temple is frequently described as a "recognized scholar"[6] or even as a "preeminent scholar of mathematics, astronomy and mythology"[7] by proponents of alternative claims, and Temple himself cites his membership in the Royal Astronomical Society[8] and several classicist organizations to bolster *Sirius*'s claims to scholarship. An examination of the case of *Temple v. Jason* will demonstrate that claims for Temple's *Sirius* scholarship are less solid than the case for the alleged aliens themselves.

Of Aliens and Argonauts

In *Sirius*, Temple makes a number of claims about Greek mythology in general and the story of Jason in particular, which he sees as a governing myth tying together all the threads of his Sirius mystery. Temple uses Jason's legendary journey as a starting point for his forays into Greek, Egyptian, and Near Eastern mythology, and there is the strong impression that he views Jason's quest for the Golden Fleece as parallel to his own search for the extraterrestrial secrets of the flying space frogs. For him, the Jason story is the one Greek myth most closely related to an esoteric tradition of alien-derived knowledge of the true nature of the binary Sirius star system—and he even views the Argonauts as the biological ancestors of the Dogon. In order to understand the scaffolding on which Temple builds his mythological claims, let us briefly review Jason's story as it has come down to us.

Jason was the son of Aeson, deposed king of Iolcus and rightful heir to the throne held by his usurping uncle Pelias. Pelias promised to restore the kingdom to Jason on condition that Jason bring the Golden Fleece from the kingdom of Colchis back to Iolcus, a quest Pelias is sure will end in

Jason's death. Jason therefore assembles fifty companions (originally un-named but later associated with the greatest Greek heroes) on the ship *Argo* and sails to Colchis, experiencing many adventures. In Colchis, Jason fails to persuade its king to give him the fleece, and he instead steals it from the dragon that guards it with the help of the king's daughter, the sorceress Medea, on condition that Jason marry her. Jason has many more adventures on the way back to Iolcus, where he presents the fleece and deposes his uncle. He then betrays Medea's love, loses the favor of the gods, and dies when a piece of the dry-docked *Argo* falls on his head.

The Jason story is cited elliptically in Homer (usually dated to c. 8th century BCE), briefly in Hesiod's *Theogony* (c. 700 BCE), and is most fully developed in Pindar's Fourth Pythian Ode (462 BCE) and Apollonius of Rhodes's *Argonautica* (c. 245 BCE). Jason also appears in some early Greek and Etruscan art, but, intriguingly, some of these images show a different version of the legend, unrecorded in the surviving poems, in which Jason apparently descends into the dragon's stomach and reemerges, aided by the goddess Athena rather than Medea.[9] Informed scholarly conjecture is that the primal Jason legend dates to Mycenaean times (c. 1500 BCE) and originally featured a voyage to the end of the world (rather than specifi-cally Colchis) to retrieve the fleece via a descent into the guardian drag-on's stomach and a triumph over death. It is possible Jason was dismem-bered and resurrected through Athena's ministrations or his own super-natural healing powers.[10] Medea may be a later addition to the original quest tale, though she must have appeared before 700 BCE, as she is in Hesiod. Such history is not considered in *Sirius*, despite at least two centu-ries of scholarly discussion about it.

For Temple, the Jason myth is much more than an adventure. His views on Jason are somewhat difficult to follow, scattered as they are through *Sirius*, but the abridged version runs like this:

Jason and the fifty Argonauts represent Sirius A (the main star we see in the sky) and the fifty-year period it takes Sirius B (the hidden compan-ion star) to travel around Sirius A. The *Argo*, their boat, is the system tak-en as a whole with its fifty oars representing each year of Sirius B's orbit.[11]

In this, the Argonauts are therefore the equivalent of the Annunaki, the fifty anonymous gods of Sumer (remember the Argonauts were originally unnamed), who therefore are also symbols for Sirius B's fifty-year orbit.[12] Jason, whose name Temple believes means "appeaser," is a feckless wimp who usurped his position in a myth-cycle that originally centered on the epic voyage of Herakles (Hercules),[13] who in turn is a later remolding of a still-earlier mythological figure, Briareus, one of the hundred-handed, fifty-headed monsters who assaulted Olympus and were imprisoned in Tartarus. Therefore, Temple concludes, Briareus was the original captain of the *Argo*.[14] Confusingly, and perhaps in partial contradiction, Jason is also identified as a version of the Sumerian hero Gilgamesh, primarily on the basis of both having fifty companions and many adventures.[15]

From this framework, Temple then branches out into increasingly fanciful excursions that are beyond the scope of this article.

Since Temple's defenders frequently cite his deep scholarship and thorough understanding of mythology and ancient history, it is only fair to ask how scholarly Temple's mythological framework is. We can begin by dispensing with one point easily enough. The "feckless" Jason was the creation of Apollonius of Rhodes, who was writing in the Hellenistic period, five or six hundred years after the Homeric age of epic poetry, and a full millennium after the Jason tale may have originated in Mycenaean Greece. Apollonius purposely recast the hero as a vulnerable but brave human in keeping with the tastes and values of the era.[16] Since this is a late development, it can have no bearing on the original myth or its supposed extraterrestrial antecedents. Similarly, I can find no support for Temple's view that Jason's name means "appeaser," as nearly every scholarly source derives his name from the Greek word "to heal."[17] Temple provides no citation beyond his own assertion, and I am unable to determine his reasoning for his claim.

Jason and the Secrets of the Space Frogs

These minor points safely dispensed with, we can move on to the meat of Temple's Jason argument. Let us begin by asking on what grounds

Temple identifies Jason as Herakles and Herakles as Briareus and/or Gilgamesh. Here, fortunately, Temple has made our job easy. In all these cases, the source of his identifications (and, indeed, it appears the entirety of his knowledge of Greek myth) is Robert Graves's *The Greek Myths* (1955), which he explicitly cites. Graves identifies Jason and Herakles thus: "Jason and Herakles are, in fact, the same character so far as the marriage-task myth is concerned ... Jason was, of course, a title of Herakles."[18] Here Graves argues that both stories reflect tasks associated with sacred kingship, and that Herakles at one point bore the title of a Jason (i.e., "healer," a meaning Temple previously rejected). This is not exactly the same as saying that Herakles captained the Argo, and Temple appears to go farther than Graves on this point.

Similarly thin is the ground uniting Herakles and Briareus. Graves holds that the Pillars of Herakles were once associated with Briareus and later assigned to Herakles after the Briareus myth "faded from memory," though he does say (without evidence or explanation) that the earliest Herakles was named Briareus.[19] Temple's troubles are compounded when we discover that Graves identifies Herakles directly with Gilgamesh[20] without the need for Briareus or reference to the Argonauts. Worse, Graves specifically identifies Achilles as another Gilgamesh "variant," and he cites the older myth of Jason's descent into the dragon's stomach (one Temple ignores) as related to the Bible's tale of Jonah and the whale, Jonah being cited as synonymous with Marduk, the Babylonian god!

As the reader may have guessed, Graves, who was a poet and novelist rather than an academic, had a particular and penchant for finding fanciful correspondences between mythological characters and for imposing his idiosyncratic views on the Greek myths. Immediately upon publication of *The Greek Myths* reviewers attacked Graves for his "defective scholarship"[21] for which there was "no conceivable evidence" to support his "inaccuracies, evasions, improbable analogies, and amateur etymologies."[22] In short, his scholarship was not to be trusted, and no reputable scholar would use Graves's theories without copious documentary support, which is not to be found in *The Sirius Mystery*. However, Temple sees Graves as "invaluable" and "superb."[23]

For Robert Temple to rely on Graves's book not just as a convenient secondary reference for Greek myths but as the foundation for his understanding of mythology and the interrelationship of myths to one another is simply unsupportable. Even when Temple began writing *The Sirius Mystery* in 1967, Graves's missteps were well-known; by the time of the 1998 revision of *Sirius,* continued reliance on these erroneous interpretations was inexcusable.

There is a further complication here for Temple's theory. Given the vast period of time over which the Jason myth was told and retold, from the Bronze Age to late versions written under the Roman Empire, it would stand to reason that prehistoric Sirius lore should best be preserved in the *oldest* versions of and allusions to the myth, those closest in time to the aliens and their teachings. But Temple does not consider this and instead takes Graves's version as "standard" (minus the apparently interchangeable heroes). All this on top of the fact that *Graves himself warns that older Argonaut stories were nothing like the story from the Hellenistic age!*[24]

Other than a superficial swipe at Herakles' and Orpheus' appearance in Apollonius, Temple makes no attempt to separate late interpolations from older traditions, thus presenting every scrap of legend from 1500 BCE to 250 BCE as part of one unified Sirius-Jason complex, as though the myth were unchanged in its details for a thousand years. This would be the equivalent of trying to study early medieval Britain using only Tennyson's *Idylls of the King* (1856-1885) and a rough idea that King Arthur lived in the Dark Ages. Obviously, one cannot claim on the basis of a modern retelling of a late version of a myth that an African tribe is the flesh-and-blood descendants of these mythic heroes.

At this point, it should go without saying that any direct relationship between Jason's fifty oarsmen and the "fifty" Anunnaki is entirely speculative. While the Anunnaki may occasionally be referred to as fifty in number (though Temple gives no source for this), their numbers vary in myth. The Babylonians, for example, considered them to be three hundred in number.[25] However, to give the devil his due, Gilgamesh *did* have fifty companions in the earliest versions of his myth (c. 2000 BCE), though these were left out of the later versions of the first and second millenniums BCE, the versions current when the Jason myth was promulgated and eventually recorded. However, as half of one hundred, fifty was an exceedingly common number in mythology, and unless we choose to read all reference to fifty as Sirius lore, there needs to be something more than linguistic convenience to justify such an interpretation of a rather standard poetic number.[26]

Conclusions

I hope this review of Temple's misuse ancient myth in *The Sirius Mystery* has accomplished two things: first, to demonstrate that an author who cannot be trusted in big things (the truth of extraterrestrial visitation) cannot be trusted in small things either; and second, to put to rest the persistent myth that even if one does not support Temple's conclusions about intelligent space-faring frogmen that his scholarship and erudition are still an important contribution to the study of ancient mythology and history.

There is a bit of poetic irony in all this, too. Robert Temple's knowledge of Jason and the Argonauts, and the story's history and development, seems to derive entirely from Robert Graves and his *Greek Myths*. Temple does not directly cite the Jason tales of Hesiod, Pindar, and Apollonius, the ancient authors from whom we derive our knowledge of the myth.[27] Had he done so, he might just have noticed a curious passage in Apollonius, who describes Medea's first glimpse of Jason at their clandestine meeting in Hecate's temple: "[H]e appeared to her as she desired, like Sirius leaping high from Ocean...."[28] There you have it: Jason is Sirius! Of course, this is nothing but a bit of poetic simile, but its omission underscores just how poorly researched *The Sirius Mystery* really is, despite its hundreds of endnotes and reputation as the thinking person's ancient astronaut book.

Notes

[1] W. E. A. Van Beek, "Dogon Restudied: A Field Evaluation of the Work of Marcel Griaule," *Current Anthropology* 32, no. 2 (1991): 139-167.

[2] Christopher Penczak, *Ascension Magick* (Llewellyn Worldwide, 2007); R. M. Decker, *35 Minutes to Mars* (Galde Press, 2004); Stephen S. Mehler, *The Land of Osiris* (Adventures Unlimited, 2002).

[3] Robert Temple and Olivia Temple, *The Sphinx Mystery* (Inner Traditions, 2009).

[4] See bibliography in *The Skeptic's Dictionary* entry for the Dogon for a partial list of skeptical critiques and rebuttals.

[5] Robert Anton Wilson, *Right Where You Are Sitting Now: Further Tales of the Illuminati* (Ronin Publishing, 1992), 78.

[6] Judy Kennedy, *Beyond the Rainbow: Renewing the Cosmic Connection* (Buy Books, 2004), 149.

[7] Lawrence R. Spenser and Carol Lee South, *The Oz Factors:* The Wizard of Oz *as an Analogy to the Mysteries of Life* (Lulu, 1999), n.p.

[8] The RAS is "open to any person over the age of eighteen" with no formal qualifications or scholarly requirements, and membership does not imply the organization's official endorsement or support of its members' views (see "How to Join" at http://www.ras.org.uk/). The same applies to the Society for the Promotion of Hellenic Studies, the Egypt Exploration Society, and the Royal Historical Society, all of which Temple listed as affiliations in the 1998 revision of the *Sirius Mystery*.

[9] Temple reproduces (reversed) one such image in the 1998 revision of *Sirius* and identifies the female figure with Medea, despite the obvious armor, aegis, and owl (not, as Temple claims, an oracular dove), Athena's symbols. He also misidentifies Athena's Medusa-head breastplate as a "serpent" and her armor as dragon scales. Temple confesses ignorance of the image's meaning, implying that he neither recalled Graves's interpretation of this image nor researched the scholarly literature, which had discussed the image since at least the nineteenth century. In another plate (again mirror reversed), he misidentifies a standard scene of Medea magically resurrecting a ram as an alchemical transmutation of a ram into gold and Pelias as Jason, demonstrating his lack of familiarity with the scholarly literature and Greek mythology in general.

[10] David Sacks, Oswyn Murray, and Margaret Bunson, *A Dictionary of the Ancient Greek World* (New York: Oxford University Press, 1997),125; C. J. Mackie, "The Earliest Jason," *Greece and Rome* 48, no. 1 (2001), 1-17. In fact, Iolcus was a Mycenaean center with an extensive shipyard, which is perhaps why the Jason legend begins there.

[11] Robert Temple, *The Sirius Mystery: New Scientific Evidence of Alien Contact 5,000 Years Ago* (Rochester, Vermont: Destiny Books, 1999), 95-96.

[12] Ibid., 120.

[13] Ibid., 154, 156.

[14] Ibid., 220.

[15] Ibid., 118-119.

[16] Steven Jackson, "Apollonius' Jason: Human Being in an Epic Scenario," *Greece & Rome* 39, no. 2 (1992):155-162.

[17] Mackie, "Earliest Jason," 2. Mackie informs me that "appeaser" is "a very secondary etymology" that does not appear in the scholarly literature about Jason (personal communication, July 30, 2009).

[18] Robert Graves, *The Greek Myths* (New York: Penguin, 1993), 602.

[19] Ibid., 497.

[20] Ibid., 451.

[21] H. J. Rose, Review of *The Greek Myths* by Robert Graves, *The Classical Review* 5, no. 2 (1955): 208.

[22] J. Macpherson, Review of *The Greek Myths* by Robert Graves *Phoenix* 21, no. 1 (1958), 17.

[23] Temple, *Sirius Mystery*, 146.

[24] Graves, *Greek Myths*, 581.

[25] Patricia Turner and Charles Russell Coulter, *Dictionary of Ancient Deities* (New York: Oxford University Press, 2001), 59.

[26] Cf. the frequent ancient practice of using a round number like 1,000 or 10,000 as a synonym for an uncountable number (as we do with "zillions"), or the frequent appearance of triads and trinities in myth. Some numbers apparently are more poetic than others and need not refer to alien sky science.

[27] Temple includes these authors in his bibliography, but while his endnotes cite passages from Hesiod and Pindar, these are not passages related to the Argonauts, a striking omission given the admitted centrality of the Argonaut story to *The Sirius Mystery*. I was unable to find a single direct citation of Apollonius (or Hesiod's or Pindar's Jason tales) unmediated through Graves.

[28] Apollonius, *Argonautica* 3.956-957; translated by Richard Hunter in *Jason and the Golden Fleece* (Oxford: Oxford University Press, 1993), 88.

43. Who Lost the Middle Ages?

I N 1685, A FRENCH SCHOLAR by the name of Jean Hardouin published an edition of the Roman author Pliny's *Natural History*. Hardouin, however, had an unusual belief about its origins. He was convinced that all of the ancient records of Greece and Rome were forgeries perpetrated by Benedictine monks, and that all of the Greco-Roman artifacts were similarly faked. By the time of his death in 1729, he had not provided a reason why the Benedictines would fake so much history, nor a shred of evidence to back up his claims.[1] Today an intellectual successor to Hardouin claims that it is not classical antiquity that was forged, but instead the history of the Middle Ages. Russian mathematician Anatoly Fomenko has devised a system he calls the "New Chronology" that he says firmly establishes the fictive nature of the medieval epoch. The University of Moscow professor published a book called *Antiquity in the Middle Ages: Greek and Bible History*, in which he argues that the written record of human history should be condensed from thousands of years into hundreds of years. For Fomenko, history unfolded not over millennia but centuries. The English edition of the book was published in September 2003, under the title *History: Fiction or Science?*, with a lurid cover featuring the crucified Christ, but it is not necessary to buy the book to learn about Fomenko's theories. Before the book's translation, he published a 29,000-word summary of his findings online. This opus, written with G. V. Nosovskij, is grandly titled "New Chronology and New Concept of the

English History: British Empire as a Direct Successor of the Byzantine-Roman Empire," and it commits as great an assault on the English language as it does on English history. Nevertheless, it is an important and illuminating look at a new wave of alternative history, a history that appeals to Russians because it is designed to restore to post-Soviet Russia some of the power and greatness of its past.

Fomenko begins by telling his readers that English history is flawed and broken. He argues that the source texts used to create our understanding of Britain from the Roman occupation to William the Conqueror are misdated: "In correct version, ancient and medieval English events am to be transferred to the epoch which begins from 9-10th cc [centuries]. Moreover, many of these events prove to be the reflections of certain events from real Byzantine-Roman history of 9-15th cc. Consequently, the Great Britain Empire is a direct successor of medieval Byzantine Empire."[2]

Say what?

According to Fomenko, there were originally four sources of historical knowledge, books which he refers to as A, B, C, and D. The latter three were imperfect copies of A—the True History. Over time as they were copied and recopied each became so garbled that the four books were eventually assumed to be four separate histories rather than flawed copies of one narrative. Therefore, when late medieval scribes set about writing history, they accidentally made history four times longer than it should have been by repeating the same history four times. Fomenko believes this accounts for "similarities" he has found in the different periods of human history. More importantly, this discovery allows him to reconstruct the True History by collapsing the four histories into a few hundred years.

He calls this compressed version the "fibred" [fiber structure] chronicle. The three chronicles B, C, and D were embedded into A by considering each one as a rigid block and shifting them forward by approximately 333, 1053, and 1778 years respectively.[3]

How did Dr. Fomenko decide how far to shift his dates? The answer goes to the heart of why his theory makes little sense. He says he decided to apply his knowledge of advanced mathematics to the study of history.

He began by studying the astronomical phenomena recorded in Ptolemy's *Almagest,* a text from the second century CE that catalogued the positions of 1,028 stars and introduced the concept of the epicycle to explain the retrograde motion of the planets. Fomenko is of the opinion that the Almagest actually records astronomical phenomena from the seventh to the thirteenth centuries CE. He detailed his reasoning in *Geometrical and Statistical Methods of Analysis of Star Configurations Dating Ptolemy's* Almagest. Without getting into the complex mathematics, the Fomenko method of analyzing the stars does not quite prove his point. Even though he assigns a small margin of error to Ptolemy's figures, he must then assume that Ptolemy's values are largely without error in order to arrive at "true" dates. A small error in value on the part of Ptolemy could—and does— throw all Fomenko's calculations to the wind.

Using this eccentric interpretation, Fomenko proceeds to declare that on this basis all historical chronology is wrong. The Roman Empire, he claims, actually began in the ninth century, and its Eastern half, condescendingly called Byzantine, was the true model for all history. ("Byzantine" was a derogatory term associated with paganism used by the Holy Roman Empire to discredit its eastern rival.) Cutting to the chase, Fomenko concludes that British history is really Byzantine history, that the English kings were British renamings of the Byzantine Emperors, and that all of this history was fabricated when refugees from the fallen Byzantine capital "returned" to England in 1453 and brought their history to the barbarian island.[4]

He counts Cenwalch of Wessex and Sussex (643-672 CE) as the first "English" king, and he says his reign is the British duplicate (or reinterpretation) of the Eastern Roman Theodosius the Great (378-395 CE), for no particular reason other than the 275-year shift in time that makes it match his "New Chronology." But to make them equivalent, Fomenko can only use Cenwalch's reign over Wessex (647-672). Even then, his 25-year reign still does not match Theodosius' 16-year stay on the throne. Nevertheless, this error of more than 50 percent is still considered a parallel.

His other parallels, even after a double reordering of Byzantine monarchs (they were themselves duplicated twice, you see), are still not very accurate. Beorhtric (ruled 16 years) is equated to Justin I (ruled 9 years), different by nearly half. Fomenko links Aethelbert (6 years) to Justin II (13 years), an error of more than 100%. He has to combine Zeno's two reigns (over a period of, but not totaling, 17 years) to match the English Cuthread (17 years).

Fomenko does manage, however, a couple of good "hits." He links Egbert, the uniter of England (ruled 38 years), to Justinian the Great, restorer of the Roman Empire (ruled 38 years). But then he combines King Edgar (16 years) with King Edward the Martyr (3 years) and claims they *both* represent Leo III the Isaurian (24 years). He concludes that the names Edgar and Edward are "similar and consequently their union is natural."[5] Of course, the eleven Emperors Constantine (and the additional Emperors named Constans and Constantius) were apparently readily distinguished by the barbarians.

His entire theory depends on his idea that history is merely the chronicle of the reigns of monarchs, and that the mathematical relationships between their reigns is as sound as the mathematically relationship of two sides of an algebraic equation. This is nonsense of the worst kind, made worse by the fact that Fomenko had to actively rewrite Byzantine history to get his correlation to match the English history he so badly wants to appropriate (requiring tolerances, as we have shown, of more than 100%).

In short, Fomenko cut and pasted the Emperors in any order he chose to make them conform as closely as he could to selected monarchs of England's past. But even more damaging to his argument claiming that there are mathematical correlations between English and Byzantine rulers is the fact that he has to discount virtually every other fact known about the two cultures. Fomenko claims that Byzantine history from 1143-1453 CE is a mistaken duplicate of history from 830-1143 CE. If this were true, then why would the "fictional" or "duplicate" monarchs of the later period all have coins prominently displaying theft names and portraits? If the rulers of two Byzantine periods and England were one and the same, why should their lives and loves, their triumphs and tragedies differ markedly through "error" and "exaggeration" while the same chroniclers doggedly preserved the length of their reigns?

For that matter, how can we expect to believe Fomenko's arguments since Imperial coinage that documents the succession of the emperors can be gathered from virtually every year from 27 BCE to 1453 CE? How do we discount written Roman history and the great reigns of the past? Further, if Fomenko is correct, we must ignore the Magna Carta of 1215, since England's King John would have been nothing more than a Byzantine fantasy. Paradoxically, Fomenko endorses the reality of the Crusades, perhaps because he thinks the Crusaders brought Byzantine history to back England. If so, one immediately wonders how feudalism, Catholicism, and every structure and artifact associated with the High Middle Ages developed spontaneously in the mere 50 years he allots between Rome and the Renaissance. To suggest that the British built medieval England from a Roman England that he claims lasted only from the ninth to tenth centuries is a feat that contradicts all known ideas about the development of civilization.

Fomenko also ignores other lines of evidence. He does not account for the chronological continuity of the Roman Catholic popes, or the well-dated series of Church Councils and Papal Bulls. He completely dismisses the radiocarbon evidence that dates artifacts from Rome and the Middle Ages to the accepted timetable and not to his own revised chronology.

Pushing his ideas still further, Fomenko argues that our confusion about the True Dates derives from the old English use of the term "Year of Grace" as a synonym for *Anno Domini*, A.D. He extrapolates: "Maybe the original (and now forgotten) meaning of a formula 'Years of Grace' differs from one which is accepted today. Maybe it was 'years in Greece.' 'Greek years' or something like this."[6] And of course, since he claims Greece was another name for the Byzantine Empire, ipso facto Christian years become Byzantine years and England becomes the Byzantine Empire, Q.E.D. To be fair, Fomenko concedes this argument is not strong, but he bases his thesis on sound-alike names, even claiming that the continent of Asia really means "Jesus-land." Grace derives from the Latin *gratia*, thanks or good-will; Greece is from the Latin *Graecia*, their word for the Hellenes. Jesus was several centuries too late to get naming fights to Asia, already called that in ancient Greek times.

None of these facts stop Fomenko from also claiming that the name "England" derived from the Byzantine dynasty of the Angeli. They are not related. In fact, the dynastic name of the three Emperors surnamed Ange-lus is Latin and is a Westernized version of its Greek original, *angeloi*. The name England derives from the Old English for "Land of the Angles," as opposed to the Saxons. The Angles derive their name from the Latin *angli* which bears no relation to the word for angel, *angelus*. *Angli* was the name given to a branch of the river Suevi in Germany. Tacitus, in his *Germania*, names the tribe so,[7] and around 450 CE the people of the Angli river unit-ed with the Saxons to invade England.

Nevertheless, despite lacking facts and evidence, Fomenko's world-view argues that history is a massive fraud: "Roughly speaking, ancient English chronicles are in fact Byzantine chronicles which were taken from Byzantine to England and then modified in a such way that they seem to speak about events in England."[8] Yet to make his case Fomenko has to massacre history and ignore the archaeological evidence from the island and from Constantinople. He has to willfully manipulate the historical record in the very way he accuses the medieval English of doing. And to what end?

Well, that answer is quite simple. Fomenko is Russian, so it is not sur-prising that Fomenko "discovered" that Russia was the source of universal empire and that its culture gave rise to England. That explains his Byzan-tine chauvinism, for the Russian czars (= Caesars) saw themselves as the legitimate successors to the Byzantine emperors through the miracle of shared faith in the (then united) Orthodox Church. If England could be shown to "really" be Byzantium, then all the advances of England, and America, are "really" Byzantine and hence Russian. In other words, this elaborate theory is nothing more than an attempt to bolster the battered and broken shell of the formerly great Russian state, and to claim for

Mother Russia a small piece of the reflected glory of a world that passed it by.

Following the publication of Fomenko's book in English his publisher, Delamere Resources Ltd, announced that it had received "innumerable venomous complaints with unprintable undertones." To respond to the critics, Delamere issued a press release in January 2004, challenging scientists to disprove Fomenko's assertions. They offered a $10,000 "cash reward" to anyone who could prove that any human artifacts existed prior to the eleventh century CE. There was one catch, however: the "proof" could not use "archaeological, dendrochronological, paleographical and carbon methods."[9] Thus having safely excluded all scientific methods of dating and most historical methods, they confidently demanded that all proof be of the same "academic level as the heretic Fomenko."[10]

Though Fomenko's theories hold no water and are easily disproved, it has not stopped the public from buying his books or indulging in speculation. Russian chess master Gary Kasparov became a willing convert, opining that Fomenko's theories were a revelation because there "were too many discrepancies and contradictions that could not be explained within the framework of traditional chronology."[11] While it is exhilarating to think that accepted knowledge could be wrong, and that humanity is on the verge of a major revision of its history, in fact the entire enterprise is constructed on a foundation of flaws, inconsistencies, and errors.

Notes

[1] Johann Burkhard Mencken, *The Charlatanry of the Learned*, translated by Francis E. Litz (New York, London, A.A. Knopf, 1937), 82-83.

[2] A.T. Fomenko and G.V. Nosovskij, "New Chronology and New Concept of the English History: British Empire as a Direct Successor of Byzantine-Roman Empire" [online], 1998, http://lib.ru/FOMENKOAT/engltr.txt

[3] Ibid.

[4] Ibid.

5 Ibid.

6 Ibid.

7 Tacitus, *Germania* 40, calling them "Anglii," i.e. people of the Angli.

8 Fomenko and Nosovskij, "New Chronology."

9 Delamere Resources, "Publisher Announces 10,000 USD Cash Reward." *PR Web* [online], January 14, 2004.

10 Ibid.

11 Gary Kasparov, "Mathematics of the Past," *New Tradition* [online], n.d.

44. Did the Hopi Predict the End of the World?

ANY ALTERNATIVE WRITERS claim that the Hopi have "ancient" prophecies that foretold the Euro-American settlement of the continental United States as well as its ultimate destruction by nuclear weapons. Such prophecies are often said to have come from a spirit being from Sirius known as the Blue Star Kachina, whom ancient astronaut writers claim is an extraterrestrial being, one of the creatures Robert Temple imagined served as the prototype for the Babylonian myth of Oannes. However, I have not been able to trace the phrase "Blue Star Kachina" back before 1963, when the novelist and New Age mystic Frank Waters used the term in his *The Book of the Hopi*. I have also not been able to find any scholarly report confirming that this name for Sirius predated the New Age movement. It seems to be the result of another "revised" chronology, one project a modern invention into the ancient past.

Where the term *does* appear, however, is in two "ancient" Hopi prophecies that have made the rounds across hundreds of alternative books and thousands of websites. The more detailed of these prophecies is attributed to a Hopi named White Feather. the prophecies foretell nine things, eight of which have happened: (1) European colonization, (2) pioneers in wagons, (3) cattle ranching, (4) train tracks, (5) telephone lines, (6) highways, (7) oil spills, and (8) hippies. The ninth seems to refer to a space station, and the coda at the end makes clear reference to nuclear war. The space station reference, however, may not be what was intended. The prophecy is so vague it could refer to a jet aircraft, or, more likely, to an event that happened in the past. In *Fingerprints of the Gods* (1995), Graham Hancock visited the Hopi elder Paul Sifki, who told him that he remembered a supernova in the early 1900s, "a star that exploded," which his grandfather had told him foretold the destruction of the earth.[1] I wonder if the prophecies' author, White Feather, wasn't referring to this or a similar event. I can't find a nova from the early 1900s, but one was observed in 1885 in the vicinity of the Andromeda galaxy; however, any number of rare astronomical events could produce similar light shows, not necessarily an actual supernova. Heck, for all I know, Sifki could have witnessed the disintegrating comet that caused the Tunguska event of 1908, when that comet (or asteroid) exploded over Siberia.

My reference to the Tunguska event, I think, clues you in that the prophecies aren't exactly what they seem. If these were truly "ancient" Hopi prophecies, this would be astonishing—and indeed many alternative writers claim them as such. (Even the 2005 encyclopedia *Gods, Goddesses, and Mythology* claims they are ancient—and accurate.[2]) However, these "prophecies" were concocted *ex post facto* in 1958, when at least eight of the nine prophecies had already happened, nuclear war was a pervasive fear, and science fiction had made space stations a probable future occurrence. The prophecies were supposedly uttered to the Methodist pastor David Young after Young picked up White Feather as a hitchhiker. The strong Christian apocalyptic themes in the prophecy make plain that Young was likely far more than the mere transmitter of the prophecies; the text was allegedly first circulated in Christian churches in 1959 in privately-printed handbills but is only known (to me at least) from the published sources, including *Something in This Book Is True* (1997) by Bob Frisell.[3] I cannot find references to the prophecy earlier than 1980, when it appeared in *Rolling Thunder: The Coming Earth Changes* by Joey R. Jochmans.[4] If this is in fact the case, the blue star referenced would therefore likely be dependent upon the blue star we are about to meet in the next prophecy.

A second Hopi prophecy, today often paired with the first, also predicts a third World War, the destruction of the United States by nuclear weapons, and the rise of a single world government. Needless to say, this prophecy dates from 1963, as recorded by Frank Waters in *The Book of the Hopi,* and is similarly not ancient. Interestingly, though, this prophecy makes explicit that the end of the world will come when Saquasohuh Kachina dances.[5] The name "Saquasohuh" means "Blue Star," the same "blue star" referred to by White Feather. As I mentioned at the beginning of this chapter, I am unable to find a clear reference to the "blue star" in any document published prior to the 1980 and 1963 texts, and it seems likely that if the White Feather prophecies are really from the 1980s, they therefore are merely expanding upon and reworking the prophecy from *The Book of the Hopi.* Jochmans' attribution of words to White Feather surrounding the prophecies seems clearly influenced by Waters' *Book of the Hopi* and its discussion of Hopi tablets and other myths, as is the nuclear apocalypse given after the common text of the prophecies ends, especially where both prophecies claim that the Hopi, by virtue of their wisdom, are exempt from destruction.

The false Hopi prophecies came to a head in the summer of 1987 at the Harmonic Convergence, an event New Agers thought signaled a change in history. Many gathered at Prophecy Rock on the Hopi mesas, but the event there had no Hopi participants and was decried by Hopi elders, especially after New Age attendees invoked aliens. At the event, the alleged Hopi prophecies from the 1950s and 1960s were appropriated by (white) New Agers as "ancient" mysteries and associated with all manner of alternative beliefs, including Robert Temple's *Sirius Mystery,* UFOs, and other unconventional ideas. As a result, the "prophecies" entered the alternative mainstream (if that's what you'd call it) in association with space beings, Sirius, and other extraterrestrial mysteries.

The association of the Blue Star Kachina from Waters' book with the star Sirius then bled back into Native American beliefs from the New Age. The crystal healer Oh Shinnah Fast Wolf, who is not Hopi (she claims to be Apache and Mohawk and was born Penny McKelvey), told Grandmother Twylah Nitsch, a Seneca, that she felt the Blue Kachina had "something to do with Sirius."[6] Oh Shinnah and Twylah Nitsch together concluded that the Hopi prophecies therefore meant that Sirius was associated with the apocalypse and with a new universal consciousness emerging when our three-dimensional world becomes "four dimensional," and this would happen in December 2012, when the Maya prophesied the end of the world. Since that prophecy is well-known to be a Euro-American imposition on Native belief, the "Hopi" prophecies similarly seem to be Native peoples reflecting back the West's own apocalyptic traditions!

The authors of these alleged prophecies were drawing on a traditional Hopi cosmology in which the current world, the Fourth World, would eventually give way to the Fifth World, in a recurrence of the periodic destruction that gave birth to new world ages. This myth, which posits the return of Pahana, the White Brother, from the East, is almost certainly related to the Mesoamerican feathered serpent legend of Quetzalcoatl and the Mesoamerican idea of successive worlds. As in the case of the Aztec god, it is possible that the whiteness of the being was ascribed to him after the contact period to help place the arrival of white men from the east into a mythic context; there are no ancient Hopi texts, only oral accounts, so we simply can't know what was believed before the first records were made. The traditional cosmology was continuously reinterpreted, however, in light of modern conditions.

Armin Geertz studied Hopi prophecy and determined that no Hopi prophecy could be traced back before the event which it describes; in fact the Hopi have continuously recreated their prophecies to justify current conditions.[7] For example, when the Hopi split around 1900, they created a "prophecy" to support the split, and new prophecies were added to reflect new technologies: the "spider web" analogy for telephone wires came about only *after* the wires went up. The most famous *ex post facto* "prophecy" is the "gourd full of ashes" that supposedly represented the destructive power of the atomic bomb. The "gourd" prophecy wasn't invented until 1956 (though some oral traditions claim 1948), long after the bomb it supposedly predicted. Thus, in short, the Hopi prophecies tell us much about the concerns of the people who uttered them, but very little about the future. Oh, and they also tell us that alternative writers will repeat *anything* they hear.

Notes

[1] Graham Hancock, *Fingerprints of the Gods* (New York: Crown, 1995), 503-4.

[2] *Gods, Goddesses, and Mythology,* vol. 11 (Tarrytown, New York: Marshall Cavendish, 2005), 124 (s.v. "Apocalypse Myths").

[3] Bob Frisell, *Something in This Book Is True,* second ed. (Berkeley: Frog Books, 2003), eBook edition.

[4] Joey R. Jochmans, *Rolling Thunder: The Coming Earth Changes* (Santa Fe, New Mexico: Sun Books, 1980), 110-115.

[5] Frank Waters, *The Book of the Hopi* (New York: Ballantine, 1963), 408-409.

[6] Sandra Corcoran, *Between the Dark and the Daylight: Awakening to Shamanism* (Bloomington, Indiana: Balboa Press, 2012), 84-86.

[7] Armin W. Geertz, *The Invention of Prophecy: Continuity and Meaning in Hopi Indian Religion* (Berkeley: University of California Press, 1994).

45. Who Really Discovered America?

ITY POOR NORTH AMERICA, a land whose history can never be her own. For centuries scholars, prophets, and cranks have tried to prove that the continent did not belong to the native peoples who populated it when the European explorers first arrived. Instead, America's ancient monuments were assigned to a "lost race," her people declared a lost tribe of Israel, and the continent's first discovery credited to ancient Europeans, Atlanteans, or space aliens—anyone but the native Americans themselves.

Today, a pair of archaeologists believe that they have found evidence that finks ancient Noah America to Stone Age Europe. Since 1999, Dennis Stanford of the Smithsonian Institution has been the most prominent spokesperson for the "Solutrean hypothesis," a theory that claims the first people to arrive in the New World came from prehistoric Spain and brought with them a distinctive way of making stone tools. In a paper presented in 2004, Stanford and his colleague Brace Bradley outlined the proposed route the Spaniards took on their trek to the Americas.[1] However, a closer look at the Solutrean hypothesis shows that the idea does not prove what its authors claim.

The Traditional View

The peopling of the Americas has been a controversial subject since Columbus. But scholars reached a rough consensus in the twentieth century that nomadic hunters from eastern Siberia came to Alaska across the Bering Strait some 14,000 years ago, during the last Ice Age, a time when sea levels were low enough to create a land bridge. These hunters followed herds of wooly mammoths and other large prehistoric animals (the wonderfully-named paleomegafauna). They traveled through an ice-free corridor in the Canadian Shield, between massive glaciers, into the heart of North America. From there they spread out across the un-peopled landscape and thereafter gave rise to the people we know as the American Indians.

Support for this idea came from an unexpected place—Clovis, New Mexico. In that out-of-the way corner of the desert in the 1930s, archaeologists discovered a distinctive type of stone point, known afterward as the "Clovis point." It was a spear tip, worked on both sides ("bifacial"). Clovis points had very distinctive characteristics. They were much taller than they were wide, had a concave base, and a long groove carved up the middle of both sides, called "fluting." This fluting allowed the point to be wedged into a slit in a wooden or bone shaft to create a spear. This innovation separated the Clovis point from nearly all other contemporary stone tool technologies, a magnificent accomplishment for the people who used these points between 10,500 and 9,000 BCE.

Clovis points were found throughout North America, although more often in the east. For over a millennium, it seems much of the continent used the same tools and hunted the same way. This became known as the Clovis culture, though whether it represented an actual cultural homogenization or just a sharing of a useful toolkit is not known. Because in the early twentieth century Clovis points were the oldest artifacts discovered, it was argued that the Clovis people were first to inhabit the New World and that America's first human inhabitants were big game hunters—exactly what the Bering crossing hypothesis suggested.

The Solutrean Hypothesis

"Clovis-first" was the default position for most of the twentieth century, and it still has supporters today. But as early as the 1930s, some began to propose that Clovis technology was not an American development. Archaeologist Frank Hibben noticed the similarities between Clovis points and the stone points made by prehistoric European people called the Solutreans. They had arisen in modern France and Spain around 25,000 years ago, during the Upper Paleolithic, and were famous for their finely-worked flint tools and their art. They were replaced by the Magdalenian culture, whose stone tools were less sophisticated.

While other cultures simply hit one stone with another to chip away flakes by percussion, the Solutrean and Clovis peoples manufactured stone tools by a distinctive technique called "pressure flaking," which used a sharp instrument for precision knapping of the stone. The Solutreans developed this technology around 20,000 BCE and spread across Western Europe before disappearing around 14,500 BCE (the dates vary slightly depending on whom you ask). Hibben believed the similarities with the later Clovis points showed that the Solutreans had peopled North America and brought their tools with them.[2] Strangely, however, little else of the Solutrean lifestyle, such as their art, came to the Americas with them.

Not long after the Solutrean hypothesis was proposed, however, archaeologists dismissed the idea with three arguments: (1) though both cultures used pressure flaking, Solutrean points were not fluted like the Clovis points—many Solutrean tools had a roughly diamond shape while Clovis points often had a concave bottom; (2) the Solutreans, who had no boats, had no way to get to North America; (3) most important, there was a gap of thousands of years between the latest Solutrean points and the earliest Clovis points—it seemed chronologically impossible for the Solutreans to have given rise to Clovis.

By the late 1930s, anthropologist Theodore McCown further noted that linguistic ambiguity created a false similarity to those trained only in the archaeology of North America or that of Europe. The very word Solutrean had come to mean both the pressure flaking technique and the culture of prehistoric Spain. Since the word now had two meanings, it was sometimes hard for non-specialists to know in which sense the word was being used. Clovis points may very well have used a Solutrean pressure-flaking technique, but that did not necessarily make them a relative of the Spanish points.[3] (There are only so many ways to make a stone tool, so perhaps it is inevitable that some techniques will resemble one another.) Only later was the term Solutrean restricted to a specific culture.

Lacking any firm evidence, the hypothesis died a quick death.

New Challenges to Clovis-First

In the second half of the twentieth century, new challenges to the Clovis-first theory began to undermine archaeology's traditional view of ancient America. Sites with anomalous findings began to appear with dates older than the oldest-known Clovis sites. Although the media would often hype these findings as overturning the established theory about the peopling of the Americas, many archaeologists rejected the sites out of hand while others cautioned that more work was needed before abandoning the Clovis-first paradigm.

Though several of the ancient sites would later turn out to be younger than first thought, a few made a compelling case for a peopling of the New World before Clovis. Meadowcroft Rock Shelter, in Pennsylvania, seemed to show continual use stretching from the colonial period back to 18,000 BCE or earlier. Many archaeologists accept the Meadowcroft site as valid, but others claim contamination has tainted the dating.

The site of Monte Verde, Chile, however, offered the best proof for a pre-Clovis settlement in America. Radiocarbon dated to around 10,500 BCE or earlier, the site was older by a thousand years than Clovis sites in the Americas. As archaeologist Brian Fagan told *Archaeology* magazine, the age of the site was "so unexpected that some archaeologists, this reviewer among them, wondered if the site really was an undisturbed cultural layer. We were wrong. Dillehay (the excavator) has proved Monte Verde is a settlement, probably at the threshold of colonization of the Americas."[4]

For people to be in South America that early implied that they must have been in North America even earlier. This pushed back the likely date for human arrival in the New World by millennia. After heated debate, a blue-ribbon panel declared the Monte Verde site valid.[5] In another blow to the Clovis-first theory, Monte Verde's evidence indicated that plant-based foods were more important than big game hunting to the early peoples, an indication that the first Americans may not have followed big game to the New World.

These challenges to Clovis-first created a rush of new theories about how and when the first people came to the Americas. A new batch of ideas proposed numerous routes from Asia to America. Many of these new theories favored some type of Pacific crossing by boat anywhere from 15,000 to 50,000 years ago. A plausible alternative to the ice corridor migration is that the first migrants arrived by hugging the coasts and sailing from Asia to America. This theory predicted the oldest sites would be found on the coast instead of the interior of North America. Ironically, this helped explain why Monte Verde was found along the coast of South America: After the end of the Ice Age, ocean levels rose, drowning coastal sites in North America, but preserving those in South America, where coasts eroded less.

By the end of the twentieth century it was generally believed that the New World was populated by waves of immigrants from Asia to America, traveling at intervals from the remote past to the very recent present. The last wave before the European conquest--the Inuit and Eskimos of the Arctic--arrived around 1000 CE. There was no one migration but instead a series of migrations over millennia. However, new controversies arose over whether at least one of those migrations came from Europe.

The New Solutrean Solution

The Solutrean connection lay dormant for almost six decades, until Stanford resurrected it at a 1999 conference. With the acceptance of Monte Verde, the time was right for challenging old theories about the peopling of the Americas. Moreover, in July 1996, a skeleton uncovered in Kennewick, Washington, raised anew the idea that Europeans had colonized the continent before the ancestors of today's Native Americans.

Initial reports said Kennewick Man, as the bones became known, had "Caucasoid" features. Confusing an obsolete technical term for skull shape for the racial category "Caucasian," some commentators and activists said

Kennewick Man proved white Europeans were "really" the first Americans. These commentators were unaware that skull shapes vary greatly both among individuals and through time. A U.S. government investigation determined that the Kennewick remains were Native American and around 7,000 to 9,000 years old.[6]

The controversy did not die down, and today several groups ranging from scholars to neo-Norse Pagans to Aryan supremacists still cite Kennewick as proof for prehistoric European colonization of America. Though the bones were dated to around 7200 BCE and were too young to be even Clovis, the door was open for new claims about Paleolithic European voyages to the New World. The Smithsonian's Dennis Stanford and his colleague Bruce Bradley seized the moment to propose the long-abandoned Solutrean solution anew.

Essentially, the two researchers repeated and expanded Hibben's claims about the similarity between Solutrean and Clovis technologies. First, they noted that no Siberian tools had fluting like the Clovis technology, ruling out Asia as a source for the Clovis culture. "Years of research in eastern Asia and Alaska have produced little evidence of any historical or technological connection between the Asian Paleolithic (Stone Age) and Clovis peoples," they wrote.[7] That the Solutreans lacked fluting posed fewer challenges, however, since other morphological evidence would serve to connect them to Clovis.

They also cited the similarity in tool kits—the scrapers and knives prehistoric hunters used to chop up big game. They argued that the Solutreans must have originated these points and tools and bequeathed them to the Clovis people. Though the Solutreans had a greater variety of tools, the Clovis people had nothing that was not paralleled in Solutrean finds. In short, because they looked alike, there must be a connection.[8]

To do Hibben one better, Stanford and Bradley incorporated the new pre-Clovis sites into their hypothesis. They claimed these new sites proved the relationship by showing that pre-Clovis technology was even closer to the Solutrean and "could represent transitional technology between Solutrean and Clovis."[9] The fluting seen in Clovis points was therefore an

American development from stone tools even more similar to the Solutrean. Thus, Clovis was not a copy of the Solutrean but an outgrowth from it.[10] Why the fluting could not be a development from earlier Asian technologies is less clear.

The Solutrean hypothesis met with immediate criticism from experts like G. L. Straus and G. A. Clark, who found it lacking, just as an earlier generation discarded it after its first proposal. But even accepting the idea on its face presented logical problems that were difficult to overcome.

Factual Problems

First, the evidence seems weighted against a European origin for early Americans. There is not a single artifact or set of human remains from the time period that is unambiguously European. Remember, Kennewick Man, even if he were European, was thousands of years too late.

Also, today's native North Americans have clear genetic origins in Asia, not in Europe. Stanford and Bradley attempt to refute this by pointing to research on a type of mitochondrial DNA called haplogroup X, a genetic marker, which is found in a higher frequency in Asian populations than either Native American or European populations.[11] Superficially, this would seem to show a link between Native Americans and Europeans.

However, since the first migrants to the Americas were likely few in number, well-known evolutionary mechanisms like the founder effect and other forms of genetic bottlenecking could have easily affected the frequency of haplogroup X. In fact, after examining the mitochondrial DNA code instead of its relative frequency, a 2002 study linked the Native American haplogroup X genetically to that found in Siberia. This clearly tied Native Americans to Asia and not Europe.[12] All other genetic data to date have confirmed the Asian link.

Second, the old questions from the 1930s about the Solutrean connection still remain unanswered. Why were Clovis points fluted when the Solutrean points were not? What were they doing for the thousands of years that separate the Solutrean and Clovis cultures? How did the Solutreans come to North America if they are not known to have boats?

Bradley and Stanford propose that the Solutreans arrived by traveling along the edge of the great Ice Age glaciers.[13] Their boats, if they had them, simply failed to survive in the archaeological record.

For the other questions, Stanford and Bradley have a convoluted explanation. Essentially, they concede that Clovis was not the first North American culture. Earlier cultures, such as that represented at Meadowcroft Rock Shelter, had unfluted points that may be transitional from Solutrean to Clovis.[14] Thus, for thousands of years the Solutreans hung out in the Americas gradually developing Clovis technology.

This raises an obvious logical problem. If Stanford and Bradley admit that there were cultures in America before Clovis, and if they concede that Clovis points may have developed from previous stone tools used in the Americas, why bother with a Solutrean origin at all? Weren't the ancient inhabitants of the Americas, known to scholars as Paleoindians, intelligent enough to invent their own tools? Unfortunately, since there are so few pre-Clovis sites, it is difficult to say how closely the earlier stone tools matched their alleged Solutrean counterparts, so a true test of this still awaits the proverbial turn of the spade.

Logical Problems

But let us accept for a moment, as a thought experiment, that Stanford and Bradley are right that Clovis stone tools are clearly derived from Solutrean predecessors. Would this prove that prehistoric Spaniards migrated to the New World and made a new life on a new continent, as the authors claim? Even accepting the identification of Clovis and Solutrean stone tools, one cannot logically deduce this conclusion.

First, technology is not identical with culture, and culture is not identical with genetic or geographic origins. To take a slightly exaggerated example, one can travel into the Amazon rain forest or the Kalahari Desert and find tribes whose members wear Nike merchandise. Does this mean that these people are from the United States? That is what the cultural origins of their clothing would tell us. But since the labels on their clothes tell us the garments were made in China, does that make these people Chinese?

Following Stanford's and Bradley's logic, we must conclude that these people are Chinese since for them cultural indicators like stone tools or Nike sneakers must travel with the people who invented them. Their logic precludes handing these indicators from person to person across a great chain of interaction, commerce, and trade. In short, if the Clovis people did use Solutrean technology, it does not necessarily make them Spaniards.

However, since there is no likely Atlantic trade route from Spain to America until the Arctic was peopled around 3000 BCE, our thought experiment forces us to consider that Solutreans did come to America. But again, assuming a Clovis-Solutrean connection does not prove that these people were one and the same.

Let us imagine Stanford's and Bradley's hearty band of Solutreans traveling along the edge of the glaciers and arriving in the Americas. These Solutreans discover a thriving population of Paleoindians and share their technology with them. The Paleoindians jump for joy that the Spaniards have brought their benighted people pressure-flaked stone tools and eagerly share the new technology with all their friends. The Solutreans, disillusioned that there are so many Paleoindians to share in the mammoths and mastodons, turn around and go home. Thus technology, but not people or genes, has traveled to the New World.

It is because of this possibility that Stanford and Bradley indirectly expose the weakness of their argument in the abstract of their recent paper: "Evidence has accumulated over the past two decades indicating that the earliest origin of people in North America may have been from southwestern Europe during the last glacial maximum. In this summary we outline a theory of a Solutrean origin for Clovis culture and briefly present the archaeological data supporting this assertion."[15]

Notice the misdirection: impersonal "evidence" shows the first North Americans came from Europe, but the authors merely suggest Clovis "culture" came from the Solutrean. The two are not the same, and the authors know that one does not prove the other, however much they wish to imply it. But since the authors previously admitted, and archaeology accepts, that Clovis was not the first North American culture, even a Solutrean origin for Clovis does not contribute to the claim that the "earliest" people in the New World came from Spain.

Under the most favorable interpretation, they can prove little more than diffusion. Under no interpretation does the theory make Europeans America's first colonists.

A More Likely Story

For the moment there is no clear evidence relating Solutreans to the Clovis people—or any earlier people of North America. Anthropologist G. A. Clark makes a compelling case that the similarities between the two cultures are coincidental, the result of two independent peoples stumbling across similar solutions when faced with similar problems in hunting ancient big game.[16] It has happened before. The bow and arrow were developed independently in the Americas and in the Old World. Writing developed on its own in the ancient Near East, in the ancient Far East, and in Mesoamerica. Witness, too, the mountains of paper devoted to supposed connections between Old and New World pyramid building and mummification. As anthropologist Lawrence Guy Straus told *National Geographic*, "One of the great failings of archaeology ... is a continuous falling back on the notion that if a couple of things resemble one another, they have to have the same source. But these similarities appear and reappear time and again in different places."[17]

The Solutrean hypothesis is simply the latest in a long string of ideas that have sought the ultimate origins of American history in other lands. Since the first explorations of the New World, researchers have tried to tie the continent's history back to Europe, as if to fulfill a need to own America's most distant past as well as its present.

The Clovis culture was likely an indigenous creation, a product of some very clever people working with what they had thousands of years ago. Until there is physical evidence that ties the ancient Americas to Europe, there can be no justification for continuing to deny Native Americans their history, their culture, and their accomplishments.

Notes

[1] Bruce Bradley and Dennis Stanford, "The North Atlantic Ice-Edge Corridor: A Possible Paleolithic Route to the New World," *World Archaeology* 36, no. 4 (2004): 459-478.

[2] Constance Holden, "Were Spaniards Among the First Americans?" *Science* 286 (1999): 1467-1468.

[3] Theodore D. McCowen, "That Magic Word, Solutrean," *American Antiquity* 5, no. 2 (1939): 150-152.

[4] "Monte Verde under Fire," *Archaeology* [online], 1999.

[5] Ibid.

[6] National Park Service Archaeology and Ethnology Program, "Kennewick" [online], May 2004.

[7] Dennis Stanford and Bruce Bradley, "The Solutrean Solution—Did Some Early Americans Come from Europe?", *Discovering Archaeology*, February 2000; reprinted in *Clovis and Beyond* [online].

[8] Ibid.

[9] Holden, "Were Spaniards," 1468.

[10] Ibid.

[11] Stanford and Bradley, "The Solutrean Solution."

[12] Ripan Malhi and David Glenn Smith, "Brief Communication: Haplogroup X Confirmed in North America," *American Journal of Physical Anthropology* 119 (2002): 84-86.

[13] Bradley and Stanford, "The North Atlantic Ice-Edge Corridor."

[14] Ibid.

[15] Ibid.

[16] G. A. Clark, "Deconstructing the North Atlantic Connection," *Current Research in the Pleistocene* 17 (2000): 12-13.

[17] Michael Parfit, "Hunt for the First Americans." *National Geographic*, December 2000, 40-67, 61.

46. The Zeno Brothers' Voyage of Discovery

AFTER EUROPEANS REALIZED that Christopher Columbus had discovered new lands, not a new path to Asia as he had claimed, national jealousies helped inspire a range of claims that other European groups had made the same journey earlier and should be granted pride of place. Many these claims are familiar: Irish monks under Saint Brendan, Welsh explorers under Prince Madoc, and the Norse. The last on that list had the virtue of also being true.

In 1558, a Venetian named Nicolò Zeno published a book and an accompanying map claiming that his ancestors, Nicolò and Antonio Zeno, brothers of the naval hero Carlo Zeno, had made voyages of equal importance to Columbus, and a century earlier to boot, earning Venice a place at the pre-Columbian table and a triumph over its rival Genoa, home to Columbus.[1] The book supposedly summarizes the correspondence of the two brothers about their adventures—correspondence which was conveniently destroyed before scholars could examine it when the younger Nicolò Zeno tore the original manuscripts to pieces.[2] Oddly, the book freely mixes supposed quotations from the letters and first person narration by the later author, all cast in the same first-person voice, as though one writer took on three personalities.

According to the younger Nicolò's book, one of the Zeno bothers (also called Zeni in the plural, or the Zen in the Venetian dialect), Nicolò, sailed to England in 1380 (which is true) and became stranded on an island called Frisland (which is not true), a non-existent North Atlantic island larger than Ireland. In the book, the elder Nicolò claims to have been rescued by Zichmi, a prince of Frisland. Fortunately for him, everyone he meets speaks Latin. Nicolò invites his brother Antonio to join him in Frisland, which he does for fourteen years (Nicolò dying four years in), while Zichmi attacks the fictitious islands of Bres, Talas, Broas, Iscant, Trans, Mimant, and Dambercas well as the Estlanda (Shetland) Islands and Iceland.

Later, after Nicolò had died in 1394, an expedition lost for twenty-six years arrives and reports having lived in a strange unknown land filled with ritual cannibals, whom they taught to fish. In fact, rival island groups fought a war in order to gain access to the travelers and learn the art of fishing. Worse, despite being the arctic "they all go naked, and suffer cruelly from the cold, nor have they the sense to clothe themselves with the skins of the animals which they take in hunting."[3] Antonio Zeno is still there and joins Zichmi on a voyage to the west in search of these strange lands. They encounter a large island called Icharia, whose residents' speech Zichmi understands. Finally, they travel to Greenland, where Zichmi remains with a colony while Antonio returns to Frisland.

On the surface of it, the story seems ridiculous—any survey of the Atlantic admits many of the islands are fakes (though defenders suggest Nicolò the younger misread references to Icelandic settlements as referring to islands since Iceland is called Islande)—but it was one of the most successful hoaxes in the history of exploration. The sixteenth century mapmakers Orelius and Mercator reportedly used it as a source, and Sir Martin Frobisher took it with him on his voyage to the Arctic.[4] One part of the reason for this is that the Zeni were real people, and they really did undertake voyages in the north. There was a foundation on which the younger Nicolò drew in fabricating the story. The other reason for the success is the infamous Zeno Map, also called the Zeni Map.

Before we look at the map, let's stipulate the Zeno narrative is a hoax. The real Nicolò Zeno (the elder) had been a military governor in Greece from 1390-1392 and was on trial in Venice in 1394 for embezzlement. He lived until at least 1402, despite having "died" in Frisland in 1394.

The map in question was drawn by the younger Nicolò, supposedly from his ancestors' now-vanished charts, and was for a long time considered the most important chart made in the 1390s, showing the North Atlantic in stunning accuracy for its day, despite the appearance of several islands that simply do not exist. Even those who denied its authenticity noted it was extremely accurate even for 1558. Of particular note is the accuracy of the shape of Greenland, better than any other fourteenth century chart. Of course, no copy of the map exists prior to its appearance in Nicolò Zeno's 1558 book.

But even from the first, there were several troubling issues. For one thing, the map showed latitude and longitude, something not included on medieval maps. Some scholars dismissed these as a later interpolation. Second, the accuracy of the map varies wildly from land to land. Greenland's shape is highly accurate, while Iceland's shape is very much inaccurate. Frisland—which does not exist—has been identified with the Faroe Islands, but only at the cost of sacrificing any claim to the map's tremendous accuracy, since the two lands look nothing alike.[5]

Martin Frobisher, in exploring the Arctic in 1577 in search of the Northwest Passage, relied on the hoax map, and as a result of its mistaken latitudes—listing Greenland's south tip at 65° north latitude instead of 60°, he mistook Greenland for Frisland—*twice!*—in 1577 and again in 1578, and extolled how accurately the map of Frisland matched the coast he reached, which was really Greenland![6]

John Davis, on his subsequent trip to the Arctic in search of the same Northwest Passage, at least recognized that the Zeni Map's Frisland did not match the coast he found, so he claimed to be the discoverer of the new island of Desolation. Sadly, it was again Greenland, which he completely misunderstood because he was using a hoax map to guide him. The island of Desolation, which never existed, was then placed on Jodocus Hondius' great chart of the world and the Molyneux Globe. The fictitious passage between Desolation and Greenland was named Frobisher's Strait, and Henry Hudson though he found it when he sailed up the east coast of Greenland at 63°, believing himself still south of Greenland proper. Also, when Spitsbergen was discovered, it was mistaken for part of Greenland for the same reasons![7]

Modern scholars, having researched the map, concluded that it is derived from a haphazard compilation of earlier charts, including Olaus Magnus' *Carta marina* (1539), printed in Venice; Cornelius Anthoniszoon's *Caerte van Oostlant* (1543); and derivatives of Claudius Clavus' early map of the North (c. 1427), including Greenland, which appears nearly identical in shape and orientation on the Clavus-derived 1467 map of Nicolaus Germanus as it does on the Zeni Map.

Many believe that the younger Nicolò Zeno faked the voyage of his ancestors to help give Venice a prior claim to the discovery of the New World, older than that of Genoese rival Columbus. Some still hold that Zeno merely garbled his ancestors' real-life voyage to the north, exaggerating or misreporting real events. The weight of evidence is that the Zeno affair is yet another episode in the chronicle of fake history passed off as the real thing. But here's the takeaway: How can we be expected to believe, as alternative writers would have it, that Europe possessed secret maps of America and Atlantis dating back a thousand years or more if they couldn't manage to determine whether Frisland actually existed?

Notes

[1] Nicolò Zeno, *The Voyage of the Venetian Brothers, Nicolò & Antonio Zeno to the Northern Seas, in the XIVth Century*, translated by Richard Henry Major (London: Hakluyt Society, 1873).

[2] Ibid., 34-35. As a result of the destruction, he "reconstructed" their content from memory, years afterward, to write his book.

[3] Ibid., 23.

[4] G. M. Asher, *Henry Hudson the Navigator* (London: Hakluyt Society, 1860), clxvi-clxvii.

[5] Ibid., clxv-clxvi.

[6] Ibid., clxvii.

[7] Ibid., clxvii-clxix.

47. Did Native Americans Discover Europe in 60 BCE?

D ID YOU KNOW that Native Americans discovered Europe in 60 BCE? No? Well, you aren't reading the right websites and alternative history books. In 2012, Cracked.com, an online humor site run by former ABC News producer Jack O'Brien, published a piece on the "Six Ridiculous Lies You Believe about the Founding of America." Cracked.com articles present humorous or satirical discussions of fact-based material. O'Brien and co-author Alford Alley claimed that their article would expose the facts behind government and media distortion and simplification of American history. The authors sparked widespread discussion online by writing that "Columbus wasn't the first to cross the Atlantic. Nor were the vikings. [sic] Two Native Americans landed in Holland in 60 B.C. and were promptly not given a national holiday by anyone."[1] Within one week of publication, more than 1.7 million people had viewed the article and its shocking report of a Native American voyage to Roman-era Europe.

When I read this, I immediately wondered how I had missed such an important ancient record of trans-oceanic crossing. Surely, such a claim must have a solid basis in fact. Well, as it turns out, the Cracked.com writers are uncritically repeating a piece of centuries-old speculation that is widespread in alternative publications and online. In the original ancient texts on which this claim is ultimately based, the people were not Native Americans, were not two in number, and did not land in Holland. 60 BCE is about right, though, give or take.

Roman around Europe

The alleged Native American encounter with Europe in 60 BCE winds its way through alternative history like kudzu. It begins, however, with a pair of ancient texts that seem almost completely unrelated to the modern claim, though they are the only facts on which the claim rests. The first of these texts comes from 43 CE and the pen of the Roman geographer Pomponius Mela in *De situ orbis*, referencing material Mela is quoting from a now-lost earlier work of the Roman writer Cornelius Nepos (c.100 BCE-c. 25 BCE) on events that took place when Quintus Caecilius Metellus Celer was a proconsul in Gaul (62-59 BCE):

> When he [Celer] was proconsul in Gaul, he was presented with certain Indians as a present by the king of the Boti; asking whence they had come to these lands, he learned they had been seized by strong storms from Indian waters, that they had traveled across the regions between, and that at last they had landed on the shores of Germany.[2]

The following parallel passage from the *Natural History* of the Roman writer Pliny the Elder from 77-79 CE also preserves the same quotation, and many scholars believe that Pliny derived his version from Mela (a source he used elsewhere in the *Natural History*) rather than from Nepos himself:

> The same Cornelius Nepos, when speaking of the northern circumnavigation, tells us that Q. Metellus Celer, the colleague of L. Afranius in the consulship, but then a proconsul in Gaul, had a present made to him by the king of the Suevi, of certain Indians, who sailing from India for the purpose of commerce, had been driven by tempests into Germany.[3]

These texts do not immediately seem to refer to America, and there is no indication that the Indians were exactly two in number. Mela, like Pliny, insisted that this event referred to a voyage from the *east*—from "beyond the Caspian gulf" in his words, not the Atlantic because both Mela and Pliny believed that there was a water route between India and the Baltic. (We could argue that this is a mistake on Nepos' part, but if so, then we have no warrant to accept any of his testimony in the affair.) The difference in accounts between Mela's Boti and Pliny's Suevi is due to Mela using the specific name of an otherwise unattested tribe[4] and Pliny using a more generic term with two distinct meanings: a Rhineland tribe, or central Germans in general.

No further information is given about the visitors—not their language, appearance, habits, or faith. All we know is that they were merchants, and as such they must have had a boat big enough for trade. At any rate, whoever the visitors were, they appear to have spoken a language known to Europeans, unless they were particularly good pantomime artists, since they were apparently able to answer Celer's questions without difficulty. Again, we could argue that we are missing essential parts of the story, such as time spent teaching the captives a new tongue, but to do so calls into question acceptance of any part of the story—how would we know what to accept as true and complete? Such are the problems when dealing with ancient fragments.

The Spanish Imposition

The story, as told in Pliny and a widely-read medieval textbook by Martianus Capella, remained known throughout the Middle Ages (more than 200 medieval copies of Pliny survive), though the story was not the subject of much interest until the discovery of America. In the mid-sixteenth century the Spanish historian Francisco López de Gómara read the story and suggested in chapter ten of his *Historia general de las Indias* (1552), that the Romans had been "deceived by the color" of Native Americans from Labrador who had been carried across the North Atlantic. He was the very first author to connect the Roman story to the New World:

> But to sail from India to Caliz by the other part of the north by a clime and regions of extreme cold, should be doubtless a difficult and dangerous thing, wherof is no memory among the old authors saving only of one ship as Pliny and Mela do write, rehearsing the testimony of Cornelius

Nepos who affirmed that the king of Suevia presented to Quintus Metellus Celer, Lieutenant of France, certain Indians driven by tempest into the sea of Germany: if the same were not of the land of Labrador or Bacallaos ["cod-fish land"; i.e., Newfoundland], and they deceived in their color.[5]

Gómara, of course, was merely speculating; he is the same man who in chapter 220 of the same book argued that the Americas were identical to Atlantis because the Aztecs had words that used the letters "atl": "But there is now no cause why we should any longer doubt or dispute of the Island of Atlantis, forasmuch as the discovering and conquest of the West Indies do plainly declare what Plato hath written of the said lands. In Mexico also at this day they call that water Atl, by the half name of Atlantis, as by a word remaining of the name of the Island that is not."[6] He did not write from evidence, merely speculation, in order to provide Classical antecedents to justify the Spanish conquest of the Americas. He was criticized even in his own lifetime for the inaccuracy of his work. In all likelihood, Columbus' misnaming of Native Americans as "Indians" suggested this passage to Gómara's mind.

Nevertheless, very shortly after the publication of *Historia general de las Indias*, the story of Native Americans in Roman-era Germany entered the English-speaking world. Gómara's text was translated in 1555 as an appendix to Richard Eden's translation of Peter Martyr d'Anghiera's *Decades* (1530), and from there it became a frequent element in discussions of early America. The suggestion seemed to carry weight because Gómara also referenced as support the quite similar story told by Aeneas Sylvius Piccolomini (Pope Pius II) in his *Historia rerum ubique gestarum* (1477) that in the time of the "German emperors," probably the reign of Frederick Barbarossa as claimed by later sources, "an Indian ship with Indian merchants was taken on the coast of Germany which evidently had been driven there from the east."[7] Again, the text directly states that the voyage came from a direction other than the Atlantic. Christopher Columbus would read Piccolomini's account and find in it, as well as those of Pliny and Pomponius Mela, the seeds of the idea that one could sail to "India" (i.e., Asia) by going west, across the Atlantic, since improved fifteenth century geography had made it impossible to believe in an imaginary eastward waterway between Germany and Asia. Some Elizabethan Britons (see Chapter 46) actually attempted arctic voyages because they were convinced the ancients had done so based on these texts.

However, we do not possess Piccolomini's source. This source was a man named Otho or Otto, whom many scholars believe to be identical with Barbarossa's uncle Otto of Friesling, though this passage does not appear in any of that Otto's extant works. Pliny's story, though, was well known in the Middle Ages, and a form of it was part of the standard educational textbook, the *Marriage of Philology and Mercury* by the Late Antique writer Martianus Capella. Capella, in turn, had completely misunderstood the entire textual tradition and transmitted to the Middle Ages the false notion that "the same Cornelius, after capturing Indians, sailed by Germany."[8] The story Piccolomini relates Otto as having given is a fairly direct summary of the three versions of the story known in the Middle Ages (Pliny's, Mela's, and Capella's), assuming Otto considered all three to be equally correct facets of the truth.

It is impossible to tell without the original text whether Otto's account is dependent upon these sources or whether by coincidence some unknown people were discovered sailing near Germany, and we can only speculate why Otto would fabricate an account, if that is what he did. We could suggest, for example, that this may have been an effort to legitimize his nephew's seizure from his cousin Henry the Lion of lands in Swabia named for the Suevi by demonstrating that events that occurred to an ancient Suevi ruler were also visited upon the new rightful ruler of Swabia. Alternately, Piccolomini may have misunderstood a reference in Otto to ancient German kings (the Suevi) as taking place in "the time of the German emperors," certainly an odd phrase given that there were still Holy Roman Emperors in Piccolomini's day. Nevertheless, it is telling that in all of these texts the "Indians"—whoever they were—were so utterly unremarkable that every author from Mela to Piccolomini used the story only to illustrate an obscure point of geography and cared not a whit about the people themselves.

Speculating about Speculation

It is only after the discovery of America that new details drawn from encounters with Native Americans begin to be grafted onto this preexisting story telling us more about these visitors and their peculiarities. Gómara began the process by naming the voyagers as Native Americans. Then, Gómara's various descriptions of Pliny, Mela, and Piccolomini were conflated in the *Discoveries of the World* (1563) of the Portuguese António Galvão, who repeated Gómara's claim that a long "canoe" (no longer a merchant ship) full of Indians had come from Newfoundland (Bacallaos) to Germany, giving the date as 1353 CE. (Later translators amended this to 1153 CE, during Barbarossa's reign). He also added the detail—unsupported by any ancient or medieval text now extant—that the Germans could not understand the sailors' speech and that these Indians were Native Americans. Galvão, who relied extensively on Gómara as his source, did make plain that he was interpreting this tale in light of modern knowledge of America.[9] The similarity between the descriptions of Galvão and Gómara makes quite clear that the Portuguese author was merely expanding upon the Spanish with details drawn from his own understanding of Native Americans, and in the process restating Gómara's suggestion as settled fact. Thus, the Flemish cartographer Cornelius Wytfliet could repeat the story of Nepos' Native Americans as true in his 1597 supplement to Ptolemy's *Geography*.

With all of these accounts of alleged Native American travelers to premodern Europe, it followed that nineteenth century scholars began working backward to search for "scientific" explanations for how these travelers got from Labrador to Germany, since many took the older texts at face value and assumed that the early modern interpretations were correct. Georg Hartwig,[10] in 1860, following the earlier work of Alexander von Humboldt,[11] suggested that the Gulf Stream could have carried some unfortunate Inuit (Eskimo) from America to Northern Europe, accounting for

Nepos' report. In 1900 Peter de Roo reviewed all of the earlier texts in his speculative and frequently inaccurate *History of America before Columbus*, and de Roo stated as plain fact that Celer (and thus Nepos) mistook the Native Americans for people from India because of their "Asiatic features," features neither Mela nor Pliny had noted.[12]

From this impressive accumulation of texts (and many more like them), the story percolated among alternative scholars before hitting the mainstream in the 1990s. It appeared for example in Ivan Van Sertima's Afrocentrist work *They Came before Columbus* (1976), where he claimed the Native Americans may have brought a South American pineapple (!) to Europe with them (see Chapter 37).[13] The late Native American scholar-activist Jack D. Forbes included the story in his *Africans and Native Americans* (1993), in which he analyzed Pliny's passage. From Pliny's scant sentences and Forbes's dim knowledge that the tribal name of the Suevi could sometimes refer to a people of the Rhine, he reinterpreted the text until he made it say that the Native Americans had landed in the Netherlands or Belgium, which he said were part of Germany in Roman times.[14] This is not true; Belgium and the southern Netherlands in 60 BCE were known as Gallia Belgica, not Germania, though the province was renamed Germania Inferior in 80 or 83 CE. The area now Holland was, though, always part of Germania. Generally, the border between Gaul and Germany was considered the Rhine.

Forbes then repeats the claim current from Gómara onward that America was the only possible place people with dark skin could have traveled from in order to reach Germany by ship. Unlike Gómara, Forbes said these travelers might have been either the Olmec (c. 1500-400 BCE) or Teotihuacan people (c. 100-700 CE), whom he mistakes for contemporaries of Nepos, whose lifespan overlaps neither.[15] And he leaves it at that, though he would discuss the topic again in greater detail in 2007's *The American Discovery of Europe*, this time with greater adherence to fact.

Forbes's relatively obscure academic text might have been the end of the story had James W. Loewen not used Forbes' book as a source (along with Van Sertima) for his bestselling 1995 book *Lies My Teacher Told Me*, in which Loewen writes, "Two American Indians shipwrecked in Holland around 60 BC became major curiosities in Europe."[16] Loewen, who in the same paragraphs credulously repeated the claim that the sixteenth century Piri Reis map shows the Antarctic coast, was sloppy in his paraphrasing of Forbes, Van Sertima, and other diffusionist authors. Forbes did not specifically call the presumed landing place "Holland," so this appears to be Loewen's misinterpretation of Forbes's mention of the Netherlands, using the incorrect synecdoche of the province for the country. How Loewen came to believe the visitors were two in number or caused "a sensation in Europe" can only be guessed.

In writing "Six Lies" for Cracked.com O'Brien and Alley turned to *Lies My Teacher Told Me* as their source for the "fact" that two Native Americans reached Europe in 60 BCE, which they cited with a link. Thus, a sixteenth century speculative argument was transformed into internet fact.

The Incredible Voyage

An actual Native American voyage to Europe is, in fact, possible, and every so often new scholars make claims that some historical tale references actual transoceanic voyages. One of the more convincing accounts of such a voyage relates that in 1508 a seven-man bark canoe carrying what seemed to be Inuit was captured by a French ship near England. Unlike Mela's Indians, these people spoke an unknown language, wore clothes made of fish skins, and drank blood.[17] They were decidedly not merchants in a trading ship, but like Mela's Indians, the one captive who survived was presented to the King of France as a gift. As we move forward in time, we find better-attested stories of an Inuit-style canoe reaching the Orkney Islands in 1682 and again in 1684,[18] though the people of Orkney thought the sailors to be Finns. A mysterious sailor arriving in Scotland due to a storm in 1700 left a canoe, now in the Marischal Museum at the University of Aberdeen, which has been identified as Inuit.[19] The people encountered in 60 BCE could not have been Inuit, however, since the Inuit did not enter eastern Canada before 1000 CE, when they began to replace the earlier Dorset culture.

However, aside from a few disputed Inuit-style harpoon heads that may have been carried to the British Isles by whales,[20] there is no physical evidence of a Native American presence in Europe before Columbus. A Native voyage is probably the least likely explanation for the event of c. 60 BCE since Cornelius Nepos and the later Roman writers seemed to find nothing particularly noteworthy about the Indians in Germany, implying they were a known people with whom Romans could communicate. Too, there are no known Native American vessels that could reasonably be confused for a cargo ship suitable for mercantile trade.

In fact, the *Journal of the American Geographical Society of New York* noted in 1891 that Pliny, writing in 77-79 CE, merely repeated the statement of his source, Mela, from 43 CE, and Mela in turn has an uncertain manuscript tradition, with several variants and possible errors. It may well be, the *Journal* suggested, that a copyist's error transformed into "*Indos*" (Indians) the original word "*Irenos*" (Irish) or even "*Iberos*" (Spanish), making this a perfectly plausible story of a Celtic shipwreck on German shores that Mela and then Pliny misunderstood.[21] Earlier scholars, recognizing the clear evidence for Roman contact with India and vice versa, argued that Nepos' account was garbled and that the Indians had arrived in Germany not by sea but by a different route. Rabelais differed, suggesting in *Pantagreul* that the Indians had circumnavigated Africa,[22] while Louis Vivien de Saint-Martin argued that they were Wends, a Slavonian people from the Baltic who could have been mistaken for Indians because the Romans believed in a nonexistent water route between the Baltic and India.[23] Several publications from India simply accepted the story as *prima facie* true via a Bering Strait and Arctic Ocean route![24] And, of course, some writers, like Edward Herbert Bunbury and James Oliver Thomson, considered the story to be nothing more than a tall tale repeated by a credulous Nepos[25]—something even Pliny seemed to suggest in criticizing Nepos' "insatitate credulity."[26]

*   *   *

Conclusion

The long and short of it is that there is no independent confirmation that Native Americans washed up in Holland around 60 BCE. We can't rule out an accidental shipwreck of Native Americans, but the evidence from the brief ancient passages now extant argues against it. All of the extant texts (depending on the independence of Otto's account) are derived from a single paragraph in Pomponius Mela that spoke of merchants in a ship sailing from the east across the Caspian to arrive in Germany. From this we simply cannot derive the exact number of two, uncontested proof they were Native Americans, proof that they sailed from the west across the Atlantic, or a clear indication they landed in what is now the Netherlands. All of these claims are interpretations, with varying degrees of evidence supporting them and many alternative explanations. Thus, on almost every point excepting the date of landfall, the claim as currently presented in alternative, Afrocentrist, and diffusionist literature is demonstrably false. Claimants would do well to make plain to their audiences the difference between fact and interpretation.

Notes

[1] Jack O'Brien and Alfrod Alley, "Six Ridiculous Lies You Believe about the Founding of America," *Cracked.com* [online], May 15, 2012.

[2] Pomponius Mela, *De situ orbis* 3.45; my translation.

[3] Pliny the Elder, *Natural History* 2.67, translated by John Bostock and H. T. Riley.

[4] Some amend this to the Boii or the Baeti.

[5] Francisco Gómara, *Historia general de las Indias*, in Richard Eden, *The First Three English Books on America (?1511-1555 A.D.)*, edited by Edward Arber (Westminster: Archibald Constable and Co., 1895), 347. (Translation adapted.)

[6] Gómara, *Historia general*, 338 (adapted).

[7] Quoted in Francesco Tarducci, *John and Sebastian Cabot,* translated by Henry Francis Brownson (Detroit: H. F. Brownson, 1893), 280.

[8] Martianus Capella, *The Marriage of Philology and Mercury* 6.621; my translation.

[9] António Galvão, *The Discoveries of the World,* translated by Richard Hakluyt (London: Hakluyt Society, 1862), 56.

[10] Georg Hartwig, *The Sea and Its Living Wonders,* 8th ed. (London: Longmans, Green, and Co., 1892), 60.

[11] Alexander von Humboldt, *Aspects of Nature,* translated by Mrs. Sabine (Philadelphia: Lea and Blanchard, 1850), 138.

[12] Peter De Roo, *History of America before Columbus,* vol. 1 (Philadelphia: J. B. Lippincott, 1900), 168.

[13] Ivan Van Sertima, *They Came before Columbus: The African Presence in the Americas* (New York: Random House, 2003), 254-255.

[14] Jack D. Forbes, *Africans and Native Americans: The Language of Race and the Evolution of Red-Black Peoples,* second ed. (University of Illinois, 1993), 12-13.

[15] Ibid., 13.

[16] James W. Loewen, *Lies My Teacher Told Me,* tenth anniversary ed. (New Press, 2007), 39.

[17] Pietro Bembo, *Rerum Venetarum historia,* book 7 (1551); translated and quoted in W. H. Tillinghast, "The Geographical Knowledge of the Ancients Considered in Relation to the Discovery of America," in Justin Windsor, *Narrative and Critical History of America,* vol. 1: Aboriginal America (Boston: Houghton, Mifflin and Co., 1889), 26.

[18] James Wallace, *A Description of the Isles of Orkney,* ed. John Small (Edinburgh: William Brown, 1883), 32-33.

[19] "Arctic Connections," *University of Aberdeen* [online], n.d.

[20] E. E. Evans and C. F. C. Hawkes, "An Eskimo Harpoon-Head from Tara Co. Down?" *Ulster Journal of Archaeology* 3 (1940): 127-133.

[21] "Type of an American Indian in an Antique Bronze of the Louvre," *Journal of the American Geographical Society of New York,* 23 (1891): 87-90.

[22] Rabelais, *Pantagreul* 4.1.

[23] Louis Vivien De Saint-Martin, *Histoire de la Géographie* (Paris: Hachette, 1873), 176.

[24] See, for example, Rama Prasad Chanda, "Indo-Aryan Expansion and the Early Relations of the Aryas with the Pre-Aryans," *The Calcutta Review* 118 (1904): 25.

[25] Edward Herbert Bunbury, *A History of Ancient Geography,* vol. 2 (London: John Murray, 1879), 172; James Oliver Thomson, *History of Ancient Geography* (Cambridge: Cambridge University Press, 1948), 199.

[26] *Natural History* 5.1.

48. Did Pagans Worship Noah's Ark?

ALTERNATIVE THEORIES OF the ancient past date back pretty much to Antiquity itself. In the eighteenth century, the rough equivalent of our modern ancient astronaut theory was "Arkism," the theory first proposed by Jacob Bryant that all ancient mythologies and religions were distortions and perversions of the story of Noah's Ark and the rest of Genesis, the only revealed truth and accurate history. Just as ancient astronaut theorists interpreted (and misinterpreted) every shred of evidence through the lens of aliens, so too did Arkite believers force all of history into the shape of Noah's Ark. However, in an important difference, Arkite worship was accepted by many scholars as a true interpretation of the ancient past for several decades surrounding 1800.

In the introduction to my translation of *The Orphic Argonautica*, a Late Antique epic poem about the voyage of Jason and the Argonauts in search of the Golden Fleece, I describe one instance in which Bryant perverted a genuine ancient text to force it into his false system.[1] Here are the genuine lines from the opening of the *Orphic Argonautica*, in which Orpheus describes the formation of the cosmos according to Orphic theology, whereby chaos eventually gives rise to creation:

> Truly, above all I disclosed the stern inevitability of ancient Chaos, and Time, who in his boundless coils, produced Aether, and the twofold, beautiful, and noble Eros, whom the younger men call Phanes, celebrated parent of eternal Night, because he himself first manifested.[2]

Contrast that with the way Jacob Bryant in his *A New System; or, an Analysis of Antient Mythology* (1774-1776) intentionally mistranslated the passage to bring it in line with the Biblical narrative of the sins of the giants, the Flood, and God's covenant with Noah:

> After the oath had been tendered to the Mustae [i.e. initiates], we commemorated the sad necessity, by which the earth was reduced to its chaotic state. We then celebrated Cronus, through whom, the world after a term of darkness enjoyed again αιθερα, a pure serene sky: through whom also was produced Eros, that twofold, conspicuous, and beautiful Being.[3]

Bryant has transformed Orpheus' discussion of the primeval formation of the cosmos from chaos into an allusion to the degradation and corruption of the antediluvian earth,[4] followed by a clear sky mirroring the rainbow that embodies God's covenant with Noah after the Flood.[5] Since ancient Greek was not widely studied in the eighteenth century, Bryant's falsified translation entered nineteenth century scholarship unchallenged and was repeated uncritically throughout that century. Christian apologists, who adopted some of Bryant's ideas, sometimes even glossed "Eros" explicitly as "rainbow" in order to support the literal truth of Genesis as witnessed by pagan records.

The Arkite theory that pagan myths, like the story of Jason and the Argonauts, were corruptions of the Genesis narrative emerged from scholars like Bryant reasoning backward from a pre-determined conclusion. In those days, it was widely accepted that the Biblical account of creation and the Flood was literally true. Since it was literally true, it must therefore be the case that all other religious beliefs were false. To the degree that they were similar to the Bible it could only be due to the pagans corrupting the Biblical truth, which, being God's Word, was the first and most excellent history ever written.

Thus, when scholars like Jacob Bryant read the fragments of the Berossus, the Babylonian priest of Marduk, that described the Great Flood in detail similar to that of the Bible,[6] it proved that the Babylonians had recorded a corrupt tradition of Noah's Flood. (We know today, of course, that the Babylonian and Sumerian flood myths predate their biblical counterpart.) From there, it was a short hop to identifying Jason and the Argonauts as Noah and the Ark (for *Argo* = Ark, they thought, assuming English to be a universal language), and seeing the Babylonian fish-god Oannes as Noah himself, Oannes being a corrupt form of Noah's name.

This belief was taken to absurd levels of spurious detail, seeing in every random word syllables related to "Noah" and the "Ark" (in English, of course) and in every boat or floating container the ship of Noah. Henry Lee outlined the theory, which he took very seriously, in his *Sea Fables Explained* in 1883, and it is laughable reading today. He first outlines the story of Oannes, half-fish and half-man, who rose up from the sea to teach the Babylonians civilization (See Chapter 25):

> In this tale we have a distorted account of the life and occupation of Noah after his escape from the deluge which destroyed his home and drowned his neighbours. Oannes was one of the names under which he was worshipped in Chaldea, at Erech ("the place of the ark"), as the sacred and intelligent fish-god, the teacher of mankind, the god of science and knowledge. There he was also called Oes, Hoa, Ea, Ana, Anu, Aun, and Oan. Noah was worshipped, also, in Syria and Mesopotamia, and in Egypt, at "populous No," or Thebes—so named from "Theba," "the ark."
>
> The history of the coffin of Osiris is another version of Noah's ark, and the period during which that Egyptian divinity is said to have been shut up in it, after it was set afloat upon the waters, was precisely the same as that during which Noah remained in the ark.
>
> Dagon, also—sometimes called Odacon—the great fish-god of the Philistines and Babylonians, was another phase of Oannes. "Dag," in Hebrew, signifies "a male fish," and "Aun" and "Oan" were two of the names of Noah. "Dag-aun" or "Dag-oan" therefore means "the fish Noah."[7]

None of this was true; it was nothing more than a figment of a scholarly imagination that had forced evidence to a predetermined conclusion in service of religious ideology. Dagon was never a fish god; his name derives from *dagan*, a Canaanite word for grain, of which he was the god. The legend of Dagon as a fish-god derives from a misinterpretation of 1 Samuel 5:4, in which the top half of a statue of Dagon breaks off and falls before the Ark of the Covenant, "and only the stump of Dagon was left to him." The phrase translated as "the stump" in the King James Version and literally reading "only Dagon" was wrongly glossed as "his fishy part" in the eleventh century on analogy with the Hebrew word for fish, *dag*, and associated in biblical commentary with the Roman poet Horace's description of the Sirens in as human above the waist and fish below it.[8] The best answer is that the Hebrew text of 1 Samuel 5:4 is corrupt and missing a word; other texts such as the Septuagint and the Syriac translation interpolate "the trunk" into the phrase. Nevertheless, from this, the myth of Dagon as the fish god (conflating him with Oannes) was born. It was from this that Lovecraft took his Dagon for the aquatic story of the same name. From a few scraps of dubious philology, false analogies, and assumed conclusions an elaborate mythology of universal Noah worship was created.

Since I think the Arkite worship theory (the "ancient ark-onaut theory," if you will) is an interesting parallel to the ancient astronaut theory, I'd like to take a look at one more case of Arkist silliness that has very close parallels in today's ancient astronaut nonsense. In Bryant's *New System*, the eighteenth-century scholar attempted to make the case that both the *Argo* of the Greek Jason myth and the chest in which the Egyptian god Osiris had been entombed were corruptions of Noah's Ark. In order to understand this, let's examine Bryant's claim point by point.

> The Argo, however, that sacred ship, which was said to have been framed by divine wisdom, is to be found there; and was certainly no other than the ark. The Grecians supposed it to have been built at Pagasæ in Thessaly, and thence navigated to Colchis. I shall hereafter *shew* the improbability of this story: and it is to be observed, that this very harbour, where it was supposed to have been constructed, was called the port of Deucalion. This alone would be a strong presumption, that in the history of the place there was a reference to the Deluge.[9]

Deucalion was the Greek flood hero, often thought of as the Greek Noah. He and his wife survived a Flood sent by Zeus in an ark. Bryant here sees the similarities, but he attributes them to the Greeks stealing the story from the Jews, and reporting on a real Flood, rather than what we know today: the Hebrew and Greek stories both descend from an even more ancient Mesopotamian original. This is almost exactly how modern ancient astronaut theorists work with ancient myths, imagining them to all report corrupt versions of real alien encounters, without consideration for the established connections between cultures and peoples. Bryant, at least, had an excuse: The Mesopotamian Flood myth wasn't discovered until after he was dead.

> The Grecians placed every antient record to their own account: their country was the scene of every action. The people of Thessaly maintained that Deucalion was exposed to a flood in their district, and saved upon mount Athos: the people of Phocis make him to be driven to Parnassus: the Dorians in Sicily say he landed upon mount *Aetna*. Lastly, the natives of Epirus suppose him to have been of their country, and to have founded the antient temple of Dodona. In consequence of this they likewise have laid claim to his history.[10]

Bryant is correct that the Greeks often localized myths to their location, but he has taken this fact as evidence that Greek mythology can be divorced from Greece and reassigned to the Holy Land. This is actually quite similar to what Robert Temple did in *The Sirius Mystery* (1976), arguing that the myths of the Dogon of Africa were "really" Greek and, in turn, therefore Egyptian and Sumerian (see Chapters 34 and 42). Before him, Ignatius Donnelly, in *Atlantis: The Antediluvian World* (1882) used the same technique to revamp Ark-ism as survivals of the history of Atlantis rather than the Ark!

> In respect to the Argo, it was the same as the ship of Noah, of which the Baris of Egypt was a representation. It is called by Plutarch the ship of Osiris, who as I have mentioned, was exposed in an ark to avoid the fury

of Typhon: "Having therefore privately taken the measure of Osiris's body, and framed a curious ark, very finely beautified and just of the size of his body, he brought it to a certain banquet."[11] *The vessel in the celestial sphere, which the Grecians call the Argo, is a representation of the ship of Osiris, which out of reverence has been placed in the heavens.* The original therefore of it must be looked for in Egypt. The very name of the Argo shews, what it alluded to; for Argus, as it should be truly expressed, signified precisely an ark, and was synonymous to Theba.[12]

Now we get to the meat of the zaniness. Bryant claims that Noah's Ark, Jason's *Argo*, and the ship of Osiris are all the same boat because all three are the constellation Argo Navis in the night sky. (Argo Navis was once the largest constellation in the heavens, representing the back two-thirds of a boat, but it was broken up in the eighteenth century into four separate clusters.) This issue is a bit complex, but the main point is that we have no idea what the earliest peoples saw when they looked up in the night sky. The most generous modern estimate places Argo Navis' invention prior to 2800 BCE (though this is *highly* speculative), but we have no evidence of what early Egyptians saw in the sky, and the suggestion that Argo Navis was known to the Egyptians before the coming of the Greeks is speculative at best.

The question of the homology of "Argo" and "Ark" is another case of silliness. The word "ark" derives from the Old English *earc*, from the Latin *arca*, a box or chest. It has no direct connection to *argos*, the Greek word meaning "swift" or "shining" or "bright." But even if it did, it is irrelevant: Noah's "ark" is the English term for a boat that was known in Hebrew as *teyvat*, a word with no connection to either term whatsoever. This is the same type of linguistic word game modern ancient astronaut writers and alternative historians have used to create false connections between ancient cultures, such as the claim that Jesus spoke Quiché Mayan while dying on the cross.[13] Nevertheless, all of this "evidence" for an Argo-Ark-Argo Navis connection reappears uncritically in Temple's *Sirius Mystery*, unchanged from when Bryant made it up 200 years earlier.[14] But back to Bryant:

It is made use of in that sense by the priests and diviners of the Philistim; who, when the ark of God was to be restored to the Israelites, put the presents of atonement, which were to accompany it, into an Argus, אֲרוֹן, or sacred receptacle.[15]

Here Bryant has joined yet another "ark" to his theory based on the coincidence of two English uses of the word Ark. The "Ark" of Noah was the *teyvat Noah*, but the Ark of the Covenant was the *ʾĀrôn Hābərît*; it is only the Vulgate's use of the Latin word for box to describe both that led to the coincidence of the English terms.

And as they were the Caphtorim, who made use of this term, to signify an holy vessel; we may presume that it was not unknown in Egypt, the region from whence they came. For this people were the children of Mizraim, as well as the native Egyptians, and their language must necessarily have been a dialect of that country. I have mentioned that many colonies went abroad under the title of Thebeans, or Arkites; and in consequence of this built cities called Theba.[16]

Just as modern ancient astronaut writers and alternative historians look for spurious connections based on similarities of language, coincidences of art, etc., so earlier did Bryant create false correlations based on shared names. For him, Egyptian Thebes and Greek Thebes had to be cult centers of Ark worship. We know today that Greek Thebes had been Mycenaean *TE-QA-DE* (*Thebasde*), while Egyptian Thebes acquired its conventional name from the Greeks, who tried to transliterate the indigenous Egyptian term *Ta-opet*, the name of the Karnak temple complex. There is no need to postulate an Ark cult of Theban priests to explain it.

In like manner there were many cities built of the name of Argos; particularly in Thessaly, Boeotia, Epirus, and Sicily: whence it is that in all these places there is some tradition of Deucalion, and the ark; however it may have been misapplied. The whole Peloponnesus was once called both Apia, and Argos. As there were many temples called both Theba and Argus in memory of the ark, they had priests, which were denominated accordingly.[17]

The "misapplied" ark tradition involves Bryant projecting one wherever he needs it. As noted before, the Greek word *argos* has nothing to do with the English word for *ark*, and neither with the Hebrew word for Noah's ship. The connection is entirely spurious, crafted out of sound-alike words, misread history, and plain ignorance. But when Bryant wrote most of this was forgivable because he did not have access to modern archaeological findings, current linguistic etymologies, or any ancient texts outside the Hebraic and Greco-Roman traditions.

Bryant had accidentally struck upon the fact that Mesopotamian and Indo-European mythologies share motifs, but lacking a sound theory to explain them, he ended up constructing a towering edifice of speculation built on foundations of quicksand. His assumption of Biblical primacy is no different than the assumption of alien intervention or of origins in Atlantis, and all these theories are equally unsound. Modern ancient astronaut theorists have access to the full range of modern scholarly findings and yet they choose to rely on the same methods and techniques that have failed so spectacularly for more than three hundred years.

Notes

[1] Jason Colavito, "Introduction," in *The Orphic Argonautica: An English Translation*, translated by Jason Colavito (Albany, New York: JasonColavito.com Books, 2011), xix-xx.

[2] *The Orphic Argonautica* 11-16; my translation.

[3] Jacob Bryant, A New System; or, An Analysis of Antient Mythology, third ed., vol. III (London: 1807), 175.

[4] Genesis 6:1-13

[5] Genesis 9:13

[6] Berossus, as preserved in Syncellus, *Chronicon* 28, 38; Eusebius, *Praeparatio Evangelica* 7, 9 and *Chronicon* 5.8.

[7] Henry Lee, *Sea Fables Explained* (London: William Clowes and Sons, 1883), 3-4.

[8] *Ars Poetica* 1.4.

[9] Bryant, *New System*, vol. 3, 54-55.

[10] Ibid., 55-56.

[11] I have replaced Bryant's quotation of a Greek line of Plutarch's with an English translation.

[12] Bryant, *New System*, vol. 3, 56.

[13] This claim is based on the alleged phonetic similarity of Jesus' words in Matthew 27:46 and Mark 15:34 to supposed Quiché Mayan words, when in fact Jesus was quoting Psalm 22:1 in Aramaic.

[14] Robert Temple, *The Sirius Mystery: New Scientific Evidence of Alien Contact 5,000 Years Ago* (Rochester, Vermont: Destiny Books, 1999), 242-247.

[15] Bryant, *New System*, vol. 3, 56-57.

[16] Ibid., 57.

[17] Ibid., 57-58.

49. Forks: The Devil's Flatware

H OW OFTEN HAVE WE heard people say that ancient history is boring, and that Atlantis, ancient astronauts, or wandering Phoenicians help to spice up the subject? Eighty years ago Lord Raglan complained that "Many educated people, however, continue to believe in [Great Zimbabwe's] fabled construction by King Solomon, merely because they like to do so, and because the truth is 'so dull,' an expression that I have often heard applied to it."[1] Many ask, what's the harm in believing something romantic and irrational? The following example is perhaps not the most important, but it is certainly a fascinating look at how a false belief can snowball and significantly impact cultural practices. Our example is the humble fork.

Our story begins with the rise of Christianity. Because Christianity is monotheistic, the early Church Fathers had to find some way to account for the pagan gods. Were they fictional? Or were they something evil? St. Augustine, drawing on Psalm 96:5, settled on declaring them "most impure demons, who desire to be thought gods."[2] Therefore, the pagan gods were actually agents of the devil. The early Christians endowed the Devil of scripture with the symbols of Pluto, the Roman ruler of the Underworld. In late Hellenistic and Roman iconography, Pluto sported a "bident," a two-pronged weapon similar to Poseidon's trident. (This was perhaps inspired by, or maybe reflected in, Seneca's *Hercules Furens*, in which Pluto uses a trident to drive Hercules from the Underworld.[3]) A

Byzantine scholiast writing on Euripides' *Phoenician Women* suggests that bidents and tridents had become interchangeable in Late Antiquity. By the Middle Ages, Pluto's bident/trident had become the property of Satan, who succeeded him as imaginary ruler of the Underworld (Hades), which, as demonstrated by Dante, had become identified with the Christian Hell.

Thus, when the Byzantine princess Maria Argyropoulina, niece of Emperor Basil II, arrived in Venice in 1004 to marry the son of the Doge and brought with her a case of golden two-pronged forks, which had been in use in Constantinople for more than three centuries, the Venetians threw a fit. The local clergy condemned the fork as decadent and as diabolical—the very instrument of the Devil. When Maria died two years later of plague, the Venetian clergy proclaimed it God's judgment on the infernal fork. St. Peter Damian preached that a Venetian princess (probably Maria, but perhaps another—she is not named by Peter) died a miserable death because she used "a certain gold prong [a fork] wherewith she actually conveys her food to her mouth, instead of using the fingers God gave her for that purpose."[4] For the next four or five centuries, Western Europe kept its forks in hiding, using them only in private, though usually because of their association with the "effeminate" Byzantine Greeks than a fear of God. Medieval texts and woodcuts demonstrate that forks were used in private homes, despite clerical and political feelings. In 1573 the Holy Inquisition investigated Paolo Veronese's depiction of buffoons in his *Last Supper*, and they specifically asked why he showed an apostle picking his teeth with a fork.[5] He was forced to rename the painting *The Feast in the House of Levi* to keep his fork and his buffoons.

"God protect me from forks!" Martin Luther is said to have exclaimed in 1518 (or 1515), although this quotation is almost certainly a modern fake.[6] Protestant clerics would preach against diabolical forks down to the end of the Thirty Years' War, symbols of unholy luxury and Italianate vice. One clergyman complained of using forks "as an insult on Providence, not to touch our meat with our fingers."[7] Before they rode brooms, European witches were assumed to ride on the large fire-forks used in early baking.

Catherine d'Medici eventually used a fork, and this vice was used to condemn her as a wicked witch of a foreign interloper in France. The fork, being Italian, was necessarily anti-French, made worse by its association with her son, the rumored homosexual King Henri III, known for his delicacy and effeminacy.[8] Eventually, Charles I of England declared it a useful device and acceptance soon followed. But even then adoption was not universal. In England, for example, the fork did not catch on until the eighteenth century, and even then more conservative types continued to denounce it as a miniature of the Devil's own utensil, or at the very least, an ungodly luxury. But by then, these critics had begun to believe medieval propaganda true. By the 1850s, the fork had become a standard eating utensil, thanks largely to aristocratic and royal patronage, so much so that by 1850 *The Spectator* could confidently write that to "eat like a Christian" was to eat with a fork, in contradistinction to the practice of the uncivilized heathens of the East, who still "lift their food with their fingers."[9] (Imagine what the Victorians would have made of McDonalds!)

But to add another layer of intrigue to the story, the tale of the devil's fork was apparently greatly embellished by modern scholars from the Renaissance to the nineteenth century as a way of casting the Middle Ages as a time of religious dogma and superstition.[10] Certainly, there was a symbolic association between the fork and the devil's bident or trident, but it was apparently the scholars of the modern era who misunderstood the subtle use of demonic symbolism in the Middle Ages as a literal belief in the diabolical origin of the fork. Thus, the fabricated Devil's fork became established as a fictious "fact" used to damn the Middle Ages as a time of ignorance, a fake history still repeated down to the present. In truth, medieval people associated the fork with foreigners, homosexuals, and women; the demonic aspect flowed from that, visual shorthand akin to drawing devil horns on the photograph of an unloved politician.

The entire process of adopting the fork, an instrument now considered a given part of the dinner service, has been colored by early Christians' decision that the "true" nature of the pagan gods was that they were demons and devils, and therefore later political and social critics were able to project religious ire as well as political opprobrium upon the fork due to its chance resemblance to the pagan/diabolical bident. Had this imagery not existed, Maria and Catherine would have been (and were) condemned on other grounds, but the fact remains: an "alternative" theory about the true nature of the ancient gods as demons impacted European dining for eight centuries. What effects would accidentally arise should we, with equally poor evidence, proclaim the gods were actually Atlanteans or aliens?

Notes

[1] Lord Raglan, *The Hero: A Study in Tradition, Myth, and Drama* (Mineola, New York: Dover, 2003), 34-35.

[2] *City of God* 7.33, translated by Marcus Dods.

[3] Seneca, *Hercules Furens* 558ff.: "He [Pluto] who as king lords it o'er countless peoples, what time thou wast making war on Pylos, Nestor's land, brought to combat with thee his plague-dealing hands, brandishing his three-forked spear, yet fled away, with but a slight wound smitten, and, though lord of death, feared he would die." (Translated by Frank Justus Miller.)

[4] *Institutio monialis,* caput. 11, quoted and translated by Darley Dale, "Flowers from Liturgica Historica," *American Catholic Quarterly Review* 44 (1919): 104.

[5] Francis Marion Crawford, *Gleanings from Venetian History* (London: Macmillan, 1907), 461.

[6] *"Gott behüte mich vor Gäbelchen."* Although this quotation is widely reported in German literature, I have not been able to verify the source for this statement. The German literature refers only to secondary sources, primarily from the 1970s-1990s. There is no evidence the quotation existed prior to then.

[7] Isaac D'Israeli, "Of Domestic Novelties at First Condemned," *Miscellanies of Literature,* vol. 1 (New York: J. & H. G. Langley, 1841), 85.

[8] Carolin Young, "Catherine D'Medici's Fork," *Authenticity in the Kitchen,* Proceedings of the Oxford Symposium on Food and Cookery 2005, ed. Richard Hosking (Prospect Books, 2006), 441-453.

[9] "A Fork," *The Spectator,* reprinted in *The Living Age,* November 30, 1850, 429.

[10] Ernst Shubert, *Essen und Trinken im Mittelalter* (Darmstadt: Wiss. Buchges, 2006), 257.

50. Final Thoughts: The Sameness of It All

HERE ARE SO MANY interesting things to explore about the past, so much exciting and fascinating history, that the so-called "mysteries" of the ancient astronaut theorists and alternative historians pale in comparison. And yet, what is that we see on television, find on bookstore shelves, and stumble across on nearly every website? Aliens, Atlantis, Chupacabra, "new" chronologies, Phoenician world travelers, prehistoric nuclear bombs, etc., ad infinitum, ad nauseam.

It's tiresome, really. The false mysteries of fake history haven't changed more than an iota in more than one hundred and fifty years. Ignatius Donnelly's *Atlantis: The Antediluvian World* (1882) set the stage for "alternative" history (though it was not the first of its genre, only the most popular), and his work is a veritable buffet of scholarship compared to the imperfect carbon copies that followed during the twentieth century. All of the basic arguments later used by Erich von Däniken in the 1970s, David Hatcher Childress in the 1980s, Graham Hancock in the 1990s, and *Ancient Aliens* today can be found in Donnelly's book. Most of the later versions are unchanged from their first presentation: that pyramids on both sides of the world are evidence of a common source; that the use of heavy blocks implies a centralized prehistoric civilization of superior organization and power; that similarities in myth speak to a common origin in real life history.

Science has demonstrated the falsity of these claims—the impossibility of a sunken continent existing in the Atlantic; the wild dissimilarities in composition, purpose, and date of the Old and New World pyramids; the elaborate evolutionary tree of Indo-European myth and other myth cycles that explains so many similarities and coincidences.

And yet... No matter how much work archaeology, anthropology, linguistics, history, biology, and every other discipline put in to explaining the human past, "alternative" theories never change. Sure, some may argue for Atlantis and others for aliens, or even an unidentified "lost" civilization in Antarctica or on the parts of continents sunken at the end of the Ice Age, but the claims and the evidence and the reasoning are always the same. They are immune to criticism. True believers will never surrender their beliefs because they are not founded on evidence.

How else can we explain why "alternative" authors still rely on sources that were out of date when Donnelly used them in 1882? How else can we explain why "alternative" authors repeat the same discredited lies over and over again? Arguments that were speculative in the 1860s do not become suddenly true against facts simply by virtue of age.

In 1882, *Nature* wrote that Donnelly made a mockery of the scientific sources he tried to marshal to his cause: "Our only reason for noticing this curious book is that the names of writers of authority which constantly appear in its pages may lead some readers astray. But the author, while quoting them, has neither assimilated their method nor understood the bearing of their facts."[1] This situation has not changed with the likes of von Däniken, Childress, et al., who ape the language of science and its pretentions without caring a whit for its methods or its reasoning.

The saddest thing is that a century from now, those who truly care about history will still be fighting the same battles against the same purveyors of false history. And I'll be willing to bet the fight will still be over the same "evidence" that Donnelly used in 1882.

Notes

[1] Review of *Atlantis: The Antediluvian World* by Ignatius Donnelly, *Nature* 26 (1882): 341.

Index

About the Author

Jason Colavito is an author and editor based in Albany, NY. His books include *The Cult of Alien Gods: H. P. Lovecraft and Extraterrestrial Pop Culture* (Prometheus, 2005), *Cthulhu in World Mythology* (Atomic Overmind, 2013), and others. His research has been featured on the History Channel, and he has consulted on and provided research assistance for programs on the National Geographic Channel (US and UK), the History Channel, and more. Colavito is internationally recognized by scholars, literary theorists, and scientists for his pioneering work exploring the connections between science, pseudoscience, and speculative fiction. His investigations examine the way human beings create and employ the supernatural to alter and understand our reality and our world.

Visit his website at http://www.JasonColavito.com and follow him on Twitter @JasonColavito.

Made in the USA
Thornton, CO
04/23/23 01:54:28

5acc6049-c4d2-4cfb-8691-cc73e6fc1e7cR01